PRAISE FOR MICHELE BORBA AND *UnSelfie*

"Parenting expert Borba (*Building Moral Intelligence*) traveled the world and researched for decades before writing this fresh and powerful primer on raising caring kids. Her thought-provoking and practical book may very well tip over the parenting priority applecart—and rightly so."—*Publishers Weekly* (starred review)

"Borba builds an excellent case for empathy, and parents concerned with the trend toward self-absorption and bullying among young people will find useful tips to counteract the negative messages children are hearing."—*Booklist* (starred review)

"Michele Borba makes a strong case for empathy as a tool that can be taught to kids, positioning them for success. . . .When you have empathy, it's like cutting through the mess and getting straight to what drives 99.9 percent of most people: a need to be understood, valued, and loved."—*New York Post*

"*UnSelfie* is an engaging and thoughtfully argued book, and its topic—teaching children to be more mindful of other people, and more in control of themselves and their own emotions—is as timely as ever. . . . Borba's book makes the case that our efforts can and will be repaid in a more empathetic world moving forward."—*NYMag.com*

"Empathy helps us develop true friendships and have a happy life, and Michele Borba's practical insights and advice are a huge help for parents who want to nurture this essential skill in their children."—**Harvey Karp, M.D., author of** *The Happiest Baby on the Block* **and** *The Happiest Toddler on the Block*

"Empathy is a gateway to success for kids across every area of life—and Dr. Michele Borba leads parents on a practical, step-by-step journey to get there. Passionately written and impeccably researched, *UnSelfie* has practical strategies on every page that you can use right away."—**Rachel Simmons, author of** *Odd Girl Out* **and cofounder of Girls Leadership**

"*UnSelfie* contains everything parents and educators need to know to give children the 'empathy advantage' and raise a new generation of caring, happy, successful kids. Nobody on the planet is better than Michele Borba at showing you how to put empathy into action. Read this book. It will change your kids' lives!"—**Jack Canfield, coauthor of** *Chicken Soup for the Parent's Soul* **and** *The Success Principles*™

"This beautiful gem of a book is a must-read for all parents who care about the quality of life of their children and the world they inhabit. I can think of no better guide than Dr. Michele Borba to teach parents exactly how to cultivate and nurture the missing ingredient in their children's success and happiness: empathy."—**Tamar Chansky, Ph.D., author of** *Freeing Your Child from Anxiety* **and** *Freeing Your Child from Negative Thinking*

"Michele Borba has written a game-changing guide showing why nurturing empathy in our children isn't optional—it's essential. This groundbreaking book is an invaluable tool for parents and educators in their quest to raise compassionate, kind, and courageous children in a culture whose only success metrics are grades, trophies, and résumés. For our children's sake, I hope parents heed her sound advice to raise UnSelfies."—**Philip Zimbardo, professor emeritus of psychology, Stanford University, and author of** *The Lucifer Effect*

"I have never, ever read a book that combines solid research on a timely and critical subject—the importance of promoting empathy—with so many amazing and creative how-to suggestions that turn this research into action. *UnSelfie* is a must-read!"—**Ellen Galinsky, author of** *Mind in the Making: The Seven Essential Life Skills Every Child Needs*

"Once again Dr. Michele Borba has written a book that is not only 'good' but *essential*. By writing about empathy in the context of our children's increased technology use, Dr. Borba penetrates the often hidden world of electronics. She does so with a science-based perspective that mirrors our own common sense. *UnSelfie* is a must-read for parents, teachers, and policy-makers."—**Michael Gurian, author of** *The Wonder of Boys* **and** *The Wonder of Girls*

"In this brilliant and timely book, Michele Borba brings into sharp relief the key skill for children making it in the twenty-first century—empathy. . . . This book offers a roadmap to a much brighter future."—**Dacher Keltner, director of the Greater Good Science Center and author of** *The Power Paradox: How We Gain and Lose Influence*

"Want your children to be both caring and successful? *UnSelfie* shows you how. . . . An engaging read with vivid stories and practical advice, *UnSelfie* is the most important parenting book you will read this year."—**Jean M. Twenge, author of** *Generation Me* **and coauthor of** *The Narcissism Epidemic*

"Dr. Borba's nine-step plan for raising successful, happy kids who also are kind, courageous, and resilient provides a revolutionary new framework for learning empathy. Empathetic kids will thrive in the future, but the seeds of success can be planted today—one habit at a time. Read this book to find out how."—**Madeline Levine, author of** *The Price of Privilege* **and** *Teach Your Children Well*

"Countless books advise parents on how to foster their children's achievement and determination. But in order to succeed in today's world, it's just as important to be kind, compassionate, and concerned about the well-being of others. If you care about cultivating these traits in your child—and you should—you'll heed Michele Borba's wise advice."—**Laurence Steinberg, Ph.D., author of** *The Ten Basic Principles of Good Parenting*

"As a parent and educator, I understand why so many of us are worried about the impact of constant connectivity and self-focus our culture so often glorifies. But Michele Borba's *UnSelfie* gives us such a powerful tool to counteract these seemingly overwhelming challenges. She has wonderful and practical ways to reconnect with our children and guide them so they can develop healthy relationships with others."—**Rosalind Wiseman, author of** *Queen Bees and Wannabes*

"This is the first book I've read that provides clear, practical, research-based steps for raising empathetic children. *UnSelfie* is an essential, enjoyable read for parents and educators, a book I plan to keep close at hand as I write, parent, and teach."—**Jessica Lahey,** *New York Times* **bestselling author of** *The Gift of Failure*

"For children of every age, Michele Borba shows parents—and all caregivers—how a focus on empathy can build moral courage, kindness, teamwork, and self-regulation. She provides a gift to us all in guiding us in nurturing the best capabilities of our most precious resources and showing how natural it is for children to focus on the 'we' and not the 'me.'"—**Maurice J. Elias, Ph.D., author of** *Emotionally Intelligent Parenting* **and** *The Other Side of the Report Card*

"Dr. Borba pulls the veil off a much-needed topic concerning the unhealthy self-centeredness existing in our world today. Her brilliant insight not only reveals the source of the problem but provides applications and skill-set training. A must-read!"—**Darrell Scott, founder, Rachel's Challenge**

"If we want our children to THRIVE through good and challenging times we must never forget that it is their ability to reach out to—and give strength to—others that will make the difference. Here is a powerful book that will make a difference for our children today as we prepare them to be the kind of adults we need to lead our world tomorrow."—**Kenneth R. Ginsburg, M.D., MSEd, author of** *Raising Kids to Thrive* **and** *Building Resilience in Children and Teens*

"If I were asked to recommend just one book to parents, caregivers, and educators that serves as an essential research-based, no-nonsense, go-to guide for raising compassionate, caring, empathic, successful, and happy children, *UnSelfie* would be my number one pick. . . . I cannot recommend this book enough!"—**Trudy Ludwig, children's advocate and bestselling author of** *The Invisible Boy*

"[A] research-based road map with practical, empowering strategies to nurture empathy in a self-absorbed world that so desperately needs it. Inspired, hope-filled, insightful, and hard to put down—a must-read for all parents."—**Amy McCready, author of** *The "Me, Me, Me" Epidemic—A Step-by-Step Guide to Raising Capable, Grateful Kids in an Over-Entitled World*

"In this era of increased technology use, *UnSelfie* emphasizes the important reminder that kindness, caring, and being genuinely connected to others is critical for children. Parents are their role models and teachers in this arena. Borba offers numerous suggestions for helping children develop and exhibit empathy and helping families find ways to connect to each other with digital-free activities. A great read."—**Tovah Klein, author of** *How Toddlers Thrive*

"In *UnSelfie*, Michele Borba boldly takes on the mistaken modern myths and practices that may lead today's young into the traps of self-absorption, and she offers us a better way."—**William Damon, Professor and Director, Stanford Center on Adolescence and author of** *The Path to Purpose*

"*UnSelfie* offers a life jacket for those swimming in a sea of selfie culture. Wade in, cast your line, and reel in a plan for raising self-regulated, empathic children. Three cheers for Michele Borba!"—**Mary Gordon, founder of Roots of Empathy**

"Luckily for us, Michele Borba has focused her attention on one of our most critical issues—how we can raise empathic, caring children. . . . She makes me hopeful that our next generation of children will be more invested in each other and more committed to creating a better and more just world."—**Richard Weissbourd, Senior Lecturer, Director, Human Development and Psychology Program at the Harvard Graduate School of Education**

"In our time, and around the world, no one is a more trusted voice on character and child behavior than Michele Borba. And no one is better equipped to help us raise more empathic, kinder, happier kids."—**Thomas Lickona, director of the Center for the 4th and 5th Rs (Respect and Responsibility) and author of** *Character Matters*

UnSelfie

Why Empathetic Kids Succeed
in Our All-About-Me World

Michele Borba, Ed.D.

TOUCHSTONE

NEW YORK   LONDON   TORONTO   SYDNEY   NEW DELHI

Note to the reader:

All the stories in this book are based on cases of children and their families and teachers whom I have known and worked with over the last years. A few stories are composite cases of children I have treated, and their actual names as well as their parents' names have been changed to protect their privacy. All examples from schools are gathered from my actual observations. The exceptions are children interviewed for newspapers or written about in books as examples of children displaying the nine habits of empathy.

 Touchstone
An Imprint of Simon & Schuster, Inc.
1230 Avenue of the Americas
New York, NY 10020

Copyright © 2016 by Michele Borba

First Touchstone trade paperback edition May 2017

TOUCHSTONE and colophon are registered trademarks of Simon & Schuster, Inc.

For information about special discounts for bulk purchases, please contact Simon & Schuster Special Sales at 1-866-506-1949 or business@simonandschuster.com.

The Simon & Schuster Speakers Bureau can bring authors to your live event. For more information or to book an event, contact the Simon & Schuster Speakers Bureau at 866-248-3049 or visit our website at www.simonspeakers.com.

Design by Maura Fadden Rosenthal/Mspace

Manufactured in the United States of America

20   19   18   17   16   15

Library of Congress Cataloging-in-Publication Data

Names: Borba, Michele, author.
Title: UnSelfie : why empathetic kids succeed in our all-about-me world /
    Michele Borba.
Description: First Edition. | New York : Touchstone, 2016.
Identifiers: LCCN 2015049137 | ISBN 9781501110030 (hardback) | ISBN
    9781501110108 (ebook)
Subjects: LCSH: Empathy. | Interpersonal relations. | Child rearing. | BISAC:
    FAMILY & RELATIONSHIPS / Parenting / General. | PSYCHOLOGY /
Developmental / Child. | PSYCHOLOGY / Interpersonal Relations.
Classification: LCC BF575.E55 .B67 2016 | DDC 649/.7—dc23 LC record available at
http://lccn.loc.gov/2015049137

ISBN 978-1-5011-1003-0
ISBN 978-1-5011-1007-8 (pbk)
ISBN 978-1-5011-1010-8 (ebook)

More than a decade ago, a dad came up to me after a speech I gave on empathy and thanked me. He handed me a photo of his son and told me that his son had hanged himself after enduring relentless bullying. The father asked me to promise that I'd never stop stressing empathy. "If someone had instilled empathy in those boys, my son would be alive today." This book is my way of keeping a promise to that dad and to all children who have endured peer cruelty.

CONTENTS

INTRODUCTION

The Hidden Advantage of Empathy and Why It Matters for Our Children

Could a greater miracle take place than for us to look through each other's eyes for an instant?
—HENRY DAVID THOREAU

In the early 1990s, a distinguished journalist named John Wallach started a summer camp in Otisfield, Maine, called the Seeds of Peace International Camp. Wallach, who had spent years reporting on friction in the Middle East, had come to the realization that the best hope for disrupting the cycle of violence is by working with the kids from these war-torn regions—and other areas throughout the world—to teach them new skills for dealing with conflict. By reaching kids early, and teaching them skills like collaborating, communicating, and peacemaking, Wallach believed he could change the tenor of the international conversation for the better.

So for the past three decades, dozens of teens have arrived each summer from Israel, Palestine, Egypt, Jordan, Pakistan, Afghanistan, India, Britain, and the United States, with the organizers' hopes that they will return home as future peacemakers and changemakers. Wallach's idea was considered idealistic or impossible by most, but by the end of each three-week session, many teens are friends with those they were taught to hate and fear. University of Chicago researchers surveyed hundreds of campers' attitudes immediately prior to and following their experience, and again nine months after returning home. They found that a significant portion of both Israeli and Palestinian teens feel more positive, closer to, and trusting "of the other" not only as they leave camp, but even a year after their experience.[1] What's more, many are committed to working for peace. Wallach's dream is succeeding, and it's because the approach is based on empathy.

I visited the camp in Maine and interviewed teens from different delegations, spoke to advisors, and closely observed. Everything I saw—the atmosphere, the activities, adult interactions, and the skills facilitators were teaching—strengthened human connection and cultivated empathy.

"We create an environment where the walls come down, so to speak: where campers are willing to try something new surrounded by people willing to support them,"[2] Leslie Lewin, the executive director, told me. "Empathy is the foundation of Seeds of Peace."

Teens eat, bunk, talk, and play together; team-building challenges help them rely on one another, and activities help them find creative solutions together. Campers also engage in daily small-group dialogue sessions led by facilitators so they learn to consider the thoughts and feelings of one another. Sitting face-to-face and sharing deep concerns with the "other side" helps dissipate prejudice, and fear is replaced by new perspectives. Then ever so slowly, these campers start to see and feel the world from the other viewpoint until they "understand as if they are the other person—as if they could step right into that person's life and know exactly how that person feels and why."[3] In short, they empathize. Empathy is the one human capacity that allows us to link minds and hearts across cultures and generations to transform our lives.[4] And that's exactly what happens to teens at that lakeside camp. These adolescents are acquiring the Empathy Advantage that they will use to guide their thoughts, feelings, and actions for the rest of the lives.

"It's impossible not to be changed on the inside after being here," a refugee from Somalia told me. "Once you see that other people have the same worries and fears, you start to feel *with* them, and everything inside you turns upside down. You never go back to the way you were before you came."

"I had beliefs that were in my mind since I was young and I couldn't accept the other side," said a camper from Palestine. "But then I realized that they [Israelis] have peaceful people just like us. . . . I believe that at the end of the day, we are all humans."[5]

That moment confirmed thirty years of research and touring the world for answers. Empathy can be instilled, and it is composed of teachable habits that can be developed, practiced, and lived. Empathy is what lays the foundation for helping children live one essential truth: *We are all humans who share the same fears and concerns, and deserve to be treated with dignity.*

"What do kids really need to be happy and successful?"

Hundreds of parents have asked me the question, and my response surprises most. "Empathy" is my answer. The trait that allows us to feel with others has the reputation of being "touchy-feely," but new research reveals that empathy is far from "soft," and it plays a surprising role in predicting kids' happiness and success. The problem is that empathy is widely underestimated by moms and dads, as well as the general public, so it's low on most child-rearing agendas.

UnSelfie introduces a revolutionary but simple idea that will transform our kids' lives: that empathy—rather than being a nice "add-on" to our kids' development—is in fact integral to their current and future success, happiness, and well-being. And what many researchers are starting to realize is that empathy is not an inborn trait. Though our children are hardwired to care, they don't come out of the womb empathetic, just like they aren't born knowing that $2 + 2 = 4$ or who the president of the United States is. Empathy is a quality that can be taught—in fact, it's a quality that *must* be taught, by parents, by educators, and by those in a child's community. And what's more, it's a talent that kids can cultivate and improve, like riding a bike or learning a foreign language. Nine essential competencies, which I will outline in this book, comprise empathy. With practice, those competencies and skills become habits that our children will use for a lifetime to maintain their caring capacities.

But why should we want our kids to empathize? For starters, the ability to empathize affects our kids' future health, wealth, authentic happiness, relationship satisfaction, and ability to bounce back from adversity.[6] It promotes kindness, prosocial behaviors, and moral courage,[7] and it is an effective antidote to bullying, aggression, prejudice, and racism.[8] Empathy is also a positive predictor of children's reading and math test scores[9] and critical thinking skills,[10] prepares kids for the global world, and gives them a job market boost. It's why *Forbes* urges companies to adopt empathy and perspective-taking principles, the *Harvard Business Review* named it as one of the "essential ingredients for leadership success and excellent performance,"[11] and the Association of American Medical Colleges identified it as an "essential learning objective."[12] In today's world, empathy equals success, and it's what I call the Empathy Advantage that will give our children the edge they need to live meaningful, productive, and happy lives and thrive in a complex new world.

Empathy is core to everything that makes a society civilized, but above all, it makes our children better people, and that's why I'm concerned. In the past decades, our kids' capacity to care has plummeted while self-absorption has skyrocketed, and it puts their humanity at stake. Today's culture values "Me" more than "We."

THE RISE OF THE SELFIE SYNDROME
AND THE FALL OF EMPATHY

"Selfies" are all the rage as people take endless photos of themselves and post them on social media for others to view, to "oooh" and "ahhh" their every "Me" and "My" accolade. The term has become so ubiquitous (the word's use increased 17,000 percent in one year; a Google search reaps more than 230 million hits) that Oxford Dictionaries chose it as its Word of the Year in 2014. A review of hundreds of books published since 1960 found a stark increase in phrases that included the word *self* or stressed personal uniqueness or being better than others ("I come first" and "I can do it myself").[13] But that "look at me looking at you" digital craze is spilling into the real world, altering our kids' offline attitudes, and creating the most entitled, competitive, self-centered, and individualistic breed on record.

I call this new self-absorbed craze the Selfie Syndrome. The condition is all about self-promotion, personal branding, and self-interest at the exclusion of others' feelings, needs, and concerns. It's permeating our culture and slowly eroding our children's character.

Self-absorption kills empathy, the foundation of humanity, and it's why we must get kids to switch their focus from "I, Me, My, Mine" to "We, Us, Our, Ours." Here are four reasons why we should be concerned.

1. **We see a measurable dip in empathy among today's youth.** Our first clue that all these selfies (and the me-centered culture that they represent) are doing irreparable harm to today's young people is the rise in narcissism among college-age students.[14] Narcissists are interested only in getting what they can for *themselves*. "If *I* ruled the world, it would be a better place." "*I* always know what *I* am doing." "*I* will never be satisfied until *I* get all that *I* deserve." The self-admiration craze wouldn't be as worrisome if a focus on others was increasing at the same time, but that isn't happening.[15] Teens are now 40 percent lower in empathy levels than three decades ago, and in the same period, narcissism has increased 58 percent.[16]

2. **We can also observe a clear increase in peer cruelty.** When empathy wanes, aggression and bullying can rise, and tormentors begin to see victims as objects, not human beings. One study showed youth bullying increasing a whopping 52 percent in just four years (2003 to 2007), and we now see evidence of bullying starting in children as young as three.[17] Another 2014 study found that cyberbullying incidents tripled within a single year.[18] Peer cruelty has become so intense that it affects kids' mental

health: one in five middle school students contemplate suicide as a solution to peer cruelty.[19] Legislators are so concerned that all fifty states have now passed anti-bullying policies. Bullying is learned, but it can also be unlearned, and cultivating empathy is our best antidote. If you can imagine a victim's pain, causing that suffering is a near impossible feat.

3. **Experts observe more cheating and weaker moral reasoning in young people today.** Kids with identities based on caring and social responsibility are more likely to consider others' needs, and the shift away from this in contemporary culture is another reason to worry. Sixty percent of adults[20] believe that young people's failure to learn moral values is a serious national problem. Over the past two decades, there's been a decline in children's moral character, and 72 percent of Americans say moral values are "getting worse"[21]: a large majority of college students say "cheating is necessary to get ahead," and 70 percent admit to cheating.[22] Not surprisingly, cheating is also on an upswing, and the most typical kind of moral reasoning among recent undergraduates is focused on personal interests, not on what's right for others.[23] Empathy is part of the antidote, but it's not the whole solution; individuals need a moral rudder to help them navigate ethical choices.

4. **Our plugged-in, high-pressure culture is leading to a mental health epidemic among young people.** One in five[24] US youth meets the criteria for a mental disorder in their lifetime.[25] Teen stress is now at higher levels than that reported by adults.[26] Our kids' well-being is at stake, but so too is their empathy. As anxiety increases, empathy wanes: it's hard to feel for others when you're in "survival mode," and that's the state of too many of our children. That creates a so-called empathy gap.

While we may be producing a smart, self-assured generation of young people, today's kids are also the most self-centered, saddest, and stressed on record. Producing caring, happy, *and* successful people will require a major change in child-rearing and teaching, one that is aligned with the latest science. *UnSelfie* offers a blueprint to show how to make that crucial shift so we apply the best, proven strategies to our parenting as well as our educational approaches.

CULTIVATING EMPATHY

So how can parents, as well as teachers, counselors, and child advocates, turn this troubling trend around and influence their children's ability to care? Which practices hinder and which help kids' caring capacities? What are the latest scientific findings we should know to raise healthier, happier, more successful, and caring kids? Those are a few of the questions that have haunted me, and I spent the past decade combing for answers and flying around the world to find out.

Teaching empathy to kids—and teaching the adults in their lives how to cultivate empathy in the children around them—is my life's work. I started out as a classroom teacher, working with kids from all sorts of backgrounds who faced myriad challenges and difficulties. Eventually, my desire to help children led me to pursue my doctorate in educational psychology and counseling. It was while working on my dissertation and interviewing hundreds of preschoolers to assess their abilities to identify emotions that I stumbled on my passion: developing children's emotional and social competencies. One four-year-old's comment set my brain twirling: "I wanna be nice, but Mommy doesn't teach me 'nice.'" Such truth! If we hope to raise empathetic, courageous, caring kids, we need to teach them how.

Soon, I was traveling the world, meeting top researchers in major universities and observing teachers to discover the best practices, and it's been an amazing trek. I was invited by the Pentagon to train counselors and educators on eighteen overseas US Army bases and serve as a consultant to educators around the world. I've presented workshops and keynotes to hundreds of parents and teachers on six continents, reported the latest child development news as a media contributor on

135 *Today* show segments, and authored more than two dozen books summarizing my findings.

But the moment when this book came into focus—the moment I realized how vital it is to cultivate empathy among all of us—was when I visited the Cambodian Killing Fields outside Phnom Penh more than a decade ago. It was where more than a million people were murdered, and it shook me to my core. All I could think about was what causes such inhumanity and how to stop it. So began a decade-long journey to find the answer. My journey took me to the sites of unfathomable horrors: Dachau, Auschwitz, Armenia, and Rwanda, where I learned that a common cause of genocide was always a complete lack of empathy for fellow human beings. I studied youth violence and school shooters. I discovered that early experiences that are seeped in warmth, model kindness, and stress "You *will* be kind" are key to reducing cruelty. I wrote a proposal, "Ending School Violence and Bullying," that was signed into California law; it stressed the need to teach children empathy-building skills. (I knew I was on the right track when a teen thanked me. "That would have kept my brother out of jail," he said. "People have to teach kids to care.") And I developed strategies to reduce bullying and trained hundreds of teachers and law enforcement officers. I also developed strategies to mobilize children's compassion to be "Upstanders," which was featured on *Dateline* (and is described in chapter 8).

Each role helped me discover powerful but simple ways parents, teachers, counselors, and communities can stretch children's "empathy muscles": Eight-year-olds in Armenia playing chess to stretch their perspective-taking skills. At-risk teens in Long Beach, California, making videos of hospice patients to give to families to preserve memories. Third graders in Canada using babies to teach them emotional literacy. Four-year-olds in San Diego stepping into different pairs of "big people" shoes to try on "Daddy and Mommy feelings." And Israeli and Palestinian teens in dialogue sessions at a lakeside Maine camp to grasp the other's side.

Most important, I saw what research confirms: empathy *can* be cultivated, and doing so transforms our children's lives. No matter what the zip code, the most effective strategies are meaningful experiences that touch kid's hearts with a caring adult close by. We can—and must—do a better job of helping our sons and daughters become good people. Failing to build their empathy capacity is nothing short of failing our children.

But nothing, absolutely nothing, has confirmed my conviction for empathy more than raising three sons. They are grown now, but when I look back and assess which quality I'm most proud of instilling in each child, my answer is a resounding "empathy." I know it's the one quality that will give my children and yours the advantage for a healthy, happy, and successful life, especially in today's digital-driven, hypercompetitive, and individualistic world.

The road to a meaningful life all starts with empathy. And the Empathy Advantage is what our children need most to succeed both now and later and in every arena of their lives.

HOW TO USE THIS BOOK

Empathetic children use nine essential habits to help them navigate the emotional minefields and ethical challenges they will inevitably face throughout life. These nine habits also guide their empathic urges and inspire them to help others. And all nine are teachable and culled from the latest research in child development, neuroscience, and social psychology. *UnSelfie* provides the blueprint to help you instill those crucial abilities that reap the Empathy Advantage until they become lifelong habits in your child.

Part 1 shows you how to help your child *develop* the first four crucial fundamentals of empathy:

- **Emotional literacy,** so he can recognize and understand the feelings and needs of himself and others;

- **Moral identity,** so he will adopt caring values that guide his integrity and activate empathy to help others;

- **Perspective taking,** so he can step into others' shoes to understand another person's feelings, thoughts, and views;

- **Moral imagination,** so he can use literature, films, and emotionally charged images as a source of inspiration to feel with others.

Part 2 is all about helping your child *practice* the habits of empathy:

- **Self-regulation** will help your child learn to manage strong emotions and reduce personal distress so he can help others.

- **Practicing kindness** will increase your child's concern about the welfare and feelings of others.

- **Collaboration** will help him in working with others to achieve shared goals for the benefit of all.

Part 3 provides ways to help your child *live* empathetically.

- **Moral courage** emboldens him to speak out, step in, and help others.

- **Altruistic leadership abilities** motivate him to make a difference for others, no matter how small it may be.

The goal is to help your child adopt each empathetic ability as a lifelong habit so he reaps the Empathy Advantage. So choose one skill a month and practice it with your child just a few minutes a day until he can use it without reminders. Even better, make empathy building a family affair and practice together. Above all, remind your child: "Just like when you practice guitar, soccer, or your multiplication tables, the more you work at being kind, the kinder you'll be."

EMPATHY STARTS WITH HUMAN CONNECTION

In writing *UnSelfie*, I had many stirring experiences, but one is etched in my soul because it confirms that the foundation for empathy is face-to-face human connection. I was in Rwanda at an orphanage for deaf and mute children who were abandoned by their parents; their grandparents had been slaughtered in the genocide. I was giving out backpacks, each filled with a pencil, a ruler, a pack of gum, a notepad, a few candies, and a note from an American child back home. Children were so excited receiving their gifts and discovering what was inside.

But I spotted one boy with an almost frantic look: he had pulled all the items from his backpack, carefully laid them out but kept searching. Another pencil? More candy? Another ruler? No, not those, and he continued his intense search. Then suddenly he found what he was looking for: the note from the child. The boy grabbed it, smelled it, and then ever so carefully unfolded the paper. I moved closer and read the words along with him.

> *Hello. My name is Jacob. I'm ten and live in Minnesota. I looked up Kigali on a map to find out where you live. I put things in this backpack and was thinking about you when I packed them. I hope you like them and have a good day.*
> *Your new friend from the United States, Jacob*

The boy devoured each word and read the note again and again. Then he put the card against his chest, held it tightly, and started to cry. He looked up at me, pointed to his tears (and mine), signed the word *love*, and pointed to the boy's note as if it were his most prized possession. That precious child just needed to know that someone cared. It's the same need for every child anywhere in our world.

I just wished Jacob had been there to see the impact his words had on his new friend. It would have helped him understand the power of empathy to transform lives.

PART ONE

DEVELOPING EMPATHY

Self-absorption in all its forms kills empathy, let alone compassion. When we focus on ourselves, our world contracts as
our problems and preoccupations loom large. But when we
focus on others, our world expands.

—Daniel Goleman,
Social Intelligence:
The New Science of Human Relationships

CHAPTER 1

Empathetic Children Can Recognize Feelings

Teaching Emotional Literacy

I was consulting in Fort McMurray, a community far north in Alberta, Canada, when the superintendent told me, "You must visit the third grade and observe the fascinating way the students are learning emotional literacy." The next day I sat at the edge of a large, round, green blanket with twenty-six eight- and nine-year-olds waiting for their most unique teacher to arrive.

"I wonder if he'll smile more?" one boy said.

"I hope he's happy to see us," said another.

"Stay still—he startles easily," a girl admonished. "Joshua needs 'warm-up time.'"

I assured the students I'd be on my best behavior, when in walked a mom carrying her baby boy and the children began singing the "Welcome" song to their young teacher. "Hello, Baby Joshua, how are you? Hello Baby Joshua, how are you today?"

The mother—a volunteer from the community—gently placed her son in the middle of the blanket. It was Joshua's third visit since the start of the school year, and the kids were amazed at how much he had changed in just a few weeks! The mom and her baby would visit six more times as part of a program called Roots of Empathy, designed by Mary Gordon. But that day I saw a brilliant forty-minute emotional literacy lesson taught by a bald, nonspeaking seven-month-old! The children were using the baby's face, body language, and vocalization to learn to read and understand emotions.

"How does Joshua seem to feel today?" a trained Roots of Empathy instructor asked. Her skillful questions helped students label the baby's emotions and then understand their own: "What makes *you* feel irritated?" "When do *you* feel frustrated?"

The instructor then flipped the question focus to help kids consider other people's feelings: "How do we know if *someone else* is upset?" "How can we help *a friend* who is anxious?"

Students were reflecting, observing, and thinking about someone else's emotional state—the ideal "UnSelfie" experience!

Then the instructor urged the class to tune in to "their baby" a bit closer. "Joshua can't tell you what he wants," she said, "but shows you with his body. What is he thinking?"

"He's trying to figure us out," said one.

"Keep watching," the instructor urged. "How do you think he feels?"

"Maybe he's worried," said another.

"Look," a child pointed out, "his hands are in fists."

"Let's smile to let him know everything's okay!"

And all the kids broke out in huge Cheshire Cat–type grins. Their caring gesture wasn't lost on that baby: Joshua saw their smiles and grinned right back.

"Joshua is learning empathy," the child next to me whispered.

I agreed, but it was clear that Baby Joshua wasn't the only one learning to "feel with others." That day a seven-month-old had helped twenty-six kids grasp important concepts such as tuning in, recognizing feelings, considering others' needs, and being kind. It was also the perfect way to help kids experience "feeling with" another human being.

I've since visited several Roots of Empathy (ROE) classes and interviewed dozens of instructors, parents, and teachers. I always left inspired: someone had discovered a powerful way to stretch children's hearts and tune in to others. And comments from student participants confirmed it.

"The program taught me that everybody has different feelings and to always respect everyone's individuality," a ten-year-old girl said.

An eleven-year-old boy had a similar verdict: "ROE has taught me to understand that just because people are different outside doesn't mean they are different inside."[1]

Since 2000, the Roots of Empathy program has been evaluated in both comparative and randomized controlled studies designed to measure changes in the behavior of participation students. Independent research has been conducted on three continents. A large study at the University of British Columbia compared Roots' students with a control group and found ROE children had an 88 percent drop in "proactive aggression" (the cold-hearted use of aggression to get what you want).[2] Phenomenal gains for sure, especially when concerns about childhood bullying are on everyone's radar. Has this program really figured out how to nurture empathy? I wanted to learn more, so I arranged an interview with the program's developer.[3]

Roots of Empathy was founded in 1996 by Mary Gordon, a warm, personable, soft-spoken woman from Newfoundland who began her career teaching kindergarten. She developed the program in response to the violence against children that she witnessed while working with families. "A realization of the devastating impact of violence or abuse on the lives of children . . . set me on a path to find ways to break this cycle," she said.[4]

Gordon also discovered the power a baby can have on transforming a child's life and told me about a boy named Darren. He was in the eighth grade, held back twice, and now two years older than his peers were. Darren's mother had been murdered in front of him when he was four years old, and he lived in a succession of foster homes. He wanted everyone to think he was tough: his head was shaved except for a ponytail at the top, and he had a tattoo on the back of his head, but deep down he was hurting.

Darren was in a Roots of Empathy class when a mother was visiting with her six-month-old baby and told students how he didn't want to cuddle. To everyone's surprise, Darren asked if he could hold Evan. The mother was a little apprehensive, but she handed him the baby.

"Darren took him into a quiet corner and rocked back and forth with the baby in his arms for several minutes," Gordon said. "Finally, he came back and asked the mother, 'If nobody has ever loved you, do you think you could still be a good father?'"

Gordon realized then that the best hope for raising caring, concerned, and humane kids rests largely in the early attachment relationship. She also understood that children must experience empathy to acquire it. And what's more, they must actively learn the language of how to describe the feelings of empathy to those around them. If some of her charges did not get enough hands-on empathetic experience at home, well then, she would bring empathy-developing experiences into the classroom through a parent and infant.

Gordon spoke to me at great length about what she terms the "literacy of feelings." "As important as it is to learn to read," she said, "it's also important to learn to relate. Without emotional literacy, to understand our feelings, to have words for them, and be able to understand others' feelings, we're basically all islands. So we teach kids emotional literacy: the words to understand what you feel based on what you've witnessed with babies." Mary Gordon had discovered an ideal way to teach children to read and understand feelings with a baby and in the process learn to feel with others.

More than 800,000 children in ten countries have been through Mary Gordon's program and have worked with a baby to help them understand feelings. I visited Maury Elementary, one of five elementary schools in Washington, DC, that now uses Roots of Empathy. The program is having an impact, particularly on one ten-year-old student. Kayne lives in one of the poorest and most violent neighborhoods in DC, and is not allowed outside his home after school due to gangs and unsafe conditions. (Several students shared concerns about their safety that day.) He admitted things had been "kind of bumpy" when he arrived.

"People weren't always so nice at this school," he said. "But things are different now."

"How so?" I asked.

"They brought this baby, and everybody changed. We just got more human or something," Kayne said. "When you get empathy, you just get better at stuff like being nice. Empathy helps you be nice."[5]

LEARNING TO TUNE IN TO FEELINGS

Your two-year-old looks at the tears in your eyes and gently pats your face. Your school-age child sees that his friend is sad and gently puts his arm on his shoulder and tells him, "It's okay. It'll get better." Your tween notices that your father's face seems strained: "Are you tired, Grandpa? Need a hug?"

All these are examples of emotional intelligence—the ability to identify an emotion in yourself or others. When working with very young children, I often call this habit "tuning in to feelings." It's the first, and arguably most crucial, of the nine essential habits of empathy that we'll be learning about in this book—the tools that will give your child the Empathy Advantage for future happiness and success. And the great news is that emotional intelligence is not just a gift; it's actually an ability that can be taught to our children, starting when they are young as toddlers . . . though the seeds are planted even earlier, by how we relate and respond to our infants.

Emotional literacy is a key to unlocking empathy. Before you can empathize, you have to be able to read someone else's, or your own, emotions so you can tune in to their feelings. ("She is smiling . . . I bet she's happy?" "Her body is slumped over . . . maybe she's tired." "I'm sad because he's sad. . . .") Emotional literacy is what motivates a child to care, and it all starts by tuning in to feelings. Identifying, understanding, and expressing emotions are the skills kids need to activate empathy.

It turns out that kids schooled in feelings are smarter, nicer, happier, *and* more resilient than children who are less literate in their Emotion ABCs.[6] The importance of emotional intelligence in future success has been proven time and time again, all over the world. Wherever this is tested, scientists have shown that kids who are able to read feelings from nonverbal cues are better adjusted emotionally, more popular, more out-going, and more sensitive in general.[7] Emotionally attuned kids are also physically healthier and score higher academically than kids who aren't coached to consider the feelings and needs of others.[8]

Tuning in to feelings is an essential part of good parenting. This most crucial empathy habit lays the groundwork for developing close rela-tionships with our kids, and it gives them the ability to relate to and feel empathy for others. We can teach children how to identify and recog-nize feelings in someone else, but it all begins with tuning in to another person.

WHY IS TUNING IN TO FEELINGS
SO HARD—FOR *ALL* OF US?

If we know what helps children tune in to feelings, then what's causing their empathy to dip so dramatically? Misguided parenting styles and a plugged-in, me-centered culture are shortchanging kids from oppor-tunities for real-time face connections and learning emotional literacy.

We Live in a "Plugged-In" Culture

The single best predictor of healthy emotional interactions is a lot of face-to-face communication; it's also the best way to learn emotions and develop human-contact skills. Staring at computer screens, texting, tweeting, and IMing do *not* teach kids their Emotion ABCs. The average eight- to eighteen-year-old is plugged in to a digital media device about seven hours and 38 minutes a day (that doesn't count time spent texting or talking on cell phones).[9] Almost 75 percent of children aged eight and younger have access to some type of "smart" mobile device at home.[10] Preschoolers spend 4.6 hours per day using screen media, and almost 40 percent of two- to four-year-olds use a smartphone, MP3 player, or tablet.[11] A new study found that 30 percent of children first play with mobile devices when they're in diapers.[12]

You do the math: if kids sleep seven hours at night, attend school and other activities for eight to nine hours, and text about a hundred messages a day, opportunities for real-time face-to-face interactions are scant.[13] And it's exactly these in-person interactions (not digital exchanges) that develop empathy. Too much online communication means that our kids will be less equipped to develop skills to navigate their social world, and it may infringe on our own relationship with our children.

A survey by the Center for the Digital Future found that the percentage of parents who say they now spend *less* time socializing as a family tripled in just two years.[14] Parents also say that the loss of family time is largely due to the increase of internet time. That's worrisome because it means that as our kids plug in more, they lose opportunities to connect face-to-face, learn emotional literacy, and practice empathizing, and we lose precious moments to connect with our kids. Those are crucial reasons why we must create "sacred unplugged times" so we do prioritize family interactions and not relinquish our parenting influence to a digital-driven world.

We Have Different Expectations of Boys and Girls

Most parents would say, "I speak the same to all my kids," but experts disagree. When it comes to "emotion instructing" we respond to genders differently, and it appears girls are getting a far better deal.

Moms tend to discuss and explain feelings more with their two-year-old daughters than with their two-year-old sons. And the differences in boys' and girls' behavior begin to show up almost immediately. Studies show that by age two-and-a-half, girls are measurably more advanced in reading facial expressions and body language ("He has a smile . . . he's happy," "She looks tired: she's rubbing her eyes") far better than their same-age male counterparts, and that gives the pink set a huge advantage in emotional literacy. We also use more emotion words such as *happy*, *sad*, and *worried* far more frequently with our four-year-old daughters than with our four-year-old sons. And the pink-blue division continues to widen from there.[15]

We also discuss more experiences that are emotional with girls ("Did you see how happy Grandma was to see us visit?" or "You noticed that your friend was scared when the dog barked. Taking her hand made her less anxious"). All this gives them more opportunities to practice "emotion talk." We also stress emotional situations and actual experiences more with our daughters. ("That girl looks sad that no one is playing with her. See how her eyes and mouth look? What can you do to make her feel better?")[16]

We discuss the causes and consequences of the emotions more with boys and leave out crucial clues that might help them learn emotional literacy: "Don't let kids see that you're upset if they make fun of you," or "You cry too easily. You have to toughen up!"[17] Small, unintended parenting responses can give our kids the wrong idea that girls should be more sensitive, while boys should control their emotions.

It isn't that boys aren't wired to tune in to feelings. William Pollack, Harvard psychologist and author of the acclaimed book *Real Boys*, points out boys as young as twenty-one months display a natural ability to feel empathy, including a wish to help people in pain.[18] But we tend to encourage girls to share their feelings while we tell our boys: "Be tough," "Hold back those tears," "Cover up your emotions."[19] Testosterone doesn't extinguish empathy and emotional literacy, but the wrong, unintended parenting reactions sure may.

We Live in a Hurried, Harried, Distracted World

"She's *always* on her smartphone. It's soooo annoying!" "I hate it when he talks on his cell. It makes me sad." "I wish he'd put down his phone when we're watching TV. It makes me feel that he cares more about his BlackBerry then me." While we criticize our children's plugged-in habits, these complaints are from our sons and daughters about us! Yep, the kids are whining about our behavior.

One national survey found that 62 percent of school-age kids said that *their parents* are too distracted when they try to talk to them.[20] The top parent distraction: cell phones. Researchers' detailed observations in a fast-food restaurant confirmed that the kids' gripes are valid. The study—published in the journal *Pediatrics*—found that when parents' cell phones were out and about, their primary engagement was on the device, not the child.[21] Each swipe and type means less talking *with, next to,* or *face-to-face* with our kids and missed empathy-building opportunities.

In another study, young children wore recording devices for several months. Researchers analyzed home sounds and found that television curtailed parent-kid interactions. For each hour of audible background television, 500 to 1,000 *fewer* adult words were spoken and heard by the kids.[22] Thirty percent[23] of households admit to leaving their television on (even when no one watches), exposing young children to 232 minutes of background television on a typical day.[24] Those minutes add up to grave implications for learning language, emotional literacy, and social development, as well as for engaging in face-to-face family interactions with us!

While there are roadblocks to nurturing our cyber kids' emotional competencies, there are solutions. In fact, new science shows babies arrive hardwired to tune in to feelings. But parents must hold those simple, old-fashioned, back-and-forth chats with face-to-face connections to nurture their children's capacity to care.

WHAT SCIENCE SAYS: HOW WE
RECOGNIZE EMOTIONS IN OTHERS

Before children can "step into someone's shoes," they must first develop the ability to read nonverbal cues in facial expressions, gestures, posture, and voice tone. In the last decade, scientists have made revolutionary findings of how much more babies and young children know about emotions than we ever envisioned. Those discoveries tell us that our babies are wired to be empathetic, almost from birth!

Most parents are surprised to learn that babies tune in to feelings far earlier than assumed, but Jenny and Bryan Masche made the discovery while filming their television show. The Masches are the proud parents of sextuplets (yes, six), and I was the "parenting expert" to help them navigate the "terrible twos" with their six toddlers on a segment of *Raising Sextuplets*.

During a film break, the proud dad showed the adults a video of one son's first haircut. We watched Grant, one sextuplet, sitting in a chair and *not* pleased about his baby book moment. Grant whimpered as Jenny cut the first wisp of hair. At the second snip, Grant wailed. But now Grant had a team of supporters: his five brothers and sisters heard their sibling's cries on the video. Suddenly, Savannah, Bailey, Molli, Cole, and Blake were bawling their eyes out because their brother was upset, and their cries made Grant sob. Six toddlers—not yet potty-trained or capable of speaking more than four words—caught each other's distress and were wailing in unison! It's called *emotional contagion* and is key to empathy because it helps children "feel with another's feelings." It turns out that even newborns recognize another's pain.

Babies Are Natural-Born Empathizers

Visit a hospital nursery and you may experience the "Wailing Room Phenomenon." If a newborn hears another baby cry, he joins the wail—and soon all the babies are wailing in sync! How do we know? Researchers played back specially designed audio recordings to newborns and found amazing discoveries.[25]

In one study, one-day-old infants were more likely to cry when they heard a tape of another newborn in distress. But when they heard recordings of their own cries or the cries of an eleven-month-old baby, the newborns didn't respond![26] At just one day old, babies show that they are natural socializers and want to connect with others. Martin Hoffman, renowned New York University psychologist, believes that the innate predisposition to cry with another "seems to be the earliest precursor of empathy."[27]

Babies also love to look at the human face, prefer people who use direct eye contact, and would rather listen to the human voice (espe-

cially their mom's) than to any other sound. To find that out, researchers presented infants with a choice of two faces: one with direct gaze,
the other with averted gaze. Babies looked longer at the face with direct
gaze: they prefer looking at people who make direct eye contact with
them.[28] (Remember to store that data: the best toy to help babies read
emotions is your face . . . and it doesn't cost a dime!)

But perhaps the decade's most intriguing finding: scientists are deci-
phering emotional understandings inside babies' brains! Thirty-eight
ten-month-old infants were each fitted with a tiny skullcap contain-
ing eight electrodes and then held by their moms. Each baby was then
shown a film clip of an actress laughing or crying. When the babies saw
the clip of an actress laughing, they smiled, and the left frontal region of
their brains crackled with electrical activity. When they watched a clip of
an actress sobbing, they became sullen—some even wailed—and activity in their right prefrontal regions spiked.[29] The now-famous study by
Nathan Fox and Richard Davidson launched the field of affective neuroscience and the brain basis of emotion. And once again, studies showed
that babies are primed to care!

Alison Gopnik, a professor of psychology at the University of California, shared a touching story in her book *The Scientist in the Crib*
(coauthored with Andrew N. Meltzoff and Patricia K. Kuhl) about her
almost-two-year-old son. She was crying from a hard day, and her son
was concerned. The toddler ran off and returned with a large box of
Band-Aids and then proceeded to put them all over his mom to try to
make her tears and "boo boos" go away. It was the best way the toddler
knew to "make Mommy all better."[30]

A caring gesture for sure, but it also showed how reading feelings
motivates prosocial behavior. The toddler understood that "tears mean
sadness"—he's felt those wet globs on his face before—and he was going
to comfort his mom.

Interpreting the subtle messages of someone's distress is another
empathy touchstone. Around two is when our children begin to show
genuine empathy for the first time. While younger babies cry if they
see or hear others in distress, only two-year-olds "try to make things all

better." They don't just feel your pain; they also try to ease it. The child realizes that not only is he a separate human being—someone besides him can feel upset—but also that the other person needs comfort, Band-Aids, or pats, even if he doesn't. It's a miraculous moment!

"Real empathy isn't just about knowing that other people feel the same way you do," Gopnik, Meltzoff, and Kuhl explain, "it's about knowing that they don't feel the same way and caring anyway."[31]

In the next years, young children will continue to expand their emotional literacy and become more proficient in reading feelings off another's face, voice tone, or body language, and learning words to describe each emotion. Language further advances their empathic capabilities. Comments such as "You look sad, Daddy," or "My friend looks scared" are clues that children are ready to move from their egocentric "Me-Me-Me" status and start feeling and caring about others to become UnSelfies.

Of course, having an emotional vocabulary doesn't assure that a child will share, care, or comfort. The right nurturance, modeling, reinforcement, experiences, and cognitive development are needed for empathy to blossom fully. But the roots of tuning in began in the nursery, where our babies first heard the cry of another and joined in to cry together.

HOW TO TEACH CHILDREN TO IDENTIFY EMOTIONS

Not every type of encounter increases children's heart muscles. Empathy stems from relationships, so the best "heart stretchers" involve kids directly so they experience emotion-charged events up close and personal. That's why babies are ideal teachers for kids: they're real, interesting, and engaging, and with the babies' repeated classroom visits, children learn to tune in and care about them. But babies aren't the only possibilities: the trick is to find what works for your child.

One such strategy called Emotion Coaching was developed by John Gottman, a noted psychology professor and author of the must-read book *The Heart of Parenting*. The adult helps the child understand the different emotions, why they occur, and how to respond as those feelings occur, so it builds emotional intelligence and empathy. Gottman's thirty-year-long research also found that kids whose parents use the strategy reap the Empathy Advantage: they are happier, more resilient, less stressed, better adjusted, and score higher in math and reading. I know the technique is simple *and* effective because I saw it in my own classroom.

Ricky was a student I'll never forget. Everyone adored him because he cared about others. If anyone had a bad day, Ricky let me know. He tuned in to feelings.

One day I found him painstakingly making a card. "It's for my mom," he said sheepishly.

"Is it her birthday?"

"Nope," he said, "I'm making it because my mom always makes my feelings feel so good."

Well, I just had to find out what this mother did to make her son's "feelings feel so good" and help him be so empathetic. My moment came the following week at a school event where I watched this mom with her son. Their entire encounter took no more than a minute—max—but her communication style was golden. She walked up to him and leaned down so the two were face-to-face. Her eyes were focused only on his eyes. While he talked, she tuned in and blocked out everything except her child. The two were in sync with each other.

Mom wasn't just listening to her child's words but also to the feelings behind them. She'd respond with a simple validation: "You're happy!" She would label his emotion: "That made you proud." Or help him reflect: "How did that make you feel?" And Ricky's entire being blossomed in front of my eyes.

Ricky's mom was helping him understand emotions by being his "emotion coach." The Roots of Empathy instructor used a similar approach by posing questions to help students reflect about "their" baby's emotional state. Here are five ways to use the strategy with your kids:

- **Be an emotion coach.** Find natural moments to connect face-to-face, to listen, and then validate your child's feelings like

Ricky's mom. For more ideas, read John Gottman's *The Heart of Parenting: Raising an Emotionally Intelligent Child.*

- **Use a baby.** If a baby is available, consider using a Roots of Empathy–type approach in your home. Could your children observe an infant sibling (or cousin or next-door neighbor) as you guide them to understand feelings? Does a parent in your child's playgroup or scout troop have a baby from whom the children could learn emotions?

- **Raise a puppy.** Are your kids begging for a puppy? Animals can be powerful subjects to teach emotions: "Watch Fido's tail. What do you think he's saying?" Or: "How do you know if Kitty is scared?" Could your older child volunteer at an animal shelter? Is there an animal your child could care for, train, and then observe its emotions?

- **Tutor a child.** Encourage your older child to tutor or coach a struggling student in reading, math, sports, art, music, or whatever else. Find a way for your child to help others and to use the experience to tune in to emotions and learn what resonates with his "student."

- **Skype with Grandma.** Skyping or FaceTiming is a great way kids can connect with loved ones face-to-face. Reflecting about their caller's emotional state *prior* to the Skype helps nurture empathy. "How will you know how she feels?" "Do you think Grandma will be tired like last time? What signs on her face tell you it's time to end the call?"

EMPATHY BUILDER: TUNING IN TO FEELINGS

Teaching your child to read feelings more accurately will boost his emotional literacy, and it's the first step toward cultivating empathy and compassion. This four-step empathy building exercise will get you started.

Take one step at a time and use it in your family's daily life until your children are ready for the next step, and then the next.

Step 1: Stop and Tune In

Empathy starts with attending to one another, so when it's time to connect with your child, hit the Pause button on everything and in your time together; tune in to each other. Don't let digital devices hinder your family connections. Set and enforce the 4T Rule: "No Texting, Tapping, Talking on a cell, or TV viewing when others talk or are present."

Step 2: Look Face-to-Face

Eye contact is how kids learn to read people's emotions, so face your child and be at eye level when you communicate. Then enforce one habit: *"Always look at the color of the talker's eyes."* The rule helps kids use eye contact and pick up facial expressions, voice tone, and emotional cues. Hint: Holding eye staring contests to see how long family members can maintain eye contact without breaking their stare is a fun way to help kids feel more comfortable looking at one another. If your child is uncomfortable using eye contact, suggest, "Look at the bridge of the speaker's nose."

Step 3: Focus on Feelings

Labeling feelings goes hand in hand with empathy and helps kids build a feeling vocabulary. Here are three easy ways to help kids focus on feelings:

- *Name the feeling.* "Looks like you're angry." "You seem frustrated." "You sound irritated."

- *Pose questions that tune in to feelings.* "Are you angry [tense, anxious, worried, frustrated]?"

- *Match the emotion with the gesture.* "You seem to be scowling. Are you tired?" "Your fists are clenched. Do you feel anxious?"

Don't judge your child's feeling; just listen empathically and validate the stated emotion.

Step 4: Express the Feelings

Once kids have an emotion vocabulary, they need opportunities to practice expressing feelings. Mary Gordon told me: "We always think we should begin our queries with 'How do you think so-and-so felt?' But you'll be more successful if you start with '*You* must have felt very upset.' The trick is to help children describe how they felt so that they have the emotional language the next time something happens. Only then can a child say, 'I'm feeling like I did when I hit Johnny.'"[32] So start by asking your child: "How do *you* feel?"

Only when your child can express his own feelings should you then switch the pronouns in your question from "How do *you* feel?" to "How does *he* [*she, they*] feel?" The small pronoun tweak takes the focus off your child's feelings and allows him to begin to consider other people's concerns.

Cynthia Ozaeta, a mom from Indio, California, helps her kids talk about their feelings with this tip: "I tell my kids if something feels bad, and you want to feel better, say how you feel," she said. "It's like medicine: you may not want to do it, but it always feels better after you do it."

HOW TO HELP KIDS ADOPT THIS HABIT

Feelings aren't learned by facing screens, texting, tapping, or talking into machines, so a first step is ensuring there are unplugged times when your family can focus on one another and not devices.

- **Take a digital reality check.** Periodically check your home cell phone records, emails, texts, tweet logs, and television, video game, tablet, and computer use. How much time is your family currently plugged in on a typical day? Is a digital "realignment" needed in your home that would allow more face-to-face connection? If so, plan it!

- **Set unplugged times.** A study by the Kaiser Family Foundation found that kids use *less* digital media in homes with firm digital rules.[33] Identify your home's sacred family times (like family meals) and places (family room), and set clear media limits for *all* family members.

- **Check your digital habits.** Placing parameters on *your* plugged-in time lets kids know that they are your priority. So fight the habit of constant phone checks. Turn on alarm features for important calls, do routine hourly checks, and make a rule: "When kids talk, my cell is off!"

- **Eat together!** Studies show that the simple act of having a relaxed family meal together several times a week—with no digital devices—can positively affect kids' social and emotional development as well as academic performance. At least one night a week, have a dinner chat that includes discussing each member's feelings during the day. A basket of emotion cards can be pulled to designate the topic. Pick a feeling—such as "proud"—and ask, "What was the proudest moment you had this week?" Everyone takes turns sharing his or her experience, starting with the opener: "I felt proud this week when . . ." Some families vote as to who had the most interesting (unusual, frustrating, exciting, different) experience. You can also turn the strategy into a fun bedtime routine or use it in the car where kids *are* locked in with you.

- **Share feelings in unplugged times.** A simple way to teach emotional literacy is to describe *how* you feel and *why* to your kids: "I'm so excited! They delivered my computer!" Thomas Lickona, author of *Raising Good Children*, started a car-ride tradition with his sons. The radio and digital gadgets were turned off, and each child was required to ask Dad how *his* day went. "It took a few times," Lickona said, "but pretty soon we were all sharing our feelings about our day." Find a time when your family can share their feelings.

AGE-BY-AGE STRATEGIES

There are dozens of ways to help children learn emotional literacy, but a favorite is from Dan Been, a math teacher in Palm Springs, California. His middle school was using strategies to boost peer sensitivity, but Been figured students should tune in to his mood as well. So he cut red, yellow, and green paper circles and taped the color signifying his mood to his class door each day.

Most days a green ("Good day") circle appeared, and the kids wouldn't say a thing. On the few days a yellow ("Caution!") sign went up, students would ask, "You okay, Mr. Been?"

And the only time a red circle appeared, his students showed concern. Been's mother was ill, and he wanted students to know that he was having a tough time. "The kids didn't know about my mom, but they sure tuned in closer to see if they could figure out what was up," he said. "I realized how sensitive kids can be and how much they tune in to us— *if* we give permission."

The teacher's colored circle system is one way to help kids understand emotions, but there are others. One mom told me she varied Been's idea by placing colored magnets to represent her moods on the refrigerator— and her kids became surprisingly more sensitive.

Another mom hangs a "Do Not Disturb" sign on her bedroom door to warn kids: "Mom having a bad day!" She said two things happened: her kids became more attuned to her, and *they* borrowed the sign to hang if *they* had a tough day. "We tuned in to each other!" she said, laughing.

Effective ways to help kids "tune in to feelings" are always practical, tailored to their ages and abilities, and meaningful. Find what works for your family!

Symbols designate the recommended age and suitability for activity: L = Little Ones: Toddlers and Preschoolers; S = School-age; T = Tweens and Older; A = All Ages

- **Build a feeling vocabulary.** Expand your children's "feeling vocabulary" gradually so they can recognize and understand an array of emotion terms and use them in context. Here are a few: agreeable, angry, annoyed, anxious, apprehensive, awful, betrayed, bored, brave, calm, capable, caring, cheerful, comfortable, confident, confused, content, cooperative, creative, cruel, curious, depressed, disappointed, disgusted, distracted, ecstatic, embarrassed, enjoying, enraged, excited, fantastic, fearful, fed up, free, friendly, frustrated, generous, gentle, gloomy, guilty, happy, hurt, ignored, impatient, insecure, interested, jealous, joyful, lonely, lost, loving, overwhelmed, panicked, peaceful, pensive, pleasant, proud, relaxed, relieved, sad, safe, satisfied, scared, sensitive, serious, shy, stressed, tense, thrilled, troubled, unafraid, uncomfortable, worried. **A**

- **Decode nonverbal cues.** Incorrectly interpreting nonverbal messages can cause serious misunderstandings. (Beware: tweens and young teens are especially prone to "misreading" emotion cues.) So point out misconceptions by naming your correct emotional state: "I know you think I'm mad, but I'm really tired." Then give clues about how body posture sends nonverbal emotion messages: "My slumped shoulders tell I'm stressed." Or, "I'm frustrated, not angry. I grind my teeth when I'm angry." **A**

- **Watch silent pictures.** Turn off the television sound for a few minutes and try guessing together how the actors feel based on their body language. Nail biting and hair twirling can mean "She's tense!" A clenched jaw could signify "He's scared!" Rolling eyes and facing away from the speaker might mean "She's not interested." Nodding and leaning in mean "She's interested!" **A**

- **Use baby books.** Drag out your photo albums and flip together to your family's baby pictures. Draw your child's attention to emotional states of the baby in the photo. "How do you think you feel here?" "What tells you so?" "What would your brother like to say in this shot?" Some parents make mini albums of their child's baby photos and slip emotion words into the plastic sleeves as their child correctly identifies the feeling. **L, S**

- **Be "feeling detectives."** Help your child associate facial expressions and body language with certain emotions by watching other people's faces and body language at the shopping mall, grocery store, park, or playground. Then try together to guess their emotional state without hearing the conversation: "How does her body look now? How do you think she feels?" "Listen to the boy's voice. How do you think he feels?" "Look how that girl has her fists so tight. See the scowl on her face? What do you think she's saying to the other girl?" **L, S**

- **Use more emotion words—especially with boys**. Our girls hear many more emotion words than boys do, so switch up your vocabulary. Talk about emotions more with your sons and give them permission to show and convey their feelings. One hint: boys are more likely to open up while doing something, so sit down *with* your son and play a game, build Legos, exercise, and talk back and forth about feelings. (Do read Rosalind Wiseman's *Masterminds & Wingmen*). **A**

- **Use emotion-charged videos.** Watching the right films can be a fun way to help kids recognize emotions. Pick ones that depict different emotions and then identify characters' feelings and how you and your child feel as viewers. A few favorites: *Inside Out*, *Bambi*, *The Wizard of Oz*, *The Lion King*, *Sleeping Beauty*, the Harry Potter movies, and *Despicable Me*. **A**

- **Make feeling flash cards and play charades.** Write the names of a few emotion words on index cards. For very young children, include only the six basic emotions: happy, sad, angry, afraid, surprised, and disgusted.[34] For older kids, slowly expand the word repertoire. Then cut and glue pictures from magazines or computer programs to depict each emotion onto a corresponding card. Show the picture while covering the word and ask your child to guess the feeling or discuss a time he experienced the feeling or to use the cards to play Feeling Charades. Each contestant pulls a card and acts it out using only his face and body with no sounds or words allowed. The aim is to guess the person's emotion and have fun. **A**

- **Read books about feelings.** Find a book about feelings, and as you read with your child pair the character's face with the appropriate emotion. Suppose you're reading *Llama Llama Red Pajama*, and you come to where Baby Llama's expression depicts his fear that Mama Llama's not there. It's a perfect spot to tune in to feeling. Ask: "How does Baby Llama's face look? Why is he afraid? Make your face look afraid like Baby Llama's. Have you ever been afraid like that?" My other book favorites are: *Glad Monster, Sad Monster: A Book About Feelings*, by Ed Emberley and Anne Miranda; *Feelings*, by Aliki; *I'm Mad*, by Elizabeth Crary; *The Way I Feel*, by Janan Cain; and *My Many Colored Days*, by Dr. Seuss. **L, S**

- **Create a "How do you feel?" card.** Rachel Simmons, author of *Odd Girl Out*, finds many adolescent girls (and, I'm sure, boys) have trouble expressing feelings to peers. Simmons's solution in her Girls Leadership Institute is giving each girl a "How Do You Feel?" card that depicts twenty faces of different emotions (like confused, panicked, anxious, betrayed, guilty, used, insecure, jealous). Each girl points to the face that depicts her feeling, and Simmons says it helps both girls "open up" and begin reconciliation. Check online for cards of "feeling faces" to print out, or have your child cut faces from magazines and glue onto cards. It also may be handy to ease a tiff or open communication with a family member. **S, T**

THE TOP FIVE THINGS TO KNOW
ABOUT TUNING IN TO FEELINGS

1. Face-to-face contact is the best way kids learn to read emotions and develop empathy.

2. Kids use digital devices at least seven and a half hours a day, which robs them of not only connecting with their family but also of developing crucial empathy habits.

3. Real, meaningful, emotion-charged, up-close-and-personal experiences work best to help kids understand feelings.

4. Kids need an emotion vocabulary to discuss emotion, and guidance for using it, to become emotionally literate.

5. Parents discuss, explain, and encourage daughters to share feelings far more than they do their sons.

ONE LAST THING

Science confirms that babies are born to be social and are hardwired to care, but there is no guarantee. The habit and skills of emotional literacy must be nurtured. Teaching children an emotion vocabulary, talking about emotions, sharing their feelings, and tuning in to others are vital for raising empathetic UnSelfies. Tuning in to feeling is what sensitizes kids to *other* people's feelings and helps them take on *another* person's perspective. The Empathy Advantage of teaching this habit is huge: kids who are adept at recognizing, understanding, and expressing their emotions are healthier, more resilient, and more popular; they do better in school; and they are more apt to help others.[35]

There are no shortcuts: deep "feeling" connection is achieved by applying timeless, unplugged parenting strategies of quality face-to-face communication with our kids. The more children connect one-on-one and the less they tap, swipe, and "friend," the greater the odds that their empathy will blossom. But it all starts with tuning in to another human being.

CHAPTER 2

Empathetic Children Have a Moral Identity

Developing an Ethical Code

The postwar 1950s was a time when kids played carefree, toys were unplugged, and they still had "childhoods." It was during that *Happy Days* era that a young boy named Chesley grew up outside Denison, Texas. His growing up even fit the *Happy Days* image: weekends spent camping, hiking, fishing, and seeing an occasional movie at the one theater in town.

Values were a staple in Chesley's home. He was respectful because his parents taught him to be deferential to his elders. They also instilled in him a strong sense of social responsibility and work ethic that remained through life. Chores were an expected part of growing up, as was getting up at seven on weekends to help his father. Chesley and his sister said that watching their father is how they learned that "anything is possible": from their mom they acquired a commitment to service.

Dinners were often served on trays so the family could watch NBC's *Huntley-Brinkley Report*. On a March 1964 evening, that is how they heard about a young woman named Kitty Genovese who was stabbed to death in front of her New York apartment. Police said that thirty-eight witnesses heard her cries for help or watched the vicious assault, but none helped, allegedly because they "didn't want to be involved."

Her neighbors' apathy had a big effect on the boy:[1] he couldn't get

the thought that "no one helped her" from his mind. It countered everything he believed and violated his sense of self. So that day he made a
pledge: "If I was ever in a situation where someone such as Kitty Genovese needed help, I would choose to act," he recalled. "I would do whatever I could. No one would be abandoned."[2]

The thirteen-year-old didn't put anything in writing. His pledge was
more of a commitment that he made to himself to live a certain way: to
care about others and never stand by.[3] Though many experiences and
people helped shape his identity, that simple promise defined his moral
identity, and remained with him as he grew up, went away to college,
began a career, and started a family. But it wasn't until forty-five years
later that the pledge would have monumental significance.

On January 15, 2009, the Texas boy's childhood dream came true:
he was now a pilot. His US Airways plane had just taken off from New
York's LaGuardia Airport when his aircraft struck a flock of geese causing the loss of both engines. His only option for a safe landing was the
Hudson River, and that's where Captain Chesley "Sully" Sullenberger,
the boy from Denison, miraculously landed his disabled plane and
saved the lives of all 155 passengers and crew.

The crash of Flight 1549 was called the "Miracle on the Hudson"
and considered one of the most remarkable emergency landings in avi-
ation history. The man who once pledged never to be a bystander was
instantly hailed a hero. And, true to his vow, Captain Sullenberger was
the last to leave his aircraft, walking twice up and down the aisle of the
disabled plane to make sure that no one was left behind. It was his way
of staying true to the pledge he made as a boy that "no one in danger
would be abandoned."

It was a remarkable tale of valor, but the integrity, courage, and compassion that Captain Sullenberger demonstrated that January day he
believes developed years before. "Both in the air and on the ground, I
was shaped by many powerful lessons and experiences—and many people," Sullenberger said later. "It's as if those moments from my life were
deposited in a bank until I needed them."[4]

LEARNING TO DEVELOP A MORAL IDENTITY

Depositing prosocial images in our children's identity banks so they can define themselves as caring, responsible people who value other people's thoughts and feelings is the basis of moral identity. If a child can imagine himself as a caring person, he is more likely to care. And if a boy from Texas can imagine himself as being responsible for helping others, he is more likely to be the last to walk a plane's aisle to ensure that no one is left behind. It's all why moral identity is such a crucial piece for raising empathetic children.

"You're such a smart boy!" "What talent!" "I'm so proud of your grades!" Of course, we're proud of our children's successes, but in trying to make them feel good, we tend to focus on their cognitive, social, and physical feats. Overlooked are their moral accomplishments like compassion, generosity, thoughtfulness, and concern for others. We even admit it: a whopping 93 percent of adults feel we are failing to instill values in children.[5] What's more, "being kind and caring" isn't even high on kids' priority lists! Two-thirds of adolescents ranked their own personal happiness as more important than their goodness.[6]

But those prosocial descriptions form our kids' sense of self. We generally behave in ways consistent with our self-image, so if we want our kids to be empathetic, they must see themselves as caring and learn to value the thoughts and feelings of others.[7] It's why we must help our kids also recognize and value their moral strengths and caring assets. A moral identity shapes our children's character and the people they become, and is a significant piece to raising empathetic children and helping them thrive.

WHY IS DEVELOPING A MORAL
IDENTITY SO DIFFICULT?

Every culture has a unique set of values and priorities that shape our children's identities. Captain Sullenberger was raised in the 1950s when a strong social responsibility and helping others were part and parcel. Today, character has taken a backseat, and benchmarks of "success" have dramatically switched. Our current idols: celebrities; our goals: wealth and fame; our priorities: ourselves; and our motto: "Just do it." And that marked cultural shift in values and priorities makes it harder for today's youth to honor the perspectives and feelings of others to form strong moral identities. Here are just a few modern-day challenges.

Narcissism Is an Epidemic in the Western World

The rise in narcissism has been growing steadily in the past few decades, with rates higher in Western than in non-Western countries. That also suggests that narcissism levels have been steadily increasing among Western youth over the past few decades.[8] The Gallup Organization compared responses to a lengthy poll of more than 11,000 young teens. Out of more than 400 items, the one showing the largest change in four decades is "I am an important person." By the late 1980s, more than 80 percent considered themselves "very important"; in the 1950s, only 12 percent of teens said they agreed with the statement.[9] The median narcissism score has also increased 30 percent in the last two decades. The biggest increases are in the number of people concurring with the comments "I like to look at my body" and "I am an extraordinary person."[10]

What's more, narcissism is *still* increasing, and that's troubling news for helping children develop solid moral identities. Kids who feel "entitled" focus on *their* needs and feelings, direct *their* perspective on *their* experiences, and see the world through *their* eyes. Left out of their picture is anyone else, and there go the opportunities to learn to value others.[11]

Parents (and Others) Dish Out Overexuberant Praise

Multiple factors can keep kids locked in "self mode," but receiving steady doses of overexuberant praise is one of the biggest culprits. These days every kid's finger-paint scribble is flaunted on our refrigerator; their trophies, ribbons, and certificates grace our mantels; and "I'm a Proud Parent of an Honor Roll Student" stickers are glued to our car bumpers. While there's nothing wrong with giving kids a pat on the back for a job well done, modern-day esteem building has risen to new heights and is endangering our children's capacity to care.

A recent Ohio State University study surveyed parents and their kids during four periods over one and a half years to identify how narcissism develops over time. The results were clear: parents who "overvalued" their children when the study began ended up with children who scored higher on tests of narcissism later. Overvalued kids were described by their parents as "more special than other children" and as kids who "deserve something extra in life." If you ever wondered whether your parenting matters, this study should put your doubts at rest. "Children believe it when their parents tell them that they are more special than others," explained Brad Bushman, one of the researchers. "That may not be good for them or for society."[12] Nor is it good for developing moral identity or empathy.

The Self-Esteem Bandwagon Goes to School, College, and the Workplace

A major switch in how we parent also trickles down to the general culture. That's why many schools are joining the "self-esteem bandwagon"—even eliminating red pencils so that teachers' red checkmarks won't derail students' self-esteem.[13] Paper Mate, the nation's major supplier of pens, stepped up their production of purple pens (a shade considered more soothing and less judgmental) to do their part in creating "a kinder, gentler education system."[14]

Coaches and the sports industry are also jumping on board. The local chapter of one national sports association spends roughly 12 percent of its yearly budget on trophies just to make sure that every kid feels special and receives a prize—even if it's just for "showing up."[15]

Overinflating kids' egos poses problems: First, the more kids hear those accolades, the more they need them. And second, kids who feel "entitled" believe the world owes them special treatment. Forget the other guy, life is all about "ME," and those "Me-first" Selfie beliefs endure. That's what's happening as our most-praised generation takes their "I am special" feelings to college and the workplace.

College professors complain that students feel they deserve special treatment, and surveys support their view. Two-thirds of students believe professors should give their grades special consideration if they explain they were "trying hard"; one-third feel they deserve at least a B for coming to class; one-third feel their final exams should be rescheduled if they hamper their vacation plans.[16]

Wall Street executives are shaking their heads as new young hires continue expecting praise.[17] Fortune 500 companies are even hiring "praise consultants" to teach managers how to compliment young employees.

It's natural for parents to want to help their kids feel good, but what we may be missing is also helping them care about *others.* Turning to science shows us how to use praise that instills in our children a strong identity and produces empathetic, caring, and altruistic kids. What's more, those findings come from a most remarkable source: people who refuse to be bystanders.

WHAT SCIENCE SAYS: HOW WE CAN CREATE A MORAL IDENTITY

For three decades, I've researched the best ways to nurture empathy. I've interviewed dozens of leading experts and combed thousands of articles, but it was while studying genocide and the darkest side of human nature that I found not only an answer, but also hope. Each genocide site I visited—Auschwitz, Rwanda, Armenia, Dachau, and Cambodia's Killing Fields—chronicled unimaginable horrors, but each one also described people who exemplify the best in humanity: "altruistic rescuers" who refused to stand by. Social scientists have interviewed hundreds of these ordinary citizens to find their motivations, and they discovered that most shared a deep belief in humanity. They cared about the feelings and thoughts of others. "I *had* to help," one rescuer explained. "It is who I am," said another. Even more intriguing was how most credited their parents for instilling those beliefs that formed their strong moral identities.

The potential for altruism exists and can be nurtured in our children. If we want empathetic children, we must help them define themselves as people who care about and value others, and we must instill those beliefs during childhood.

Parents Instill a Moral Identity in Their Children

Nazis killed Samuel Oliner's family, but a Polish peasant woman named Balwina saved him. Sam Oliner and Pearl Oliner, his wife, spent three decades interviewing more than 1,500 non-rescuers and rescuers from Nazi-occupied Europe to determine why some, like Balwina, put themselves at great personal risk without external rewards. It is one of the most extensive studies of people who rescued Jews during the Holocaust and why some people care so deeply. Their results, published in *The Altruistic Personality*, offer insight as to how significant parents can be in raising children with moral identities.[18]

The Oliners found several distinctions in rescuers, but three are especially important. First, most rescuers were deeply empathetic: they simply could not stand by and watch others suffer. Many also had a strong sense of self-efficacy and believed they could make a difference and help others.[19] And the majority had internalized a strong identity based on caring values and an ethic of social responsibility that they learned from their parents.[20] In fact, when asked which values their parents taught them, 44 percent cited "caring or generosity." In contrast, non-rescuers were far more centered on their own needs or felt obliged to help only a small circle of others.[21] Their parents were more likely to stress monetary values ("Be thrifty," "Get a good job") than caring, moral concerns.

Altruists Feel an Obligation to Others

University of California professor Kristen Monroe also conducted in-depth interviews of altruists, including philanthropists, rescuers of Jews during the Holocaust, and Carnegie Medal recipients who performed exceptional heroism. Then Monroe did a psychological analysis to determine what motivated their heroic behavior. Foremost in her findings: altruists simply have a different way of seeing the world. "Where the rest of us see a stranger, altruists see a fellow human being," Monroe wrote in her book *The Heart of Altruism*.[22]

Monroe believes that a strong identity based on caring not only influences our behavior, but is also a critical component for altruism. And she is convinced that the potential for altruism exists in all people. But whether we act on our concerns rests largely in how we view ourselves in relation to others.[23] Because altruists' self-perceptions are based on much stronger obligation to others, it leaves them no choice but to help. Even so, those guiding beliefs don't happen by chance: their moral identities must be developed.

Their Values Are an Extension of Themselves

Developmental psychologists Anne Colby and William Damon pondered another altruism conundrum: how caring commitment forms. The eminent researchers identified twenty-three "moral exemplars," or highly dedicated Americans with a long-standing commitment to moral purposes who have struggled to make the world better.[24] Drawing on in-depth interviews and biographical accounts, Colby and Damon traced their extraordinary lives from childhood, and wrote about their discoveries in *Some Do Care: Contemporary Lives of Moral Commitment*.

One finding has a familiar ring: all the exemplars had a strong moral identity based on a sense of responsibility for their fellow human beings.[25] Their caring values were so deep that they became an extension of themselves. In fact, Damon and Colby believe that a key reason for the exemplars' unwavering dedication to caring lies in that close connection between their identity and their beliefs in goodness. "The exemplar's moral identities become tightly integrated, almost fused, with their self-identities," explain the researchers.[26] As one exemplar explained: "It's hard for me to separate who I am from what I want to do and what I am doing." And the formation of their moral identities usually began in childhood.

Altruists Think of Themselves as "Someone Who Cares"

Sam and Pearl Oliner, Kristen Monroe, William Damon, and Anne Colby, as well as a growing number of social psychologists, believe that an "altruistic disposition" exists and can be nurtured from early in life.[27] While no guarantee, when a child believes "I am a kid who cares," he is more likely to reach out and help others. But keeping self-centered attitudes from clouding the identities of our most-praised generation could be a challenge, especially when parents continue to pour on those accolades.

HOW TO STRENGTHEN CHILDREN'S MORALITY

The parents of four young children in Santa Maria, California, sent a plea to the *Dr. Phil* show. Their four kids were defiant, the three-year-old was in constant meltdown, and the parents wanted help. So Dr. Phil sent me with a film crew on a house call. I was drained within minutes of walking into the home. The parents' negative comments were relentless, especially to three-year-old Trinity. Craving notice from her mom and dad, the little girl was acting up, using attention-getting behaviors, and continuously in time-out. Trinity was suffering. I spent the day offering positive behavior alternatives and ways to cut parental negativity.

A review of the crew's taping showed one scene that was chilling. There was Trinity lying in her bed repeating her mother's words to herself over and over and over: "You're a bad girl, Trinity. You're a bad, bad girl." Her parents' words had become Trinity's inner voice: she had internalized their destructive messages and believed them. I've never witnessed such devastating proof that our children become what they hear.

What we say about our children helps define who they are and the type of people they believe themselves to be. Too much praise can make kids *more* self-centered, *more* competitive, and *more* prone to cut others down.[28] Too little encouragement can erode self-esteem. But the right words can help children see themselves as kind, considerate, caring people and want to act in a way that supports that image. In fact, using positive labels such as "You're the kind of person who likes to help" can lead kids to see themselves as helpers and be more likely to lend a hand.[29] Positive labels also help children deposit those images to use in forming their moral identities. Try these five proven strategies:

1. **Take a reality check.** Notice how your child responds to your encouragement, and then watch for signs that you may be *over*-praising.

   - *Self-centered and forgets other people's contributions:* "I did great!"

   - *Dependent on praise and needs constant approval:* "Do you like it, Mommy?"

   - *Expects or demands accolades:* "Aren't you going to tell me, 'Good job'?"

   - *Tears others down to feel better about himself:* "But I'm better!"

   If you notice repeated signs of entitlement, it may be time to switch *your* style.

2. **Align praise with character.** In one ingenious experiment, children gave away some of their game winnings after watching a model do so. And those children who were told that they made the donation "because you're the kind of person who likes to help other people" were far more generous in the future than

those told that they contributed because they were "expected to do so."[30] So help your child see himself as a "good person" by pointing out how his behavior "matches" his identity: "Randy, you're the kind of person who always lends a hand to help." "You're my 'caring girl': you always make people feel good." "Sally, you're always so thoughtful—you're a considerate person." Just make sure the praise is deserved.

3. **Use nouns, not verbs.** Adam Grant described two experiments in his must-read *Give and Take: Why Helping Others Drives Our Success*, carried out with three- to six-year-olds to see if a subtle change in grammar could make a difference in children's behavior. In one, *helping* was referred to with a verb ("Some children choose to *help*"). In the other, *helping* was referred to as a noun ("Some children choose to *be helpers*"). Kids invited to "be helpers" were far more likely to help than kids who heard the verb wording "to help." It turns out that even a simple grammatical switch in our messages can affect our children's behavior. Researchers surmise that "using the noun 'helper' may mean that helping means something positive about one's identity, and that image may motivate children to help more."[31] So if you want your child to see himself as a caring person, use nouns!

4. **Focus on character, not behavior.** A study with seven- to ten-year-olds found that praising children's characters rather than their behaviors helped them internalize altruism as part of their identities.[32] The character-praised kids were also more likely to be more generous than those children who were told that they had donated because they were expected to do so. The takeaway here: use labels that stress your child's character, not her behavior. Here's the difference in wording:

- *Character-focused praise:* "You're the kind of person who likes to help other people." Or "You are a considerate and helpful person."

- *Behavior-focused praise:* "It was nice that you sent some of your pencils to the orphans." Or "Sharing your toys was a considerate thing to do."

5. **Model it!** In this experiment, 140 school-age children received tokens for winning a game and then were told they could either keep or donate their winnings to children in poverty.[33] But before deciding, the students watched their teacher decide what she would do with her tokens. When the adult told students to donate the tokens but kept them herself, the children were less likely to be generous. When she lectured the kids on the value of giving and then donated her tokens, children were generous at first, but there was little impact on their future generosity. But when she cut the lecture and simply donated all her tokens (as they watched), the children donated their own tokens and were generous in later opportunities. Remember to model the behaviors you want your child to adopt.

EMPATHY BUILDER: HOW TO REFUSE TEMPTATIONS AND STICK UP FOR YOUR BELIEFS

Standing up for important principles can be difficult. And peer pressure can make kids doubt themselves and waver from their moral identities. So teach these refusal strategies to help your children stick to their beliefs and buck temptations. The acronym REFUSE helps kids recall the six tactics. Your child should rehearse one skill at a time until it becomes a habit, and then add the next.

- **R = Review who you are.** Ask yourself: "Is this person telling me to do something that isn't safe or kind, goes against our family mantra, rules, and what I stand for? If so, I should REFUSE."

- **E = Express your belief.** Prepare a short comeback line like: "It's not my style," "I promised my dad I wouldn't," or "It's not nice." Or use your parents or teacher as an excuse: "My mom will ground me for life if she finds out."

- **F = F̲irm voice.** State your views using a strong—not yelling—tone to get your point across.

- **U = U̲se strong posture.** Use assertive body language so you can be taken seriously: shoulders back, feet slightly apart, hands by side, head high, look eye to eye.

- **S = S̲ay no and don't give in.** Remember, your job is *not* to try to change the other person's mind, but to stick to *your* beliefs. If you start to waver, say no again and again. Your confidence will boost each time you say it.

- **E = E̲xit.** Sometimes the best option is to leave the scene. (Set up a policy that you will pick your child up with no questions asked in tricky or unsafe situations.)

HOW TO HELP KIDS ADOPT THIS HABIT

Captain "Sully" Sullenberger made a pledge that defined his core beliefs at age thirteen. But the pilot isn't alone in creating a personal mantra or vow to match his beliefs.

John Wooden, the famous UCLA basketball coach, carried a folded paper given to him by his father in the eighth grade listing a seven-point creed for life. It included "Be true to yourself," "Help others," "Count and give thanks for your blessings every day." "I tried to live by this, and I tried to teach by it," Wooden explained.[34] And Wooden carried it with him his entire life.

Abraham Lincoln memorized passages from Shakespeare to fortify his character. His son, Robert, said Lincoln constantly carried a volume of Shakespeare's plays while president.[35] Robert Kennedy found enlightenment in Shakespeare's character Henry V. Dorothy Day, the social activist, turned to passages in Tolstoy or Dostoyevsky.[36]

The right words can strengthen your moral identity and sustain you in difficult times. James Stockdale, one of our greatest military heroes, endured extreme torture during seven years of imprisonment by the Viet Cong, but never wavered from his beliefs. He credits part of his survival from learning the words of Epictetus and Seneca in high school.[37] And our children need words to live by as well.

How to Create a Family Mantra to Boost Kids' Moral Identities

Mantras can help children define who they are and adopt those messages as part of their selfhood. You can use the same premise to help your family define your core principles. That's what bestselling author Bruce Feiler and his wife, Linda Rottenberg, did one Saturday night. They planned a family pajama party (complete with popcorn and s'mores) with their two girls to create their "brand." The foursome took turns writing answers to questions like "What words best describe our family?" and "What is most important to our family?" They jotted their comments such as "We bring people together" and "We help others to fly" and turned them into their family mission statement.

Feiler says that the process "forces you to conceive, construct, and then put in a public place a written ideal of what you want your family to be."[38] It also helps children develop moral identity. (A must-read is Bruce Feiler's *The Secrets of Happy Families*.)

Use these steps to develop your family mantra and instill moral identities in your children.

- **Call a special family meeting.** Make it special: block your schedule, order pizza, turn off digital devices, and have everyone in attendance. The mantra doesn't have to be written in one sitting, so gauge session times based on your kids' attention. Keep it fun!

- **Review meeting rules.** Everyone is listened to. No putdowns allowed. You may disagree, but do so respectfully. Everyone gets a turn. Assign a recorder to jot key ideas to help create your mantra.

- **Discuss who you are as a family.** Explain that this is a chance to talk about your beliefs and the kind of family you want to become. It's also a chance to hear your kids describe how they see themselves and your family. These kinds of questions that Feiler suggests can start your conversation; the answers can determine your mantra.

  ▷ What do we stand for?

  ▷ What kind of family do we want to become?

  ▷ What kind of feeling do we want in our home?

  ▷ What principles do we want to follow?

  ▷ How do you hope people describe us?

  ▷ What do we want to be remembered for?

  ▷ How do we want to give back to others?

  ▷ How can we make our world a better place?

- **Identify your core values.** Brainstorm the values that mean most to your family or you hope to see in your children. The clearer you identify the values you deem most significant, the likelier your kids will adopt them. Those that help instill moral identity include virtues like acceptance, appreciation, charitableness, citizenship, compassion, consideration, cooperation, courage, courtesy, empathy, fairness, generosity, gratitude, helpfulness, integrity, justness, kindness, peacefulness, respect, responsibility, and service.

- **Create a motto that describes your family.** A family mantra is a short phrase that expresses your core values and guiding beliefs. It also helps children to define themselves. Develop a short phrase that best describes your family. A few:

  ▷ "Our family steps in to help."

  ▷ "We treat others the way we want to be treated."

▷ "We are helpful, not hurtful."

▷ "We are kind even if no one's looking."

▷ "Our purpose is to care."

- **Make it memorable.** Kids need to hear the mantra often to internalize it, so find ways to weave it into your daily life. I've heard of many variations. The Galvins hang their mantra on their refrigerator, where it's remained for twenty-five years. The Perlyns do a morning family huddle and recite their pledge. A teen told me that her family said, "We're the caring Feys" so often that the motto "became me. I see myself as a caring person."

- **Create personal mantras for your children.** Now use the same steps to help each child develop a personal mantra such as "I'm a caring person," "I know it's nice to be nice," or "I reach out to help others." The motto can also be a quote from a book, person, or film, just as long as it resonates with your child. Keeping it visual helps kids remember it. Some kids make a poster and tape it to their wall. A tween has his as a screen saver. My girlfriend needlepointed a pillow of her daughter's mantra: it was the first thing she packed for college.

AGE-BY-AGE STRATEGIES

When I first taught, I was working on my doctorate in educational psychology and was fascinated with Lawrence Kohlberg's cognitive theory of moral development. The Harvard psychologist believed that moral growth develops in stages, and that it can be stretched with moral dilemmas. I incorporated Kohlberg's ideas in my lessons, and I was ecstatic when several students responded with higher-level moral reasoning. But my excitement faded when I caught my two best "moral talkers" throwing rocks, one of which hit a neighbor on the head. They also showed little concern for the man, who needed several stitches.

"We didn't know he was inside," one told me. "We aimed for his wall." "It couldn't hurt that bad: it was just a rock," the other said.

I was bewildered: these were the same boys who impressed me with their "moral" replies, so how could they have so little empathy? They also gave textbook answers to my next questions: "How do you think the man feels?" ("Sad.") "How would *you* feel if someone did that to you?" ("Mad.") They may have mastered emotional literacy (the concept we discussed in the previous chapter), but they were stumped when I asked, "How do you feel causing the man such pain? Do you care?" They were dumbstruck. But then came their honest and oh-so-enlightening comment: "I guess we're not caring kind of kids."

That was how I learned that moral reasoning and emotional literacy don't guarantee caring behavior (nor, for that matter, does understanding another's perspective or even feeling with another). To respond empathetically, kids must see themselves as people who care and value others' thoughts and feelings. What each lacked was a moral identity to guide their actions. Missing that crucial piece leaves a huge void in a child's empathy quotient.

Symbols designate the recommended age and suitability for activity: L = Little Ones: Toddlers and Preschoolers; S = School-age; T = Tweens and Older; A = All Ages

- **Share your beliefs.** Parents who raise kids with strong moral identities don't do so by accident. They ensure that their children know what their family stands for. State your values again and again, so your child understands the "why" behind your beliefs. "In our family we don't watch violent movies because we're against violence." "I don't care if your friends use four-letter words. In this family we stand for respect." "We believe in giving back, so please find two gently used toys to give to a needy family." **A**

- **Be a role model.** What you do in those ordinary moments may be powerful images for your child to deposit in his identity bank.

How you treat your family, friends, neighbors, and strangers; what movies you watch; the kinds of books and television shows you choose; how you react to conflicts, your child swearing, his friend's cheating, the neighbor littering: these are decisions kids closely watch. One of the greatest questions to ask yourself each day is "If I were the only example my child had to learn moral identity, what did she learn today?" **A**

- **Hold family debates.** The best place for kids to learn to find their voice is at home. So why not start family debates? Topics can range from family issues such as your rules, allowances, and curfews; to real-world issues such as the welfare system, voting age, or current headlines. Whatever the topic, encourage your kids to speak out so they'll be more comfortable defending their beliefs in public. Debating also helps kids define who they are and strengthens their moral identities. **S, T**

- **Develop your "best possible self."** Laura King, professor at the University of Missouri–Columbia, had study participants write a brief description of their "best possible self" each day and found a dramatic boost in their optimism.[39] Try it with your children at bedtime or dinner: "What did you do today that was your 'best self'? Play the scene in your mind to the part you feel proudest of. Imagine yourself doing something like that again tomorrow." Your child can also keep a diary of his "best self." **A**

- **Make a virtue scrapbook.** Create a scrapbook to help your kids realize their character traits and caring qualities, not just their academic achievements. One mother filled a small album with photos and drawings depicting her child's moral self (his kindness to friends, compassion with animals, sportsmanship on his team). "There's so much competition, I wanted him to see that there's more to life than test scores," she said. "Whenever he has a hard day, he 'reads' about the 'Good Jeffry.'" **A**

- **Write a birthday letter.** A special way to help kids develop moral identities is writing an annual birthday letter. Highlight the year's special moments and also describe your child's caring qualities like her kind spirit, thoughtful nature, giving heart. Enjoy it together and then store it. They're a great twenty-first-birthday present, treasured mementos of your child's emerging identity. A

- **Capture caring moments.** We're quick to snap photos of our kids' academic successes, athletic prowess, or cute looks. But those shutter clicks convey to children that those images bring us the most pride. Make sure to display prominently photos of your kids engaged in kind and thoughtful endeavors so they recognize that "caring matters." Also let your kids overhear (without them thinking they're supposed to) you describing those qualities to others as well. A

- **Teach "Is that me?" tests.** Teach a few conscience tests to help your child stick to her identity in trying times. Tell her to first think about the dilemma ("Should I go along with Klara and not let Carole sit with us?"), ask herself the test question, and then review whether the situation fits who she believes herself to be. (If not, she can use the REFUSE tactics in the previous section.)

  1. *Golden Rule Test:* "Would I want people to do this to me?"

  2. *Who I Am Test:* "Does this go against my beliefs and our family's mantra?"

  3. *Assembly Test:* "Would I do it if the principal announced it at the assembly?"

  4. *Newspaper Test:* "Would I do it if it made front-page headlines?"

  5. *Family Test:* "Does this go against our family mantra and rules?"

6. *Grandma Test:* "Would I do it if my grandma heard about it?"

7. *Helpful or Hurtful Test:* "Is this helpful or hurtful? I only do helpful things."

8. *3Rs Test:* "Could it damage my relationships or reputation, or might I regret it later?" **S, T**

- **Encourage self-talk.** Verbal taunts can make even the most confident kid doubt her beliefs. So teach your child a statement to say inside her head (called "self-talk") to help counter the taunt if someone picks at her identity. A few: "I know who I am, and that isn't me," "I am a good person, and don't deserve this treatment," "This is his problem, not mine." Then practice the line until it becomes internalized. Do help your child realize that the problem rests with the perpetrator, not her. **S, T**

- **Use the "KIND Rule."** Teach your kids the KIND Rule to guide their inner moral compass both online and off. "If in doubt, ask yourself four questions. Is it kind? Is it inspirational? Is it necessary? Is it definite? *If not, don't say, text, or send it.*" Post the rule on your refrigerator and computer! **S, T**

THE TOP FIVE THINGS TO KNOW ABOUT DEVELOPING MORAL IDENTITIES

1. Moral identity can inspire empathy, activate compassion, and motivate caring behavior.

2. To respond empathetically, kids must *value* other people's thoughts and feelings.

3. Overpraising can make kids competitive, tear others down, and diminish empathy.[40]

4. Entitling and "overvaluing" kids may increase narcissism and hamper moral identity.

5. If a child can imagine himself as a caring person, he is more likely to care about others.

ONE LAST THING

Justin was constantly in trouble for bullying. Educators had tried numerous intervention strategies, and the principal wanted to expel him. But his health teacher asked for one more reprieve. "There's no one at home who cares about Justin," Beth Simmons said. "Expelling him will only increase his anger, and we'll lose him forever." The principal agreed to give him one more chance, but with the caveat that Justin would mentor a kindergartener during his sixth-period class under the health teacher's supervision. Her hope was that the service project would help Justin see himself differently and activate his empathy, which she thought had shut down because it never was nurtured.

Simmons met Justin each day for a few weeks to help him create a simple "reading" lesson for five-year-old Noah and role-played ways he could encourage the child. Then following each session, she'd debrief Justin as to how the session had gone and what he learned about Noah. The teacher said she didn't know if the approach would work, but she felt that Justin never had the opportunity to see himself as a person who *could* care. Deep down, she saw a caring heart that Justin couldn't imagine.

Then one day the magic happened: the kindergarten teacher noticed that Justin was showing that he cared about Noah: he began to smile when Noah looked happy, to listen when the child talked, and to encourage him when he tried. A relationship between a young boy and his "big friend" had opened. His teachers also saw the change and commented that Justin wasn't so withdrawn and that his behavior was improving. For perhaps the first time, the teen was seeing himself as a caring person, and his empathy was opening.

Noah also saw the change and told his teacher as much. "Justin's a good guy. It just took him a while to figure it out," Noah said. And then added wise advice: "You can't give up on kids, ya know. Sometimes it takes them a while to come around."

William Damon, author of *The Moral Child*, tells us that forming a moral identity is a lifetime journey that evolves from a variety of sources such as receiving feedback, observing others that either inspire or appall, reflecting on our experience, and responding to cultural influences such as family, school, religious institutions, and the mass media."[41] But at the helm must be parents who inspire their children to see themselves as good people. Whether the culture is *Happy Days* or *Modern Family*, one thing has not changed: parents must help their children view themselves as people who care. Instilling this second crucial habit is one more way to give kids the Empathy Advantage.

CHAPTER 3

Empathetic Children Understand the Needs of Others

Instilling Perspective Taking and Learning to Walk in Another's Shoes

It was April 1968, and Martin Luther King Jr. was the third-grade's class "Hero of the Month" in Riceville, Iowa. So when King was murdered in Memphis that same month, the students wanted to know why their hero was killed. They had never experienced racism, living in an all-white community. Their teacher, Jane Elliott, felt there had to be a better way to help her students understand what discrimination felt like than merely talking about it, and by morning she decided to conduct a most unique lesson.[1]

"I don't think we really know what it would be like to be a black child unless we actually experienced discrimination ourselves," she told students. "Well, would you like to find out?" And the class agreed.

The teacher divided her twenty-eight students into two groups: those with blue or green eyes and those with brown. Then she declared all brown-eyed students to be "superior" and entitled to preferential treatment: extended recess, early lunch dismissal, choice of lunch-line partners, second food helpings, and being line leaders. Blue- or green-eyed students' class rights were withdrawn including drinking from the water fountain, taking second lunch helpings, playing on the big playground, and using recess equipment.

The difference in the students was quickly evident: brown-eyed children were happier, more alert, and doing far better work than previously. And the blue- and green-eyed kids were miserable: their posture, expressions, and attitudes took on the inferior role, and their class work regressed.

On Monday, the teacher reversed their roles. "The truth is that blue-eyed people are better and smarter than brown-eyed people," Elliott told students. Once again, the role-taking exercise began, and again the children's behavior transformed.

On Tuesday, when the experiment was over, the teacher asked children to describe their experiences and was surprised how deeply they were affected: "I felt dirty," "I felt like I was tied up," "I felt like crying," "I felt left out." Several parents also noticed a change.

"What have you done with my son?" one mother asked. "He's a different boy at home. He even treats his little brother and sister kinder."[2]

Elliott also saw the difference. The once-belligerent boy had become a more thoughtful, pleasant child almost overnight. In fact, the teacher noted that all her students seemed to be more caring.[3]

The exercise was so successful that the teacher repeated Discrimination Day with succeeding classes. But it wasn't until fourteen years later that she realized the exercise's true impact. Eleven of her former third graders returned for a class reunion and for the first time told their teacher how the experience had changed their lives.[4]

"It's something we're going to carry with us, in our minds, in our feelings," one said. "We're more open-minded," said another.

"Our children won't learn to be prejudiced from us."[5]

The experience had changed even the way they were raising their own children.

While academicians debate the controversial lesson's merits, Elliott's now-adult students may have the final word. Almost four decades after the exercise, a reporter tracked down fifty of Elliott's students and published their recollections in *Smithsonian* magazine. "Everyone who took part in it seemed to recall the exercise as though it had happened yesterday," the reporter wrote. The former third graders' verdicts are hard to dismiss.[6]

"You cannot underestimate the impact that such an experience has had on us."

"I don't know how anyone who went through the experience can say that they have not been changed."

"When I see someone being treated differently than someone else, I remember what it felt like the day the brown-eyed people were [discriminated against]."

The teacher's role-taking exercise was not only memorable, it also altered her students' perspectives. It's a rare lesson that has such power.

Watching, helping, doing: children's empathy is sparked by active, face-to-face experiences—not from worksheets or lectures. It's why Jane Elliott's exercise was so unforgettable and is still in the minds and hearts of her students forty years later. When trying to enhance children's perspective-taking skills we should look for real, meaningful activities that tug their heartstrings and help them imagine what someone else might be thinking or feeling. The reason for our efforts is lofty and noble: it's all about helping our kids become good people. Jane Elliott's description of her former students is the brass ring for parenting: "They have turned into the kind of people I would have wanted them to be."[7]

LEARNING TO WALK IN ANOTHER'S SHOES

Perspective taking is the ability to understand another person's thoughts, feelings, wants, and needs. I like to call this essential habit the "gateway to empathy," because it helps us step into another's shoes, feel what another human being is feeling, and understand the world from his or her point of view. Mastering perspective taking is an important part of instilling a deep, caring connection with others. It's also a habit that children need for every part of life—from handling playground disputes today to mastering boardroom debates tomorrow.

When children can grasp another's perspective, they are more likely to be empathetic, handle conflicts peacefully, be less judgmental, value differences, speak up for those who are victimized, and act in ways that are more helpful, comforting, and supportive of others. Studies also show that kids who understand others' points of view acquire the Empathy Advantage: they are better adjusted,[8] more popular,[9] and even have healthier peer relationships. And perspective taking pulls kids out from "Me" absorption, since it turns their vision toward *other* people's concerns. It's a powerful Selfie antidote.

And here's good news: As with all the other aspects of empathy, perspective taking can be taught to kids as young as toddlers and reinforced to kids from middle school and high school—and beyond. New research shows that by "simply putting ourselves in another person's shoes," we can significantly reduce our unconscious biases—and markedly improve our real-life interactions with people who look different from us.[10] Developing perspective taking can help reduce racism and bullying as well as make our children's world more caring and humane. How do we develop this habit in our kids? Read on.

WHY IS TEACHING PERSPECTIVE TAKING SO HARD?

So it's clear from the research that the best way to teach kids about perspective taking is to find ways for them to step out of their own shoes and experience the "other" side. There are dozens of ways to do so—Jane Elliott's classroom exercise was a particularly memorable one. But there are many other ways to help children learn perspective taking in teachable moments throughout the day.

- *Do it over.* "Joshua, your words made your brother feel sad. Try that again, but say your words in a way to make Tim happy."

- *Role-play from the other side.* "Let's stop and do this again, but this time think how Kevin feels not being invited to play. I'll pretend to be you. 'Kevin, you can't play with us.' Now you be Kevin and act how he feels and thinks being left out."

- *Freeze and think.* "Stop and don't go further. Take a look at Dad's face and ask yourself how you'd feel if your daughter just spoke that way. What do you need to say to Dad?"

The trick is to look for those discipline moments when we can help our children grasp how their actions affect others so it stretches their empathy and one day they can act right without our guidance.

But one of the big conundrums parents and educators face is that we must model empathy to our children while simultaneously setting limits and, yes, disciplining them when they step out of line. Discipline is a very personal issue for families, and I'm not here to tell you what's right or wrong. But if we're telling our kids not to hit another child one minute, and then turning around and spanking that same child the next minute for an infraction, how does a child make sense of that? How do *we* make sense of that?

When it comes to disciplining our kids, the first thing to know is that American parents do it frequently. We discipline our two- to ten-year-olds about every six to nine minutes on average—or roughly fifty encounters each day. That adds up to more than 15,000 discipline inter-actions a year![11] How many of these involve one kid not considering another's feelings? If that's the case, we're missing a lot of empathy-stretching opportunities. Here are our typical discipline approaches, and how they may actually hinder kids from empathy and specifically from learning this critical habit of perspective taking.

Spanking. Ninety-four percent of US parents admit to spanking their kids by the time they reach age four, and that's troubling news for empathy.[12] Tulane University researchers tracked 2,500 youngsters and found that those spanked frequently at age three were much more likely to be aggressive by age five.[13] Of course, other factors weigh in (like how the punishment is delivered and by whom), but it's hard denying that six decades of research link spanking to ten negative child outcomes, including aggression, antisocial behavior, mental health problems, diminished moral development, and decreased empathy.[14]

Yelling. Many parents are realizing the detriments of spanking, but lack another effective discipline response. So when misbehavior continues, parent frustration builds and we yell.[15] We don't feel good doing it (two-thirds of parents named "yelling" at their kids as their biggest guilt inducer).[16] But at a loss for a discipline alternative, "yelling" has become the modern-day spanking. Certainly, shouting can cause kids' emotional distress, but *what* we shout also is harmful. Brain imagery confirms that "spanking with words" by shaming, disdaining, or ridiculing could in fact damage children's brain connections.[17]

Continuing to rely on yelling endangers empathy on three counts:

1. **Yelling damages the parent-child relationship.** The seeds for empathy are planted in our relationship with our child. Research shows that empathetic individuals tend to have closer, warmer, and more supportive relationships with their parents.

2. **Shame is a proven empathy killer.** Shame is far more painful and less productive to learning to care than making kids feel guilty or embarrassed about their wrongdoing. Shame degrades kids, makes them feel inferior and personally distressed, and heightens their preoccupation with other's evaluations ("Mom thinks I'm a bad person"). Studies show that shame-based discipline also makes kids *less* likely to feel for those they may have wronged.[18]

3. **Yelling creates a poor model.** No contest here: screaming parents make horrific examples for kids to copy. And the research is clear: parents who raise empathetic kids model caring behavior with their children and with those outside the family. They also strongly emphasize kindness and expect their kids to apply the value to all people.[19]

Time-Out. Another discipline tactic is removing a child from an activity to sit alone. "Decades of research in attachment demonstrate that particularly in times of distress, we need to be near and be soothed by the people who care for us,"[20] says Daniel Siegel from the UCLA School of Medicine. But when children lose emotional control, parents often put them in their room alone to calm down and try to figure out what they did wrong. Experts worry that time-out does not help children learn acceptable behavior or consider the feelings of those they hurt. What's more, brain scans show that relational pain caused by rejection or isolation is similar to brain images of kids suffering from physical pain or abuse.

Rewarding. "If you're nice, you get a treat!" "Another star on your chart and you earn a toy!" "Good behavior charts" and enticing their kids "to be good" with toys, candy, or money is another common discipline practice. But Alfie Kohn, author of *Punished by Rewards*, cites more than seventy studies that show that the approach can backfire—especially for empathy—because kids can start believing that getting the reward is the reason to be kind. What's more, kids are *less* likely "to act prosocially once the extrinsic reward for acting that way is withdrawn."[21] So the hook loses its lure to help kids want to care, and the chance to "step into another's shoes" is lost.

Of course, I'm far from implying that kids should get away with inappropriate behavior. A child needs to understand what's acceptable and what's not, and a parent or teacher must have tools to communicate those expectations. So that leaves us with a dilemma: "What is the best response to stop misbehavior and help kids realize that their actions affect others?" Luckily, science has an answer.

WHAT SCIENCE SAYS: HOW TO SET LIMITS

"My toddler bites kids. Is he too young to be punished?"

"How do I stop our daughter from picking on her little brother?"

"The school says our son bullies kids on the bus. How should we punish him?"

There's so much conflicting advice on discipline, it's natural for parents to be confused. That's why we should turn to science for solutions.

For more than four decades, the New York University psychology professor Martin Hoffman has investigated children's empathy, specifically as it relates to discipline and limit setting. Hoffman found that parents who consistently react to their children's misbehavior by highlighting the distress of the one harmed and who help them understand the impact of their actions tend to have more empathic children.[22] He calls the discipline approach "induction," and many studies verify its effectiveness in not only improving behavior but also enhancing perspective taking, encouraging kids to lend a hand, and building their empathy muscles.

Toddlers Care What Other Toddlers Think

For more than three decades, Carolyn Zahn-Waxler and Marian Radke-Yarrow have been studying empathy, and they found that focusing the child's attention on the effect of their behavior on another person (or "induction") is surprisingly effective, even with very young children. In one ingenious study, they enlisted moms as quasi research assistants to collect data about their fifteen- to twenty-nine-month-olds. The mothers recorded their toddlers' reactions to other children's distress (sorrow, pain, discomfort, anger, fatigue) and their own responses before, during, and following each event. But when Zahn-Waxler and Radke-Yarrow analyzed nine months of the reports, they found that the mothers who used induction influenced their child's perspective taking *and* prosocial behavior significantly more than moms who didn't. Here is one mother's report on her twenty-two-month-old son, John, his play date, Jerry, and her empathetic parenting skills:

> "Today Jerry . . . started completely bawling and he wouldn't
> stop. John kept coming over and handing Jerry toys, trying
> to cheer him up so to speak. He'd say things like, 'Here, Jerry,'

and I said to John, 'Jerry's sad; he doesn't feel good; he had a shot today.' John would look at me with his eyebrows kind of wrinkled together, like he really understood that Jerry was crying because he was unhappy, not that he was just being a crybaby. He went over and rubbed Jerry's arm and said, 'Nice Jerry,' and continued to give him toys."[23]

So how does this work in the "real world"? Suppose you discover that your child grabbed a toy from a friend and won't let him play with it. The inductive technique is to help your son or daughter imagine how it would feel to be in the victim's place, so that he might understand the impact of his behavior on the other child. Doing so can enhance not only your child's perspective-taking skills but also his moral growth. One strategy is to role-play how the other child might feel using one of your child's favorite toys. After "grabbing" the toy from your child, ask, "How would you feel if somebody grabbed a toy from you? Would it be fair? Why not? What can you do to make things better?"

But science says there are caveats: inductive discipline must be delivered using the right tone for results. A verbal warning or simple explanation ("Stop that!" "You pinched Johnny.") had little effect eliciting an altruistic response from their child. And moms who frequently explained *why* the behavior was harmful ("See what you did! Do you see that you hurt Kelly? Don't ever pull her fingers!") were more likely to have their children help or comfort their distressed peer. Kids don't want to hurt other kids, and if you show them—clearly, concisely, and without judgment—how their actions affect other children, they will take that to heart. This is the basis of the induction discipline technique.

The Parent Science Lesson: Make sure to "plainly explain" to your child why his behavior was hurtful and draw attention to the victim's distress. And use the Goldilocks Response Model with your tone: Not *too* harsh ("Don't act like that. You're grounded for a month"), not *too* soft ("It's okay. Things like that happen"), but *just* right ("You made your friend cry. I expect you to treat people kindly. What will you do to make your friend feel better?"), so your child understands the behavior you expect.

Express Disappointment, Not Anger

But your child doesn't care just about what his peers think; he is also looking to *your* reaction for clues. It turns out that a parent's emotional reaction to a child's behavior can be just as powerful as the reaction of another child, and this influence *grows* (not diminishes) as kids age.

Another study in this vein analyzed parental discipline responses to their eleven- to thirteen-year-olds' misbehaviors in order to determine how different discipline types affect empathy and behavior. First, researchers asked the children's mothers how they would respond to various kid misbehaviors.[24] Next, they queried the kids on how they *thought* their parents would respond. Finally they gauged each child's level of empathy on five tests. The result: children whose parents used induction—who discussed how a child's misbehavior made them, the parent, feel—showed higher levels of empathy, perspective taking, and prosocial behaviors than kids whose parents relied heavily on power-assertive discipline such as taking away privileges, or on physical punishments like spanking. The fear of disappointing their parents was both a powerful deterrent from bad behavior and a driver of empathy.

The Parent Science Lesson: Don't shy from telling your child you are disappointed in their behavior. Research shows that it is one of the best ways we can react to kids' bad behavior. The trick is to stress the child's misbehavior and not the child. ("I never want to hear that language. That's not who you are!" "In this house, we care about people. I'm disappointed in how you behaved!") Sharing your disappointment is an opportunity to emphasize the values you stand for as well as to convey that you expect your kids to act in a kind and caring way.

Teens Care What You Think, Too

Pointing out the impact of behavior is also effective for older kids, according to a study of fifth, eighth, and tenth graders and their moms. Students completed surveys about their mothers' most common discipline response and whether they thought the strategies were fair and appropriate. Researchers also assessed the strength of each child's moral self-concept. Mothers were then asked to describe their discipline responses and how frequently they used it. The results showed that mothers who used induction *and* expressed disappointment to their teens about uncaring behavior raised children with stronger moral identities and perspective-taking abilities.[25]

If the teen did an egregious deed, like stealing something from a store, these moms used discipline that pointed out the impact of their teen's behavior on the other person.

> *Mom: Okay, Jordan, let's think about the man who owns the video store. How do you think he feels about his property being taken?*
>
> *Jordan: I guess he'd be kind of upset.*
>
> *Mom: But why?*
>
> *Jordan: Because people are taking things from his store.*
>
> *Mom: Sure, but who do you think has to pay for the missing items?*
>
> *Jordan: I don't know . . . the man?*
>
> *Mom: Yep. How would you feel if you had to pay for things someone took from you?*
>
> *Jordan: I'd be angry.*
>
> *Mom: Would you feel it was fair if you had to use your own salary to pay for it?*
>
> *Jordan: No. Sorry. I'll return it.*

The Parent Science Lesson: Keep using "impact statements" and inductive-type discipline during the teen years. Doing so helps your kids internalize your caring values and form strong moral identities even as they age and the struggles they face get larger. Also, express your disappointment regarding any uncaring act and stress how your child's behavior affected the victim's feelings so he can grasp other's perspectives.

HOW TO TEACH CHILDREN TO SEE THINGS FROM SOMEONE ELSE'S PERSPECTIVE

So if inductive discipline is so effective in enhancing children's behavior and their perspective-taking skills, how do we as parents actually implement it? The four steps of the inductive discipline method are described below. The acronym CARE will help you recall the four crucial parts of the approach.

Step 1: C = Call Attention to Uncaring

The step has two parts: naming *what* your child did that was wrong and describing *why* it was uncaring. Many parents skip this and jump into giving the heavy-handed lecture or dispensing punishment that Martin Hoffman calls "power assertion." Of course we're upset, frustrated, or mystified by our kid's misbehavior, but if we don't review *why* the behavior was wrong, there goes a missed opportunity to teach perspective taking and stretch empathy. Our kids must grasp how their actions affect others. The second your child is uncaring, call attention to it. Discuss privately why his act was uncaring and the reason you disapprove.

- "Yelling out that Jeb couldn't make a basket was mean."

- "Telling Bert to leave so you could play with Sally was inconsiderate."

- "Texting when Grandpa tried to talk to you was rude."

Step 2: A = Assess How Uncaring Affects Others

Perspective taking doesn't come naturally, and kids don't always grasp how the behavior affects others. Nancy Eisenberg, author of *The Caring Child*, says that one of the best empathy-building practices is pointing out the impact of the child's behavior on the other person ("See, you made her cry") or highlighting the victim's feelings ("Now he feels bad").[26] Doing so stretches perspective taking so kids focus on the victim's thoughts, feelings, or needs, and it can be effective even with very young children. The trick is to guide your child to imagine what it would be like to be in the victim's place so he "feels their pain." A place to begin is by asking your child to think about how she would feel, think, or need if treated the same way. Once a child understands the issue from her perspective, help her step into the victim's shoes and focus on another's feelings, thoughts, and needs.

- *Younger children:* Suppose your child grabbed his pal's toy. Ask "How would you feel if Tim took your toy? Make your face look like Tim feels. How does he feel?"

- *Older children:* "Pretend you're Sara and discover somebody sent that text about you. How would you feel? What would you say to the sender? What is Sara thinking?"

Step 3: R = Repair the Hurt and Require Reparations

Helping a child understand how his actions caused another distress is an essential part of discipline and perspective taking. Once a child makes that connection ("I made the other person feel [sad, humiliated, scared] and I know just how he feels"), conscience usually kicks in. Repairing the victim's hurt is also how to relieve the offender's guilt. But reparations must be heartfelt (not contrived), age-appropriate, and "fit the crime." Here is how one father helped his son "repair the hurt" when his son made fun of his friend, Mark:

Dad: How do you think you made Mark feel?

Son: He feels sad—that's how I'd feel.

Dad: So what will you do to let Mark know you're sorry and care about him?

Son: I'll ask if he wants to come over.

Dad: Yes, but your friend might not know that you regret what you did.

Son: I'll call and say I'm sorry.

Dad: That's not easy, but it's a caring thing to do.

Step 4: E = Express Disappointment
and Stress Caring Expectations

The final step is explaining how you feel about uncaring actions and expressing your disappointment in your child's behavior. Don't feel guilty about doing so: science says one of the most effective discipline responses is sharing disappointment for bad behavior.[27] It's a potent way to let your kid know that you believe he can do better. Stating your disappointment also "enables children to develop standards for judging their actions, feelings of empathy and responsibility for others, and a sense of moral identity, which are conducive to becoming a helpful person,"[28] explains Adam Grant, author of *Give and Take*. The step has two parts: first, expressing disappointment in the behavior (not your child); second, stressing your expectations for caring and belief in your child that he can do better.

- "I don't like hearing you talk behind your friend's back. You're a good person, and I expect you to consider people's feelings."

- "That tone is disrespectful and upsets me. I expect you to treat all people with respect. You can do better."

EMPATHY BUILDER: UNDERSTANDING SOMEONE'S THOUGHTS, FEELINGS, AND NEEDS

Teaching kids to tune in and listen to the "other side" is a potent way to boost perspective taking and stretch empathy. After all, tuning in to others is how we help our children understand the feelings and needs of others, and become less "self-absorbed" and more "other" conscious. Developing this empathy skill involves four steps that are learned in sequence. Work on one step at a time until your child is ready to take on the succeeding step. You might play listening games, practice at dinner and family meetings, and model each step as you listen to your kids. Hint: This empathy builder is composed of skills addressed in other chapters, such as eye contact, listening, managing feelings, focusing, and emotional literacy. If needed, review the "Empathy Builder" sections—particularly in chapters 1 and 3—to help your child master the ability.

Step 1: FOCUS "Pay Attention to the Other"

The first step to perspective taking is paying attention to the speaker. Teach your child five key listening skills that boost empathy and classroom success by teaching the acronym SOLER:

1. S = Sit or stand still so you pay attention to the speaker.

2. O = Be open to the speaker's view and feelings.

3. L = Lean in slightly to convey interest.

4. E = Look eye to eye. To help stay focused, use the skill you learned in chapter 1: "Look at the color of the talker's eyes or the bridge of the speaker's nose."

5. R = Recognize the speaker's views. Acknowledge by nodding and smiling to show you care.

Step 2: FEEL "Look and Listen" for the Feeling

Emotional literacy plays a part in perspective taking, so teach your child to "Look and Listen" for the emotion. Say, "The person may not say how he feels, but his body, face, and voice give clues. Pretend to be a detective and ask yourself: 'How does he feel?'"

- *Ask for clarification if unsure.* "Are you . . . ? " "Did that make you feel . . . ?"

- *Name the feeling.* "You sound [feeling]." "You look [feeling]."

Step 3: IMAGINE "Put Yourself in Their Shoes"

One way to help kids figure out another person's perspective is to teach them to step into the person's shoes with their imagination. "While the person talks, try to imagine what he's thinking or feeling on the inside so you'll know what he wants or needs." The trick is to find a strategy that helps the child imagine the other person's perspective.

- A younger child can pretend to wear a magic cape that allows him to "see" inside someone's mind and gives him super powers to read what another person is thinking or feeling.

- Encourage an older child to ask himself: "If it were me, I'd feel/ think/want . . ."

Step 4: SHARE "Describe Their Side"

The last step is for your child to paraphrase the speaker's perspective and strengthen empathy. Explain: "One way to let someone know you care is telling what you heard him say. It means you understand their feelings, thoughts, or needs."

- *Repeat it:* "You said . . ." "I heard you say . . ." "One thing you said was . . ."

- *Paraphrase thoughts, feelings, or needs:* "You think . . ." "You feel . . ." "You need . . ." "You want . . . because . . ." "You feel . . . when . . . and you need . . ."

- *Offer support:* "Sounds like you need . . . " "I could . . ." "May I help?"

Explain to your child in age-appropriate terms that listening to understand someone's perspective doesn't mean you have to agree with the view. People will have different opinions, and that's what makes us human. So listen to the person without judging, giving your opinion, or debating the view. It lets people know you care and are empathizing.

HOW TO HELP KIDS STEP INTO OTHERS' SHOES

Fire crews were working nonstop to curtail a 200,000-acre San Diego wildfire. But the preschool teacher was dealing with another issue: many of her students' parents were those firefighters. In the brief time they could go home, they were exhausted, and their children couldn't understand why "Daddy can't play." Their teacher wanted to help her young students grasp their parents' perspective, so she plopped firemen boots on the floor and began.

"Who wants to put these on and pretend to be a fireman like your daddy?"

Little hands were flying: the kids were eager to play "make believe."

The teacher called on a child who was missing his father terribly. Unable to express his fears for his parent's safety, the four-year-old was acting up and having nightmares. The boy threw off his shoes, jumped into the oversize boots, and was ready to play "fireman."

"Ready?" she asked. "Imagine you're your daddy. You're working hard to stop that bad fire. You're sleeping on the ground, wearing dirty, smelly clothes, and you're so tired. You're away from home a long time and miss your family so much. But most of all, you want to hug your little boy and feel his arms around you."

The adults sat mesmerized watching the preschooler literally "become" his daddy. The child's expression, demeanor, and entire body changed within seconds as he imagined how his father felt.

"How do you feel?" the teacher asked.

"I'm tired and sad," the boy quietly said. "I want to go home."

"What would make you feel better?"

The boy froze, and then something clicked. He jumped out of the boots, ran to the playhouse, grabbed an object, and returned.

"Quick, give this to Daddy," he said. "It'll make him feel better." And he pushed his teddy bear into his teacher's hands.

Well, there wasn't an adult with a dry eye: we knew we'd witnessed a powerful moment. An empathetic teacher found a way to comfort a young child by helping him imagine his father's horrific predicament. She also proved what science says: even little ones can be taught to "step into someone's shoes."

Perspective taking can activate empathy so children want to help others, and that's what happened that day. By imagining his father's discomfort, the son wanted to comfort Daddy, and did it the best way a four-year-old knew how: giving him his teddy bear.[29]

How Perspective Taking Activates Empathy

Dr. Ezra Stotland, from the University of Washington,[30] was one of the first researchers whose work demonstrated the power of perspective taking. He asked subjects to watch as "intense and painful" heat was applied to a person's hand strapped to a machine. The victim was actually Stotland's assistant, who was taught to act as if he were feeling pain: the "heat" didn't exist. Some subjects were told just to focus on the assistant's movements; some were instructed to put themselves in the person's place and imagine his feelings; some were told to imagine the heat on their own hands. Each subject's physiological responses were monitored, and these indicated their empathy levels.

When the subjects were told to focus only on the assistant, they had little empathy for his "pain." But when instructed either to imagine having the heat placed on their own hands, or the victim's feelings, their empathy increased significantly. And Stotland discovered that "imagining how another person feels" is a powerful way to nurture perspective taking.

Studies show that we can increase children's desires to lend a hand by encouraging them to focus on the *other* person's thoughts, feelings, and needs—not their own.[31] There are many ways to help kids step into another's moccasins. The preschool teacher's young student put on fireman boots and played make-believe to understand how his father felt. Jane

Elliott's third graders experienced discrimination through role-playing. Ezra Stotland's subjects imagined a person in pain. But perspective taking can also be a tool to help kids work out sibling conflicts, change uncaring behavior, understand another's side, grasp why their friend is miffed, or solve dozens of day-to-day issues and give them the Empathy Advantage.

Six Ways to Help Kids Walk in Another's Shoes

1. **Try props.** Liam had difficulty understanding anyone's feelings but his own. So when he couldn't grasp the distress he caused a classmate, I knew I needed to dig deeper to tweak his empathy. I spotted a wire hanger, bent it into a circle, and improvised: "Liam, put your head up to the hole and imagine you're Stevie. I'll be you." And our role-play began: "That haircut makes you look dumb. How do you feel, Stevie?" Pretending to be Stevie is what helped Liam finally understand his classmate's pain, but the hanger was key. Try props, puppets, action figures, stuffed animals, or costumes. You can also tape photos on pencils to create stick puppets so younger kids can role-play the "other side."

2. **Switch places!** Ken, a dad, shared a great way to help kids understand *our* perspective. His twelve-year-old couldn't understand why Ken was upset when he didn't call to say he was late. When he finally arrived home, Ken made him see things from *his* side: "Sit in my chair: it's warm from sitting and looking at my watch. Pretend you're me: You don't know where your son is. It's dark, late, and he didn't call. What thoughts are going through your mind?" Ken said his son apologized, promised he'd never forget to call home, and has kept his word. Try having your child "step into your shoes" and imagine experiencing a situation from *your* perspective.

3. **Use imagineering.** Suppose your child sent a "get well" card to Grandma. Use the opportunity to help her imagine how Grandma feels receiving it. "Pretend you're Grandma and you

receive this card from your granddaughter. How do you feel reading what it says?" Broaden your child's perspective taking by including people he hasn't met: "Pretend you're that new boy and don't know anyone. How do you feel? How can you make him feel welcome?" "Imagine you're that child in Iowa who just lost her house in the tornado. What are you thinking? What do you need? What can we do?"

4. **Redo uncaring behavior.** Help your child "redo" an uncaring action by role-playing a behavior that considers the other person's feelings. "Let's do that over and say what your friend might want to hear." "Try again, but this time, think about how your team would feel if their teammate put you down." "Start over and ask me in a way that makes my feelings not hurt."

5. **Ask, "I wonder."** Encourage your older kids to ask themselves: "I wonder: What does [Uncle Fred, Bart, Coach] think/feel/need?" Encourage your kids to use the "I wonder" question whenever they encounter someone new like the new girl, woman in line, child on the swings, man lying on the street.

6. **Reverse sides.** Next time there's a sibling battle or friendship tiff, don't offer advice. Instead, make your kids "reverse sides" to see things from another perspective. You say, "I know you're upset, but you two can figure out how to solve it. Both of you tell me what happened but from your sibling's side." They listen to each version, and then you ask: "Now that you know both sides, how will you work this out so it's fair to both of you?"

AGE-BY-AGE STRATEGIES

I was visiting a Kansas school when I happened upon two boys engaged in serious conversation with their principal. The eleven-year-olds were suspended from class for another heated debate over their shared locker.

Each accused the other of "messing with my stuff," but the principal was using a different discipline ploy. She handed each a Think Sheet, which required the boys to answer from the other's perspective. Questions included "What happened?" "How do you feel about what happened?" "What would you like to tell the other person?" "What is the best way to solve this problem so both of you are satisfied?" Listening to their reactions was priceless:

"I'm not him, so how do I know how he feels?"

"This is too hard," said the other. "I can't figure out what he wants."

And that was their problem: neither thought about how the other felt because each was seeing only "their side."

The principal's perspective-taking strategy was a brilliant way to help the boys figure out the feelings, thoughts, and needs of someone besides themselves. Here are strategies to help your child understand what it feels like to walk in someone else's shoes.

Symbols designate the recommended age and suitability for activity: L = Little Ones: Toddlers and Preschoolers; S = School-age; T = Tweens and Older; A = All Ages

- **Use the formula "feels + needs."** Look for occasions to draw attention to people's feelings, and then ask your child to guess what the person might need in order to change his mood. **A**

    Parent: See that boy with his face looking down? How do you think he feels? [Now guide your child to use the appropriate feeling word.]

    Child: I think he's sad.

    Parent: What do you think he needs to feel better?

    Child: Maybe he needs someone to sit with because he's lonely.

    Parent: Is there something you can do to help?

- **Use real events, books, and news.** Help stretch your child's perspective using everyday moments. *In the news:* "That girl won the spelling bee. How do you think she feels?" *In books:* "Take the bears' side. How would you feel if Goldilocks used your beds and chairs without asking?" *On TV:* "The cyclone destroyed most of the children's homes in Vanuatu. What do you think those kids are feeling and thinking?" *In your family:* "How does Dad feel hearing that his mom is so sick?" Don't overlook asking: "I wonder if there's a way we can help?" **A**

- **Use shoes, hats, and scarves.** Laurie Coon, a Dublin, Ohio, counselor, teaches an empathy activity with shoeboxes filled with ice skates, cross-trainers, slippers, army boots, stilettos, and so on. Students pull a shoebox, step into the shoes, and describe who might wear them. My friend, Mary Grace Galvin, filled a trunk with hats and scarves so that her kids could spend hours pretending to be "different people." **L, S**

- **Make a face.** Researchers asked subjects to imitate certain facial expressions—such as disgust, sorrow, fear—and detected changes in their brains that were characteristic of that emotion. It seems that making a facial expression synonymous with an emotion can make us *feel* that emotion.[32] So ask your child to "make a face" that shows how he thinks the other person feels: it may enhance his perspective-taking skills. **L, S**

  Child: Danny got kicked off the team.

  Parent: Make your face look how he feels. (Child makes sad face.)

  Parent: Imagine what he's thinking.

  Child: He thinks nobody likes him. I should call.

- **Introduce disadvantages.** A scout leader gave an unusual task to her troop: "Identify a disadvantage you've never experienced like living in a homeless shelter, being blind, or motor impaired. Now find a way to understand what it feels like to be that person." Some teens did a twenty-four-hour hunger strike (with parental blessings) to understand famine. Not only did they gain a new perspective, but the activity also activated their empathy. Many now volunteer to feed the hungry. Other ideas:

Blind: Wear a blindfold and try to move around your house. Younger kids can play "Pin the Tail on the Donkey."

Mute: Sing but cover your mouth.

Deaf: Put in earplugs and headphones *and* try listening.

Learning challenged: Attempt writing backward or while looking in a mirror.

Physically challenged: Try navigating your surroundings from a wheelchair. **S, T**

- **Stretch perspective.** Have your child experience a challenging situation: visit a homeless shelter, a center for the blind, a nursing home, or a soup kitchen. When you return, ask, "Is your view the same or different from before you went?" Consider volunteering together at the same place to help your child really get to know the people. Then ask, "What happened to your feelings about the people now?" **A**

- **Try theater.** Role taking is a tool actors use to understand their characters. Meryl Streep said that developing empathy has given her the ability to "feel the exquisite living pleasure of transmitting [a character's] feelings to an audience."[33] Actors also testify that role taking strengthens their empathy muscles. Children's theater and acting classes can enhance their perspective-taking abilities. Might acting be an experience to consider for your child? **A**

- **Use books.** A few young reader favorites: *Paper Bag Princess*, by Robert Munsch; *The True Story of the Three Little Pigs*, by Jon Scieszka; *The Bedspread*, by Sylvia Fair; *The Pain and the Great One*, by Judy Blume; *Through Grandpa's Eyes*, by Patricia MacLachlan. Perspective-stretching questions include "What's the perspective of [character]? Whose view is missing? How would you feel? What would you do differently?" **A**

- **Watch flicks.** In the Disney film *Freaky Friday*, a mother and daughter don't get along. Then one freaky day they mysteriously switch bodies, and each is forced to learn the other's perspective.

It's a great film to discuss role taking with kids. For older kids and teens: *Dances with Wolves*; *The Elephant Man*; *Roll of Thunder, Hear My Cry*; *The Man Without a Face*; and *Watership Down*. **S, T**

- **Take your kid to work.** On the fourth Thursday of each April, more than 37 million American employees participate in Take Our Daughters and Sons to Work Day. In schools students become "Principal for a Day," in police departments kids become "Chief," in cities kids become "Mayor for a Day." Find a way to help your child step into other people's roles including your own. **S, T**

- **Widen your child's "social hub."** It's easier for children to empathize with people they know, or are similar to, so widen your child's perspective by exposing him to people of different backgrounds including race, ideology, gender, culture, religion, and age. Then stress: "They may have different skin color [speak another language, etc.], but they have the same thoughts, feelings, and needs as you." **A**

THE TOP FIVE THINGS TO KNOW ABOUT INSTILLING PERSPECTIVE TAKING

1. Mentally stepping into someone's shoes is a way to build kids' empathy muscles.

2. Understanding what another thinks, feels, wants, and needs takes practice and ability.

3. Perspective taking is composed of teachable skills such as emotional literacy, managing feelings, imagining other's thoughts and feelings, solving problems, and empathizing.

4. Helping kids consider others' feelings, thoughts, and needs is an effective way to boost empathy.

5. Focusing your child's attention on the effect his behavior has on another person boosts perspective taking.

ONE LAST THING

Debbie Parks, principal of Aukamm Elementary in Wiesbaden, Germany, is an empathetic educator who understands kids' needs. Hers is a Department of Defense school on one of our overseas army bases, so when seventy-five of her students' parents were deployed to Afghanistan, she found a unique way to use perspective taking to comfort those children. Parks flew the school's mascot, an oversize stuffed bear named the Duke, overseas to be with their parents to help students step into the shoes of their moms and dads. Once the Duke arrived, he (aka the soldiers) immediately began sending pictures via internet to the school of his adventures that Parks posted around the school. There were photos showing the bear performing feats of heroism, visiting orphanages, saving the lives of hospital patients, and flying helicopters with their deployed parents, as well as eating in the chow hall, doing physical training, and celebrating Thanksgiving and Christmas in Afghanistan with the troops.

"When the children saw that the Duke was doing things alongside their fathers—and in two cases their mothers—it gave them a calming reassurance," Parks told me. "The stuffed bear became a mechanism for resiliency that the children latched on to and needed at that time in their lives." The Duke also was a way for those deployed moms and dads to connect with their children and allow them to step safely into their world.

Finally, after eleven months in Afghanistan, the soldiers returned home, and their children were there to welcome them with open arms. The Duke was also given leave, flying home with the parents, who returned the bear to the students safe and sound.

While boosting perspective taking is crucial for our kids, let's not forget the importance of seeing the world through the prism of our sons and daughters. Successful parents have a good sense of what's going on in their children's lives, and this third essential habit of empathy will help us—as well as our kids—thrive.

CHAPTER 4

Empathetic Children Have a Moral Imagination

Reading to Cultivate Empathy

Books can transport children to other worlds and transform their hearts. I learned that lesson while visiting a school where I saw a hall bulletin board that was covered from floor to ceiling with student-made paper hearts. The caption over them read, "Changing the World One Heart at a Time." The hearts were lovely, but how the board came about was what made it so moving.

The principal told me the board had been empty until Ryan, a fourth grader, passed it on his way home one day. Ryan rarely spoke and, unbeknownst to anyone, his home was in turmoil. His father was an alcoholic who frequently beat up Ryan's mom while the fourth grader hid in his closet. Fearing his dad would severely injure his mom if he told anyone, he played it safe by distancing himself emotionally from his teachers and classmates and remaining quiet.

His unstable mother wasn't able to do his laundry, so Ryan wore the same unkempt shirt and pants every day. It wasn't hard for kids to pick up on this child's vulnerabilities, so he was often excluded by peers and tormented by two school bullies. "Nice shirt, Ryan," they'd taunt. "Can't your parents buy you something else to wear? No wonder you're always by yourself."

That afternoon, though, another classmate saw Ryan eating by himself and recognized something everyone else had missed: Ryan looked lonely. So Danny, ignoring his friends' admonishments, asked Ryan if he could sit with him. Ryan later told the principal that he was so amazed that somebody wanted to eat with him, he couldn't stop thinking about it the rest of the day. He wanted to find a way to thank Danny for his kindness. It was still on his mind as he passed a bulletin board in the hall. He picked a paper off the floor, quickly tore it into a heart shape, and then jotted a note—"Danny, thanks for having lunch with me today. It made me happy. Ryan"—and pinned it to the board.

The next day, another student read the note and, copying Ryan's gesture, tore a paper heart and wrote a note of appreciation to another classmate. Then another student repeated the gesture, and another, and by the time I got to the school, over four hundred student-made hearts filled the board and the hall as well. And it was all started by one child's empathy. I stood there soaking up these children's gestures of kindness and then looked back at the heading, "Changing the World One Heart at a Time." It was the perfect caption to describe what had happened: the kindness momentum spiraled, other kids' hearts opened as well, and they started sticking up for their pal Ryan. The bullying stopped, and Ryan found friends and became a happier and changed child.

But the most interesting twist was hearing what had motivated Danny to feel for his classmate. It turns out that his teacher had read *The Hundred Dresses*, by Eleanor Estes, as a class read-aloud. The book tells the stirring story of Wanda Petronski, a poor, quiet, third-grade girl who always wears the same faded blue dress. Like Ryan, Wanda has no friends and often sits and plays alone. She also must endure a few classmates who constantly taunt her about her one dress. "What are you going to wear tomorrow?" the girls would dig, knowing she has only one dress.

Finally, one day Wanda blurts, "I have a *hundred* dresses at home—all different colors!" Well, the torment spirals to such a level that Wanda's parents can no longer endure the cruelty their daughter faces, and the Petronski family moves to a different location. The girls later realize

Wanda has remarkable artistic talents: she did have a hundred dresses at home—but they were all drawn on paper, and guilt sets in. By then Wanda is gone and the girls can never make amends for their cruel actions.

Over the years I've read my now well-worn book to countless classes as well as to my children, and its haunting tale never fails to stir their emotions. I ask, "Have you ever had someone make fun of how you dress or look or made fun of another kid or excluded them because they looked differently?" and hands always rise slowly or the children will look down at their feet. Danny was no different. "When my teacher asked what the girls could have done to help Wanda, I thought of Ryan," he told me. "He was lonely and had kids picking on him just like Wanda. That book made me feel differently about Ryan and me. It made me want to do something to help."

READING TO DEVELOP A MORAL IMAGINATION

It's a rare parent who doesn't believe that reading is crucial for their children's success, and widespread data support those views. Students who are good readers are more likely to do well in school, obtain higher grades, and pass exams than are those with weaker abilities. Those achievement gains can add up to big advantages to help teens get those college acceptances, scholarships, and even higher job wages—all big reasons why tutoring is a billion-dollar industry. Parents know reading is key to academic success, but new findings give "book power" a surprising added value: *Reading can make our kids not only smarter, but also kinder!*

Research following more than 17,000 people from birth to age fifty discovered that their reading level at age seven was the most important indicator of their future socioeconomic status.[1] Another study found that reading for pleasure at age fifteen was the most important indicator of the future success of the child.[2]

In fact, it turns out that reading—and specifically, *enjoying* reading—has profound implications for every part of our children's success, both now and in the future.

WHY IS GETTING KIDS TO READ SUCH A STRUGGLE?

Sounds simple enough: all we need to do is have our kids read, and they'll become more successful *and* empathetic. But today's digital-driven and faster-paced culture doesn't make it easy to instill literary habits in our children.

Getting Digital-Driven Kids to Read Is Tough

Our most pressing challenge may be getting a book in our kids' hands! A survey of thousands of eight- to sixteen-year-olds found that kids today are clearly reading less.[3] Peer pressure is also a problem: one-fifth of our kids admit they'd be embarrassed if a friend saw them with a book! Not so comforting if you're trying to instill a passion for reading in children. Reading rates aren't just declining as kids grow but also have plummeted significantly over the past three decades. Forty-five percent of seventeen-year-olds admit they read *by choice* only once or twice a year.[4] What's more, we're reading to our kids less than ever. In 1999, children two to seven were read to for an average of forty-five minutes a day; in 2013, that number dropped to just over thirty minutes per day.In 1984, 64 percent said they read once a week or more.[5]

More than half of kids said they preferred watching television to reading[6] (their daily screen preference has switched to viewing television on a mobile device[7]). Watching videos on YouTube, playing mobile games and apps, and text messaging are the most popular activities after watching TV.[8] As digital entertainment choices rise, our kids' reading habits will continue to decline unless we become more intentional about carving in reading time and setting unplugged family time.

Overscheduled Kids

"I have so much homework and activities, there isn't enough time to read," one child told me, and he's not alone. The Overscheduled Kid syndrome continues to affect families, with agendas so tightly filled with academic and sports activities there is no time left for reading.

Despite parental concern over the kid reading dip,we read less to our children than did previous generations,[9] and the cherished tradition of bedtime stories is waning as well. Only 64 percent of parents say they read bedtime stories to their children (though 91 percent had bedtime tales read to them when they were young).[10] One recent study found that 28 percent of parents say they use a mobile device to put their young children to sleep[11] and there goes vanished memories of hearing us read *Goodnight Moon* and other cherished bedtime tales). Grown-ups cite their "lack of time" for the decline of the family nighttime reading habit.

Picture books—like *Madeline*, *Stellaluna*, and *Enemy Pie*—are no longer a childhood staple for our younger set, and sales are dragging in the publishing industry.[12] It appears that parents are leaving the picture book behind and moving quickly to text-heavier chapter books, believing that these will give their kids a stronger academic boost. That view doesn't stand up: picture books are richer in emotion-charged content than chapter books are, and it's this emotionally charged content (particularly in the first several years of life) that's crucial to empathy development.

Digital Screens Reduce Reading Pleasure

Kids who do read prefer to do so on electronic devices. "That's good news," you say. "The kids are reading!" But there's a drawback: those new digital screens don't seem to be improving our kids' reading experience. In fact, evidence shows that children who read exclusively onscreen are three times less likely to say they enjoy reading, a third less likely to have a favorite book, and far less likely to be strong readers. So while electronic books are convenient and "all the rage," they don't necessarily help our kids fall in love with reading, and that's the very habit we hope they acquire.

The current educational focus on Common Core standards has big implications for what our kids are reading, too. There's a much greater emphasis on nonfiction starting at younger grades but particularly at the high school level,[13] with reasoning that nonfiction reading improves students' writing abilities. Maybe so, but the new curriculum emphasis poses a potential drawback: literary fiction—*not nonfiction*—is what science says is better at nurturing empathy, perspective taking, and appreciating and understanding those not "like us" (or what I call "otherness.")[14]

While these are all stumbling blocks to cultivating literary habits, there *are* solutions. There are also new findings about the impact of reading on children's development that have surprised even scientists.

WHAT SCIENCE SAYS: WHY READING MATTERS

Many of us can recall a cherished story from our childhood that tugged at our heartstrings. How can we forget the passion of John Steinbeck's Joad family in *The Grapes of Wrath* and their struggles to survive the Great Depression? Books can inspire us as well as offer us strategies to handle life. Maurice Sendak's *Where the Wild Things Are* helped my youngest get through his fear of the dark. Zach would just yell, "BE STILL!" to a dark corner, just as his hero Max did to those wild things, and the strategy worked. Max helped Zach cure his fears!

Books can be portals to understanding other worlds and other views, to helping our children be more open to differences and cultivate new perspectives. We've always assumed that a good story can make us feel more deeply, but now several studies prove it.

Researchers in Canada at York University and the University of Toronto found results that startled even them: people who read fiction[15] are more capable of understanding others, empathizing, and seeing another person's point of view than those who read nonfiction. What's more: adults who read *less* fiction report themselves to be *less* empathic.

Other studies[16] have found that books affect young children as well. In fact, Raymond Mar, a psychologist from York University, found that the more stories young children had read to them, the stronger their ability to imagine what other people are thinking and feeling. That effect was also found when the preschoolers watched movies—but not television.

Researchers at New York's New School for Social Research[17] set out to find what type of reading material is most effective in empathy building. Participants were divided and given excerpts from different genres to read: award-winning literary fiction writers (like Louise Erdrich, Alice Munro, or Wendell Berry); bestselling popular fiction (such as Gillian Flynn's *Gone Girl*, Danielle Steel's *The Sins of the Mother*, or a Robert Heinlein science fiction tale); nonfiction (excerpts from *Smithsonian* magazine that were well written but not literary or about people), while one group read nothing. And then participants were given paper-and-pencil tests to measure their empathy levels as well as take part in four other experiments.

The results were interesting: participants who read nonfiction, popular fiction, or nothing had unimpressive results, but those who read literary fiction improved significantly in their abilities to understand what others are thinking and feeling. Those gains were true though they read for only three to five minutes *and* if participants admitted to not enjoying reading literary fiction! Reading literature—even for short periods—can enhance empathy, and proof of that is showing up not only on paper-and-pencil tests, but also on images of our brains!

This Is Your Brain on a Book

Remember when we watched a film or read a great book and were so stirred that for a least a few seconds we couldn't move? We now know that it wasn't just our heart that was affected. Data show that when we recognize an emotion in someone else, our brains actually generate that same feeling. In short, "we are actually simulating the other person's emotional state."[18] Those neural changes in our brains even show up on magnetic images and may be altering our children's brain chemistry!

Neuroscientists at Washington University[19] watched fMRI (functional magnetic resonance imaging) scans of volunteers as they read words from selected material. The images from their brains mimicked the brain activity related to the actions of the characters they read about! If in the passage the character was "pulling on a light cord," the region of the brain associated with controlling grasping motions would activate. If they read that the character changed location ("he went through the front door and into the kitchen"), the region responsible for spatial abilities would light up. When we read literary fiction, we not only feel "with" the characters, but also we "do" what they do—and our brains mirror their actions! Another study at Michigan State University[20] monitored brain images of volunteers as they read Jane Austen. As readers analyzed key passages, blood flow increased in their brain. The right reading passage—especially from literary fiction—not only can make us think deeper, it also transports us into a different world, helps us feel for the character, and literally lights up our brain! But why is literary fiction more effective in stretching our empathy muscles than, say, those trendy popular teen sellers with vampires and zombies?

Why Literary Fiction Transports Us to Different Worlds

Science theorizes that strong literary fiction focuses more on characters' lives and trials, while popular fiction is more concerned with the plot. The more effort we make trying to figure out a character's intentions, emotions, or thoughts, the greater the odds that our empathy muscles are stretched as well. That's why the right passage or scene from, say, To Kill a Mockingbird or Charlotte's Web can make us grip the chair a little tighter or wipe away those tears. We really feel for Scout, Wilbur, and the other protagonists on the page. We've stepped into their shoes—emotionally at least—and identify with their discomfort and feel their pain.

Some authors just have a knack for helping kids get into the shoes of their characters and speaking to their imagination. Beverly Cleary is one of those special writers, which explains why her books have sold more than 91 million copies. Her characters are wonderful, but Ramona Quimby, star of Cleary's *Ramona the Pest*, is plain unforgettable. She also exhibits all those qualities that science says are so important in empathy stretching. In short, she has experiences that her young readers can relate to.

Five-year-old Ramona has waited *her whole life* to go to kindergarten, and she's thrilled finally to be there. She's also a bit rambunctious, is called a pest (without knowing why), and finds herself in trouble a lot. When her teacher sends her home until she can learn to behave, Ramona just flat-out refuses to go back to school, and *nothing* anyone says can change her mind. After all, she says, "If they don't like me, why go?"

I've read *Ramona the Pest* to countless students over the years as well as to my sons. My first graders would relive their own concerns about going off to kindergarten, finding friends, and trying to fit in. And more than a few would feel uneasy when Ramona got in trouble—yet again and again—because it felt like *they* were getting in trouble alongside her! Each time I came to the part when Ramona is sent home "until she learned to behave," I'd feel their distress.

"She doesn't think the teacher likes her," they'd mumble. "She doesn't want to come back 'cause everyone thinks she's a pest!" Cleary's words never failed to create emotional friction in my young listeners. After all, everyone—even Ramona—wants to be liked, and my students felt for her. So they'd lean in a little closer so as not to miss what—if anything—would change Ramona's mind about coming back to school. *Ramona the Pest* became a yearly tradition, but one year it had a special impact on a student.

A new student, Molly, had just moved to the school I was consulting at. She knew no one, and her father had deployed to Afghanistan the same week. So it wasn't surprising that this six-year-old would have a hard time adjusting. But Cleary's book struck a chord with Molly. She didn't want to miss a word: she was tense, focused, and so concerned when Ramona decided not to come back to school. After all, she knew how it felt when you thought no one cared, and she hurt for Ramona. I heard her give a little sigh and whisper, "It's okay, Ramona. Come back! You'll find a friend!" It was all I could do to keep reading.

But Molly's angst didn't go unnoticed. Annie, another student, was sitting nearby and saw Molly's distress. I could see she was trying to decide what to do. I caught Annie looking again at Molly, and then came the moment: her empathy was stirred. She knew Molly needed a friend, so she moved in a little closer and put her arm around her new buddy. Two girls listened together, side by side, arm in arm. Here were two children in sync with a character's feelings as well as each other's, confirming what science says can happen with the right book at the right time.

HOW TO CULTIVATE EMPATHETIC READING IN CHILDREN

"You'll be that one," the five-year-old would say to her companion, "and I'll be this one." [21] It was a pretend game the daughter of Keith Oatley (who also happens to be a renowned cognitive psychologist) would play with her friend. They were preparing to watch a movie together (one they'd obviously seen a few times already) and were assigning each other roles from the movie. The father recognized that the children's make-believe play activity would also let them step outside themselves and imagine the thoughts and feelings of their chosen actor. Of course, to the five-year-olds, the activity was just a fun game, but it was also a science-backed way to boost empathy.

There are numerous variations to the children's make-believe game to instill the habit of reading for feeling. An Oregon high school English teacher helps her ninth graders understand characters' perspectives by using six paper shoe cutouts. Her test for Shakespeare's *Romeo and Juliet* is for students to take turns stepping onto each cutout and describing that character's views and feelings (Romeo, Juliet, Lady Capulet, Tybalt, Mercutio, Friar Laurence). The teacher told me that the exercise not only enhances her students' perspective for each character, but it is also their favorite test.

A mom in Liverpool said she conducts a similar exercise—using real shoes! When her family finished reading *Charlotte's Web*, she printed each character's name (Charlotte, Wilbur, Fern, and Templeton) on a sticky note and stuck them on her husband's shoes. Her kids were delighted to jump into each big shoe and pretend to be the character.

For a younger child, capitalize on his imagination by using puppets, dolls, stuffed toys, or action figures to portray the character. His beloved teddy bear can be Dumbo, while other stuffed toys such as his Bunny, Puppy, and Kanga can represent the elephants and crows in the movie. Now have fun playing out the parts in the scene in which the elephants and crows make fun of poor Dumbo while gently posing those great questions like: "You be Dumbo. How would you feel if that was you being left out?" The right question posed at the right moment can help your child understand the emotions and needs of others. It's never too early—or late—to stretch empathy.

Role-playing and acting can also expand perspective taking, so if you have a little drama queen under your roof, encourage her to act out the part of a character from a film or book. You don't have to put on a Broadway performance to activate empathy! A few hats, scarves, or even towels can help kids get into the creative spirit of pretend and transport them into the minds and feelings of others. As your child matures and his empathy muscles strengthen, you can put away the shoes, hats, and puppets, and encourage him to enroll in an acting class or neighborhood theater production. The secret is finding meaningful ways and the right reading material to help your child imagine another world.

EMPATHY BUILDER: POSING QUESTIONS TO STRETCH MORAL IMAGINATION

There are dozens of ways for kids to learn to read with feeling to increase moral imagination. Here is the one practice that will help children step vicariously into someone else's place and see the world from another perspective. The strategy has three steps, so choose which is most appropriate to your child's current ability until he can use the technique without your reminders.

Step 1: Pose "What If?" Questions

Using "What if?" questions is a first step to helping kids step into another's shoes and think about the character from their own perspective. Here are a few ways to pose the questions to stretch empathy:

- "What if you were that character?"

- "If you were the character, would you have made the same choice?"

- "If that were you, what would you do next?"

- "If that were you, what advice would you give?"

- "If you were a fortune-teller, what do you think [character] is going to do now?"

- "If that were you, would you do the same thing?"

This technique works best if you push the video Pause button or stop reading one or two times in key places and then ask the question. Caution: don't abuse that Pause button or post too many queries or your kids will not want to watch movies or read with you!

Step 2: Ask "How Would *You* Feel?" Questions

The right questions can also help your child reflect if he's had similar feelings or experiences as the character has. The pronoun "you" in the query is still directed toward your child's feelings and thoughts, but with a gentle nudge that helps the child feel and think more about where the character is coming from.

- "Have you ever had that same experience? How did you feel?"

- "Look at the character's face . . . how do you think she feels? Have you ever felt like that?"

- "What's happening to [character]? What do you think is going through her mind? Have you ever had the same thoughts?"

Step 3: Switch the Focus from "Me" to "You"

The ultimate goal is helping children imagine the thoughts or feelings of others. You can nudge your child to switch from "me" thinking to "you" thinking with the right questions. Here are a few ideas:

- "Pretend you're the character. How do you think she feels right now? What does she need to feel better?"

- "Be a mind reader . . . what do you think he's thinking?"

- "Imagine you are that person. How does she feel about being [homeless, unhappy, bullied, ignored]?"

As your child's role-switching abilities increase, remind your child that whenever she reads or watches a special movie to use the "me to you" reading habit. "Remember as you read, ask yourself: 'How does the character feel?'"

HOW TO HELP KIDS BOOST THEIR MORAL IMAGINATIONS

There are dozens of ways to use literature and movies to cultivate children's empathy, open their hearts to care about others, as well as to expand their cognitive development and enhance academic achievement. A big secret to cultivating this habit is to make the activity fun as well as meaningful to children while matching material to their abilities and interests. Do ask your child every once in a while: "When's the last time you read a great book?" If your son or daughter has a blank look, then you know you need to work harder to make reading pleasurable. Here are a few ways to instill a love of reading in our kids:

- **Make books available!** Studies show that the more books you have in your home, the greater the chance your kid will become a reader. You don't have to break the bank, but you should have available the type of reading material that elevates empathy. Dig out that library card. Take advantage of garage sales and buy gently used books. Set up a book exchange with the neighbors. Listen to audiobooks and then read the book as a family! Always stash an extra book in your child's backpack and your car for those "just in case" reading moments.

- **Tailor material to your child's passions.** A big secret to engaging kids in reading is to find material with a theme your child identifies with. If your daughter loves horses, *Black Beauty* or *National Velvet* might be the perfect match. Films like *The Boy in the Striped Pajamas*, *The Book Thief*, and *Extremely Loud and Incredibly Close*, or books like *Where the Red Fern Grows* or *Bridge to Terabithia*, can cause even a tough-skinned older kid to melt. To find the right selection for your teen, consider these online resources: Your Favorites: 100 Best-Ever Teen Novels (http://www.npr.org/2012/08/07/1577955366/your -favorites-100-best-ever-teen-novels), which is based on over 75,000 votes on best young adult novels, or the Empathy Library (http://empathylibrary.com), the world's first online guide full of recommended empathy-building books and films.

- **Match the book to your child's reading level.** If your goal is to instill a love for reading, don't push a book too hard. Most educators suggest you choose books for kids' reading pleasure that are slightly *below* their academic level. Check the last report card or reading achievement scores for his or her reading level. Or at the next parent-conference ask the teacher what your child's current reading level is. The back of many children's books lists the reading level: for example, RL 2.1 means "Second grade, first month," and RL 4.2 means "Fourth grade, second month." You must match the reading level so it is geared to your child's tested reading ability, not his age or year and month in school.

- **Find a good reference!** If you have difficulty finding a selection for your child, ask a children's librarian. They are wonderful resources for this kind of information—and they love to be asked! Also, check resources of great books kids like to read such as Scholastic's national yearly survey of six- to seventeen-year-olds, "Kids and Family Reading Report," http://www.scholastic.com/readingreport/what-kids-want-to-read, which is a portal leading to many guides of many books from all publishers, not just those of Scholastic. *Quick-Picks* (http://www.ala.org/yalsa/quick-picks-reluctant-young-adult-readers) is another resource, or ask other kids for book ideas. You might also treat yourself to a great reference that lists kids' top reading choices, such as: *Best Books for Boys: How to Engage Boys in Reading in Ways That Will Change Their Lives: K–8*, by Pam Allyn; *Best Books for Kids Who (Think They) Hate to Read*, by Laura Backes; *Books Children Love*, by Elizabeth Laraway Wilson; *How to Get Your Child to Love Reading*, by Esmé Raji Codell; and *The Read-Aloud Handbook*, by Jim Trelease. Just be sure to let your child have a choice in the selection: 89 percent of kids say their favorite books are ones *they* pick out![22]

- **Don't stop reading out loud!** Around the age of eight is when our children generally stop reading for enjoyment. Ironically, it's also when we typically stop reading aloud to them, so don't stop reading aloud to your child. Find a book your whole family enjoys and use it as an ongoing read-aloud. Also, make sure your child sees *you* with a book in hand. Children who are more apt to be good readers have parents who read for pleasure.

AGE-BY-AGE STRATEGIES

A father took his son to see the movie *Pay It Forward*, hoping to spend time together. The film is about a teacher who assigns students to think of a way to change the world and put it into action. One student conjures the notion of paying a favor not back, but forward—repaying good deeds not with payback but with new good deeds done for three new people. The efforts of Trevor Ferrell (discussed further in chapter 9) make the world a better place not only in the lives of those close to him but also to those of an ever-widening circle of people completely unknown to him.

"I read the reviews, and thought it might be something Mark would enjoy," the father told me. "I just never dreamed a film would affect him so much. But when the house lights came back, he was so deep in thought that I knew that the movie had hit a chord. Mark told me that he *had* to do something to help homeless kids in our town. He was so emphatic that by the time we pulled into our driveway, he had a plan on how he was going to get shoes to those kids, and he did."

We never know what will resonate with our children. In fact, the best empathy-stretching moments are often unplanned, so if you see that your child is connecting deeply with a book or film, capitalize on that moment. Here are everyday ways to help kids develop the habit of reading for feeling as well as enjoyment. Remember to keep your strategies fun, and like Mark's dad, follow your child's lead.

Symbols designate the recommended age and suitability for activity: L = Little Ones: Toddlers and Preschoolers; S = School age; T = Tweens and Older; A = All Ages.

- **Carve out time to read.** Kids say the biggest reason they don't read for fun is "there isn't enough time," so check your child's calendar. Is there one thing you can cut? Eliminating just *one* television show, video game, or extracurricular activity can free up thirty minutes a week to read. Just a few minutes a day can increase this habit. **A**

- **Get cozy!** One of the best ways to bond with your child is with a good book. My kids (and I!) used to love covering our card table with a sheet, crawling into our special sanctuary underneath it, and reading on Saturday afternoons. Find a reading ritual that works for your family—whether it's curling up with books by the fireplace, sitting on the lawn on a lazy Sunday afternoon, or finishing the day with a bedtime story. Such routines help instill the message that "book are comforting," plant seeds of empathy, and nurture a love of reading. A

- **Start family movie nights!** Family favorites such as *The Wizard of Oz, Charlotte's Web, The Shawshank Redemption, The Book Thief,* or *The King's Speech* can activate our children's hearts. So why not initiate a regular family movie time? Just set a date, rent or stream a stirring film, pop the popcorn, and make memories. Some neighborhoods hold Summer Movie Nights: families take turns tacking a sheet outside, plugging in the DVD, spreading blankets on the lawn, and showing a great flick such as *Into the Wild, The Blind Side, The Outsiders, October Sky, E.T. The Extra-Terrestrial,* or *The Breakfast Club* for the neighborhood kids to watch. (Do view the film first to ensure suitability for your crowd.) Check out websites such as Teach with Movies (http://www.teachwithmovies.org) and Common Sense Media (http://www.commonsense.org), which offer reviews and age-by-age child ratings of current movies. A

- **Ask your child to make up the ending.** One way to expand perspective is to have kids make up the ending before hearing the writer's version. Pause the movie or put your finger in the book seconds before the finale and ask questions like: "Imagine you're the character right now, what would you do?" "What do you think will happen?" "If you were the author [or filmmaker], how would you end it?" Then finish the book or film and vote as to which version you all prefer: your child's or the writer's. A

- **Share *your* feelings.** Did you know that a simple way to help children understand the feelings, thoughts, wishes, and knowledge of others is if parents[23] talk about their own feelings? Suppose you're reading *The Velveteen Rabbit* and see that the two of you are getting teary-eyed. Don't hide your emotions: grab a tissue, cuddle up, and share your feelings! Not only are you connecting, but you are also using the moment for "feeling instruction." So don't be shy: share your emotions with your child. "It makes me so sad how they're treating Dumbo. What about you?" Or "I'm so upset the way those girls treat each other. My heart hurts. What about yours?" Talking about emotions[24] with our kids is one way they learn the skills of emotional intelligence, and tying those chats to a book or movie scene is one more way to stretch their empathy muscles. **A**

- **Play feeling games.** Children's picture books with emotionally charged illustrations can help kids develop a feeling vocabulary, which will improve their abilities to imagine another's views and mental state. Suppose you and your child are reading Molly Bang's *When Sophie Gets Angry—Really, Really Angry*: point to the illustrations that depict different emotional states and play feeling games: "How does Sophie's face look? Yes, she does look angry. What made her so angry? Make your face look angry like Sophie's face." Or maybe you're reading Judith Viorst's *Alexander and the Terrible, Horrible, No Good, Very Bad Day*. Use the illustrations: "Look at Alexander's face! What's that feeling called? Can you imagine how he feels right now? Make your body look the way you think Alexander feels." **L, S**

- **Read with emotion!** Kids must learn to recognize emotions not only on a character's facial expressions and body language but also in voice tone. Reading with feeling will help your child recognize that tone of voice also conveys moods. So you might read the same short passage, but each time give your voice a different tone (bored, excited, tired, sad, angry). Pretend you're actors: ask each other to guess the tone you're trying to portray. **L, S**

- **Use audiobooks.** Don't overlook listening to audiobooks with your kids. They are a great way to boost comprehension and auditory processing skills as well as make memories as the whole family listens in. You might download audiobooks onto your child's MP3 player or car tape deck; just gear the listening time to your children's attention span. While your teen may love *The Vampire*

Diaries or *The Hunger Games*, be sure that she still has the opportunity to listen to gripping classics such as *To Kill a Mockingbird*, *Wonder*, *Brave New World*, and *The Giver*, which are more apt to stir our emotional imaginations. **A**

- **Start book clubs!** One-fifth[25] of children say they read less because they "would be embarrassed if a friend saw them with a book," so consider having your child's friends join a book club! Clubs have gained popularity in recent years, in a wide variety of types: for mothers and daughters, fathers and sons, and "kids only." They're a fun way for parents to connect with their kids while also helping them develop a love of reading and language, literacy skills, and the ability to read with feeling. Most important, many kids love book clubs and get hooked on reading because they're doing so with peers. A few resources about how to get started include *The Mother-Daughter Project*, by SuEllen Hamkins and Renée Schultz; *The Kids' Book Club Book*, by Judy Gelman and Vicki Levy Krupp; and *The Parent-Child Book Club*, by Melissa Stoller and Marcy Winkler. **S, T**

- **Read novels together.** Check the teacher's website for your child's required reading list (or look at the bottom of his backpack!), and then get two copies of each school reading requirement: one for you and one for your kid. Though you each read the book alone, the experience creates discussion opportunities to share your thoughts and hear your child's views. Think of how many parents and kids read Harry Potter books and then watched the movies, together. **S, T**

- **Check reading material for content.** In our quest to get our kids to read, we sometimes lower our standards for reading material, but beware: a new study found that a typical teen bestselling novel contains thirty-eight[26] instances of profanity (which translates to almost seven instances of profanity per each hour a teen reads). So read those reviews or do the old-time but still valuable test: just flip open to a few random pages and review the content. **S, T**

THE TOP FIVE THINGS TO KNOW ABOUT
CULTIVATING MORAL IMAGINATION

1. Today's children are reading less than previous generations. Igniting their passion for the printed word may be our first challenge to instilling this crucial habit.

2. As digital entertainment choices (such as apps, videos games, social media) increase, children's literary habits shrink, making unplugged time for family reading essential.

3. Reading literary fiction—even for short periods—nurtures empathy and perspective-taking ability, at least temporarily.

4. Children who read exclusively on digital screens are three times less likely to say they enjoy reading, a third less likely to have a favorite book, and far less likely to become strong readers.

5. Part of the secret in helping children step into the shoes of a character with literature is offering material that matches their interests as well as reading abilities.

ONE LAST THING

Books stir our emotions, spark our curiosity, create lasting memories, and become portals to other worlds. In some cases, a book can whip our conscience, shift our perspective, or activate our feelings so we stand up and change the world for the better. The right book can stir a child's empathy better than any lesson or lecture ever could. And the right book matched with the right child can be the gateway to opening his heart to humanity. Raising a generation that would rather text than read, we have our work cut out, for as reading declines, so too will one of the proven tools to expand our children's capacity to imagine another's feelings and needs, as well as reap the Empathy Advantage and thrive.

PART TWO

PRACTICING EMPATHY

It is one of the beautiful compensations of life that no man can sincerely try to help another without helping himself.

—Ralph Waldo Emerson

CHAPTER 5

Empathetic Children Can Keep Their Cool

Managing Strong Emotions and Mastering Self-Regulation

Ten minutes beyond San Diego's lush beaches is City Heights, a community with one of the highest number of low-income and ethnically diverse families in the area. And right in the middle of City Heights is Epiphany Prep Charter School. The staff is committed to educating their students for college and a career as well as preparing them for life. I was there to see how they were educating the "whole child."

Many of these students witness violence in their neighborhoods, and it can exact a heavy cost. Untethered stress reduces children's focusing abilities, resilience, and emotional health, and all this jeopardizes their academic achievement. But stress also affects empathy. It's tough to feel for others when you're in "survival mode." Witnessing others' distress can also trigger "compassion fatigue" and shut down empathy because you're too distraught from seeing their pain.

While teachers can't change students' home environments, they can teach ways for the kids in their classrooms to cope. And it's true for us as parents, as well: while we can't oversee what happens beyond our front doors, we can offer our children tools to handle whatever comes their way. Self-regulation is one of those essential tools, and it's composed of skills like self-awareness, self-management, emotional literacy, and problem solving.

Second-grade teacher Mayra Reyes was teaching those skills in a unique process called restorative justice (RJ) where everyone—victim, offender, and community—talks out a problem together and offers solutions. The goal is for offenders "to repair the harm done by apologizing or somehow making amends," thus restoring their relationship with victims.

I became a RJ "believer" while observing Hutus and Tutsis in Rwanda listen calmly to one another's perspectives after experiencing the horrors of genocide. "If they can, anyone can" became my mantra. I realized that restorative justice is a powerful empathy-building practice, and that day I saw it work with young children.

Conflicts were frequent when school began. "The children didn't know ways to resolve issues other than physically," Reyes told me. And so the teacher adapted the RJ model so her second graders could learn self-regulation, conflict resolution, and perspective taking. She first taught them emotional literacy skills, so students could identify feelings and calmly talk through problems. A Calm Down Corner was also available for students to decompress. Then she taught three simple problem-solving steps to help students resolve conflicts peacefully:

1. **Identify the Problem.** "Today I had a problem when . . ."

2. **Identify Your Feelings.** "I feel . . ." or "I felt . . ."

3. **Seek Solutions.** "A possible short-term solution is . . ." "A possible long-term solution is . . ."

Short-term solutions could be apologizing, doing an activity like making a card together, and modeling the positive behavior in a skit. Long-term solutions might include creating a behavior contract with the student or becoming a class restorative justice expert. Students slowly learned the skills with repeated practice and were ready to apply them.

"Does anyone have a problem they need help solving?" Mayra Reyes asked. I was about to see a Restorative Justice Circle, and students gathered eagerly around the rug.

Juanita raised her hand, and Reyes handed her a talking piece to hold, a red gift box to remind students that "speaking is a gift, and the person talking is imparting important knowledge." Circle rules mandated that a classmate's name be used only if present, language must be professional ("as if you're speaking to the principal"), and just the person holding the talking piece may speak. Those are great rules for family meetings as well.

"Today I had a problem," Juanita began. "Pedro called me a name in the computer lab." She was asking her classmates to help her find a solution.

Next, it was Pedro's turn. (Students may opt out of the circle and request a private meeting, but Pedro was willing.) "Today I had a problem with Juanita," he said. "She was kicking me under the table, so I told Juanita she was stupid."

Pedro and Juanita then voiced their feelings: "It made me feel unsafe," Juanita said. "I felt very upset with Juanita," Pedro said.

Now Pedro and Juanita would each ask two peers to share either a long-term or short-term solution.

Juanita chose Kristina and Raul. Kristina suggested Pedro apologize to Juanita for calling her stupid. Raul suggested that they shake hands and say, "I'm sorry."

Pedro called on two classmates for ideas. Isaac proposed that Pedro or Juanita request a seat change, and Iliana advised Pedro to sit farther back, "So he doesn't get kicked."

Then Pedro and Juanita must decide their solution. The onetime adversaries whispered together and then announced their decision while jointly holding the talking piece to show they were "one voice."

"Our short-term solution is to apologize to one another, since we both did something wrong," said Juanita.

"Our long-term solution is to request a seat change so we stop fighting," said Pedro.

Classmates erupted in claps, elated that the twosome had solved their problem. And as promised, Pedro and Juanita shook hands in front of their peers.

These kids managed their emotions, communicated their needs, understood other's perspectives, and created win-win solutions. As one eight-year-old told Reyes: "Just because we are little doesn't mean we can't do big things."

"At the beginning solutions are one-sided, because students want to solve 'their' issue," Reyes told me. "But then they start to listen, put themselves into each other's shoes, and develop a deeper understanding of one another." [1]

The school's name, Epiphany, means "a moment in which you suddenly understand something in a new or very clear way." Reyes's Restorative Justice Circles were creating such a moment for her students. They were learning not only self-regulation, but also how to solve problems peacefully and expand their empathy: an epiphany every child needs.

LEARNING TO DEVELOP SELF-REGULATION

In Part 1 of this book, we discussed four basic tenets of developing empathy: teaching emotional literacy, moral identity, perspective taking, and moral imagination, each of which increases the odds that our children will be kind and helpful and acquire the Empathy Advantage. But developing empathy is just part of the equation. The next step is for children to *practice* empathy in their day-to-day lives, and in order to do that they must learn additional habits—the first of which is self-regulation. Self-regulation allows kids to keep their emotions in check so they can recognize others' feelings and then calmly think of how to help. If kids don't know how to manage emotions, their empathy is jeopardized. If they are too distressed by another's pain, they either cope by shutting down their compassionate instincts to care for themselves or can't think clearly enough to help. Anxiety and stress can sabotage empathy.

Managing emotions helps children to look beyond themselves, put aside what would feed their urges, and "do for others." It helps kids become UnSelfies. And it's the habit kids tell me that they need most: "Nobody tells us *how* to calm down!" "I'm so upset when kids bully

Kevin, that I can't think *how* to help!" "Somebody needs to tell me *how* to keep my mouth shut so I don't gossip."

Cultivating self-regulation builds kids' empathy muscles, but it also has additional surprising advantages. The ability to manage emotions is a better predictor of academic achievement than IQ,[2] it dramatically increases your adult child's health and financial stability,[3] and it strengthens resilience so your child can bounce back from setbacks.[4] And it helps fill in the empathy gap (feeling another's pain but not acting on urges to help), so kids are more likely to *feel* empathy and *respond* compassionately.

This chapter offers proven ways to boost your child's self-regulation abilities. Best yet, learning these habits will enhance *every* area of your child's development—cognitive, moral, social and emotional—both now and forever.

WHY IS IT SO HARD FOR KIDS TO KEEP THEIR COOL?

Peace Chairs, Quiet Time, Calm Down Corners, and Restorative Justice Circles are popping up in schools from coast to coast to help "the most stressed generation on record." Educators recognize that poor self-regulation skills reduce academic achievement *and* empathy. Here are reasons why today's kids struggle with self-regulation and how it widens the empathy gap and derails them from helping others.

Stressed-Out Kids

Forget those images of carefree childhoods. Today's teens are experiencing stress at an all-time high:[5] one in three say they feel "overwhelmed." Especially sobering is that our kids' stress now tops *our* stress levels.[6] One in six college students has been diagnosed or treated by a professional for anxiety in the past twelve months; childhood anxiety is up 25 percent.[7] The reasons include economic hardship, trauma, make-or-break testing, bullying, and pressure to perform day-to-day. But one fact remains: when stress rises, kids suffer.

Untamed stress impairs not only judgment, memory, and impulse control but also our compassionate instincts.[8] Anxiety makes us oblivious to others' feelings, reduces perspective taking, increases egocentrism (aka the Selfie Syndrome),[9] and widens the empathy gap. It's hard for kids to tune in to someone else's pain and help if they're in distress themselves. And it's why we must build in time for our kids to decompress, and learn their stress triggers, and teach them healthy ways to manage destructive emotions.

Glorification of Violent Behavior

Our media is called "the most violent in the world" for good reason.[10] By the end of elementary school, the average child will witness 8,000 murders and, by age eighteen, 200,000 other vivid acts of violence, on all screens including video, television, and online streaming.[11]

Then there's the gaming industry. In-depth studies from Canada's Brock University found that overexposure to violent images also slows moral growth and weakens a child's ability to feel for others.[12] For many children their plugged-in time—about seven hours a day—is basically like having a full-time job. "The more kids see and experience violence (whether at school, home, on TV, computer, video games, or as a victim), the more they think it's 'normal, common, and acceptable.'"[13] And the more it lowers kids' inhibitions against aggression toward others.

Viewing aggression may also change our children's brains. Brain scans found that just one week after playing violent video games, even kids who were not frequent video game players showed decreased activity in the parts of their brains that regulate emotion, attention, and concentration.[14] Time to keep a closer eye on our children's media diet and keep the empathy gap in check.

Parents Behaving Badly

The most effective way kids learn self-regulation is by watching others, and it appears their parents aren't the best models. News stories repeat-edy warn us of parents behaving badly at their kids' sporting events and even at high school graduations. In fact, parental misbehavior has become so troublesome that Soccer America now instructs refs in how to deal with "spectator abuse."[15] Other organizations, including Little League for baseball, Pop Warner for football, and the United States Tennis Association, are also concerned about poor adult sportsmanship, and are revising their policies to deal with "big people" misbehaving at their events. Make no mistake, kids are watching our behavior both on screen and off, and it *is* impacting their character.

For proof, try this: a survey of a thousand children—whether parents worked outside the home or not—gave their moms the lowest grades for controlling tempers when they made them angry.[16] If parents aren't modeling self-regulation or empathy, how will kids learn it? So ask yourself: "What kind of grade would my kids give me for managing my behavior?"

The Age of Multitasking

Today's kids are whizzes at texting, friending, and swiping while studying, eating, or chatting. Even on their best behavior, most kids can't focus on their school assignments more than two minutes without using social media.[17] But dividing attention means that their brain must shift focus between two, three, or four things, and there are "switching costs" including lessened cognitive abilities, mental fatigue, and *reduced empathy*. Simply having a cell phone nearby—without even checking it—can reduce empathy.[18]

The plain fact is if kids are focusing on that text or counting Facebook followers, they're not tuning in to people. If they "don't build up the neural circuitry that focused attention requires," says Daniel Goleman, "they could have problems controlling their emotions and being empathetic."[19] And a large survey of tween-age girls found that their multitasking hours and electronic diversions were associated with diminished social and emotional skills.[20]

Multitasking is another trend that might be widening the empathy gap. It's time to revive that parental admonishment "Turn it off, and please look at me when I'm talking to you." And then make sure you're applying that same rule to yourself.

Despite a multitasking culture, violent media, stress upsurge, and adults behaving badly, self-regulation is *not* genetically bound and *can* be taught. This is one habit we can't afford to put on the back burner: our kids' academic achievement, mental health, *and* empathy quotients are at stake.

WHAT SCIENCE SAYS: HOW TO TEACH SELF-CONTROL

Tulita Elementary School is located in Redondo Beach just blocks from the Pacific Ocean and serves a diverse population of students. I was visiting Jennifer Bell's first-grade class to see her lesson on mindfulness— which has been getting quite a bit of attention these days, including millions of Google hits. Today she was teaching the neuroscience of mindfulness, and her students were enthralled, as was I. Bell sat holding up her arm (bent at the elbow, hand in a fist with her thumb tucked under four fingers) to explain to seven-year-olds how the brain works.

"This part is your spinal cord [rubbing her elbow to her wrist] that sends messages to your brain. The brain stem [pointing to her palm] controls things like your breathing and tummy when you feel nervous. Close by is your amygdala [pointing to under her fingers] that wants to 'fight, flee, or freeze' when it feels stressed. When it feels a threat, it quickly calls out an emergency signal, and our body goes on alert mode. How do you know when you're upset?" she asks.

"When I'm mad, my head gets a headache," one boy says.

"I feel it in my heart," adds a girl with long pigtails.

"Our body sends out stress signs we should listen to," says Bell. "And here is your prefrontal cortex [four bent fingers] and your 'wise leader.' When we get agitated and our amygdala isn't happy, we breathe faster and faster, our heart pounds harder and harder, our prefrontal cortex can't think, so we 'pop' our lid." [Her fist pops wide open.]

"What can we do if we're feeling upset to help our prefrontal cortex think and our amygdala from sending out a crisis alert?" she asks.

Every seven-year-old chimed in: "Just breathe!"

"That's right!" Bell says. "All we have to do to calm down is to breathe in . . . and breathe out. Then your prefrontal cortex can be your wise leader again. Just breathe!"

I had just watched one of the best descriptions on the emotional brain, and it was taught to first graders. Bell was adapting her lesson based on the work of Daniel Siegel, a clinical professor of psychiatry and codirector of the UCLA Mindful Awareness Research Center. The content was resonating: her young students "got it."

I realized a frequent parenting mistake: failing to explain the science behind learning a skill. So why would children put in effort to make it a habit? These kids told me why they should exercise their breathing muscles ("It helps me calm down," "It clears my brain," "I don't flip my lid and hit my sister"), and took Bell's lessons seriously.

The children were also eager to share the breathing exercises they'd practiced all year. Bell reminded them: "Find a quiet place and lie down. Close your eyes, breathe through your nose, and let it out. Focus on each breath. Remember, just breathe." Within seconds, the room was still: students were lying flat on the rug, eyes closed and breathing deeply. I swore two boys were asleep, and I was reminding myself to try this at night.

As I left, students were busy gluing images of favorite breathing strategies on paper headbands, so they would remember to use them at home: "Just Breathe!" was printed in huge letters across the top. "I want to help my students learn tools that they can use for the rest of their lives," Bell told me.

I had no doubts that those breathing strategies and this teacher would be imprinted in these students' memory banks for a long time.

The Mistaken "Cognitive Hype"

"Mindfulness" (or "being aware of what is happening as it is happening")[21] is the hot buzzword. It has gained extensive popularity in psychology, business, medicine, and education alike as research confirms its wide-ranging benefits for adults and kids. But it was the surprise discoveries about the power of emotions that started the revolution. The general belief was that skills like emotional literacy, empathy, self-regulation, and focusing abilities were locked in by genetics. Besides, emotional and social skills were "nice to have" but not too important in the big scheme of "what children need to succeed." So we put our energy into what we believe helps give our kids "the résumé edge"—piano lessons, robotics, Mandarin classes, special tutors—because we'd been fed the "Cognitive Hype." After all, school achievement, Ivy League acceptance, and career advancements all depended on "cognitive" capabilities. Right?

But then a fresh stream of research began to put holes in the cognitive theory. While it was important, our one-sided endeavors to help our kids overlooked the surprising power of emotions and empathy to boost our children's success and happiness. We were actually shortchanging our children's futures.

Self-Regulation: A Secret to Success

Rethinking the "Cognitive Hype" started with marshmallows, preschoolers, and a legendary Stanford University study.[22] In 1970, Walter Mischel, now a renowned psychologist, invited a group of four-year-olds to a "game room" where they were shown a tray of marshmallows (and other treats) and asked to choose one. Then came the challenge: "Do you want the marshmallow now, or can you wait until I come back and you can have two?" Waiting is hard for any kid, but especially for preschoolers. Still, about a third of the children waited and received a larger reward for demonstrating their self-restraint.

When researchers followed the children they found significant differences. By high school, those who could halt their "gotta have it now" emotions had significantly higher SAT scores—an average 210 points higher—than those who couldn't wait at age four. Forty years later (Mischel is still tracking the original kids), those with more self-restraint were far more socially competent, self-assertive, and better able to deal with the frustrations of life. Mischel recently announced to the world his own epiphany: for over four decades, he thought that preschoolers' "waiting" abilities were due to inborn temperaments. But scientific advancements have revealed that self-regulation is teachable.

Next came a long-term study in Dunedin, New Zealand, that followed 1,037 children—all the babies born over a period of twelve months—for forty years. It found that ability to put the brakes on emotions is essential to success. Lead researcher Terrie E. Moffitt said: "Childhood self-control strongly predicts adult success, in people of high or low intelligence, in rich or poor."[23] Those who showed early signs of self-regulation not only were less likely to develop later addictions or commit a crime but also were healthier and wealthier adults than were their more impulsive peers.[24] In fact, a child's self-regulation ability is a better predictor of their academic achievement than IQ is.[25] Self-regulation also correlates with better health, greater wealth, lowered risk of substance abuse,[26] and increased financial stability. The "Cognitive Hype" took another ding, but could we really impact our children's self-regulation skills?

Then came another study whose results stirred not only the scientific world but also revamped educational curriculums and parenting toolkits—and the subjects were Buddhist monks.

Lessons from Monks' Brains

Richard Davidson is a prominent neuroscientist at the University of Wisconsin–Madison, and he is fascinated with how meditation and emotions help us lead lives that are more meaningful. So Davidson turned to unusual subjects: Tibetan Buddhist monks lent to him by the Dalai Lama for a series of groundbreaking studies. One by one, they were led to Davidson's lab and hooked up to an electroencephalograph (EEG) that would record their brain activity as they meditated.

In one study, the brain activity of monks who had practiced meditating for ten thousand to fifty thousand hours, and that of college students with little meditative experience, were monitored. The scans shocked researchers: the records of the monks' brain activity differed significantly from those of the student volunteers. Monks who spent the most years meditating produced exceptionally powerful gamma waves (brain waves associated with peak concentration and higher mental activity): up to 30 times stronger than the college students did and on a scale never previously reported in a healthy person.

Davidson had discovered that the brain is not fixed but rather that it has an ability called "neuroplasticity." And the years of meditating had rewired the monks' brains. What's more, Davidson proved that the brain can change not only in childhood but also throughout life.[27]

The research team also had the monks and students meditate on compassion (for instance, wishing loved ones well or thinking about other people's suffering and not just their own). While all subjects showed activity in the parts of the brain that generate positive emotions and happiness, the monks had much greater activation in areas linked to empathy and recognizing others' emotions. Extensively practicing compassion meditation had dramatically changed the areas of the monks' brains that detect feelings.[28]

Davidson's extraordinary discoveries have enormous implications for parenting: self-regulation as well as kindness and compassion can be learned in the same way as playing a cello or being proficient in hockey. While we've trained our children to be violinists, math whizzes, spelling champs, and gymnasts, we can also train them to be good human beings. One way is by helping our children practice compassion and managing emotions more diligently.

The Mindfulness Revolution in Schools

Science shows that practicing mindfulness—even minutes a day for a few weeks—can reap such positive benefits as boosting immune systems,[29] reducing stress,[30] increasing resilience, enhancing focus,[31] stretching attention,[32] and improving memory.[33] But mindfulness can also nurture empathy[34] and compassion[35] as well as increase children's willingness to help others.[36] It's why thousands of educators, like Jennifer Bell, are adding mindfulness to their class routines. It also seems to help youth growing up in challenging environments.

When Visitacion Valley Middle School in San Francisco introduced Quiet Time as a twice-daily, fifteen-minute ritual—a time when students may choose to sit quietly or meditate—it became the first public school in the country to adopt the practice. Violence in the neighborhoods (nine shootings in one month) was spilling into the school and affecting the students.[37] The staff had tried numerous strategies, but none was effective. In the first year of the new approach, suspensions were reduced by 45 percent.

Within four years, suspensions decreased 79 percent; attendance rates climbed to 98 percent, grade point averages and test scores improved. What's more, students said they are calmer and less angry, and their "happiness levels" (recorded on the annual California Healthy Kids Survey) skyrocketed.[38] Burton High School, just a few blocks away (and once dubbed "Fight School"), implemented Quiet Time, and found similar results.

Yes, students in high-risk areas do face enormous stress, but *all* kids— regardless of zip code—can benefit from self-regulation. In fact, "privileged teens" reared in upper-class environments now have higher rates of depression, anxiety, and substance abuse than any other socioeconomic group of young Americans today.[39] Mindfulness is really a way to help children keep stress at bay and respond without instantly reacting.

Research on the effectiveness of school mindfulness programs shows promise in everything from improving kindness to math, and proving to be a game changer for *all* kids:

- Fourth and fifth graders regulated stress better, were more optimistic, kinder, helpful, and improved in math.[40]

- At-risk third graders showed significant improvement in behavior and focusing.[41]

- British teens showed lower depression and stress levels and improved well-being.[42]

- Elementary students improved significantly in paying attention, self-control, classroom participation, and respect for others.[43]

Practicing mindfulness just a few minutes a day is making a difference in children's lives. It turns out that best solution for self-regulation is literally right under our nose. All kids need to do is "Just breathe!"

HOW TO TEACH CHILDREN SELF-REGULATION

I was on-air with Alexandra Barzvi, host of *Doctor Radio*, and parents were calling in on how to reduce tantrums. "Stress comes *before* the anger," I told one parent. "Helping your child learn to calm down *before* the meltdown is your goal."

The next caller had advice. Her eight-year-old son was exploding after school until Mom realized that he didn't know how to decompress. So she put a beanbag chair in a quiet corner with a CD player and a few of his favorite books.

"The next day, I asked him to sit with me because 'I had a bad day and needed to relax,'" she said. "It became our new after-school ritual, and his meltdowns slowly faded. Two weeks later, I found him in the beanbag listening to music. He told me 'I'm relaxing.' Now he does it daily: he just needed me to show him how to calm down."

I'm sure every listener bought a beanbag chair that day. But that mom reminded everyone that helping our kids manage emotions starts by showing them how.

- **Model calmness.** Your child's best template for learning self-regulation is you. So how do you act in front of your kids after a hard day? When you're driving with your children and another car cuts in front of you? When the bank says you're overdrawn?

Your kids are watching, so make sure your behavior is what you want them to copy.

- **Tune in to your child.** How does your child handle stress? If he has a stressful experience or sees another in distress does he:

  ▷ Develop physical ailments like a headache, stomachache, or heart palpitations?

  ▷ Try to avoid the person or the scene?

  ▷ Become distressed and try to block out the person's pain?

  ▷ Have trouble bouncing back and need a long time to recover?

  ▷ Need help calming down to recover?

  Learn your child's emotional needs so you can empathize and know how to help.

- **Identify body alarms.** Say: "We have little body signs that warn us we're getting upset and need to calm down." Help your child recognize her body alarms such as flushed cheeks, clenched fists, tightened muscles, pounding heart, churning tummy, dry mouth, and quicker breaths. Then point out her sign quietly when she *first* gets frustrated: "Your hands are in fists. Are you feeling yourself getting stressed?" The more kids are aware of early stress, the better they'll be at regulating their emotions.

- **Create a quiet space.** Find a place to help your family decompress. Size doesn't matter, but it should have a soothing feel. It might have a beanbag or rocking chair, soft pillows, stuffed animals, or a CD player. Introduce it as a "place to calm down for every family member." Hint: Kids should equate the spot as a place to decompress, *not* for discipline or time-out.

- **Make a Stress Box.** My friends at the Thompson Child and Family Focus developed a Stress Box to teach students self-regulation. It includes an MP3 player with soothing music, a Koosh ball, a bubble blower, and a notepad and pen or crayons to "write away their anger," and books about feelings. Younger kids: *Glad Monster, Sad Monster*, by Ed Emberley and Anne Miranda; *On Monday When It Rained*, by Cheryl Kachenmeister. Older kids and teens: *Fighting Invisible Tigers*, by Earl Hipp; or *Hot Stones & Funny Bones*, by Brian Luke Seaward. Make a family stress box, teach everyone how to use each stress reducer, and then put it in your quiet place for your family.

- **Teach a self-regulation strategy.** Each child needs a calming strategy that works for him. This chapter offers numerous self-regulation techniques, so find one that appeals to your child. Then help him practice until it becomes a habit.

EMPATHY BUILDER: USING MINDFUL BREATHING TO MANAGE FEELINGS

Science proves that teaching children to be mindful of the moment can enhance self-regulation as well as compassion. Here are four steps to help your family become a more mindful family.

Step 1: Teach Yourself to "Just Breathe"

Practice mindful breathing first alone, so you can teach it to your family. Find a comfortable, quiet spot, keep your shoulders as relaxed as possible, and then focus on taking deep, slow breaths by breathing in through your nose and exhaling through your mouth. The exhales should be twice as long as your inhales to maximize the relaxation response. When your mind wanders—which it will—gently tell yourself to think about your breathing. Increase the session lengths as your comfort level improves.

Step 2: Explain the Benefits

Tell your child, "Taking slow, deep breaths helps you relax and calms your brain so you can think clearer and stay in control. You can use it before taking a test, to get to sleep, or any time you're frustrated, worried, sad, or just need to chill. And you can use it anywhere. The more you practice, the easier it is to calm and relax."

Step 3: Teach Belly Breathing

Sit straight in a chair or lie flat on the floor with hands low on belly. Inhale deeply through your nose, gently hold it, and then let the air out slowly through your lips. "Feel your tummy rise and fall with each breath. Try to keep your mind on your breaths, but if it wanders, just tell yourself to focus on your belly breaths."

In the beginning, you might sit next to your child and softly count and breathe as he breathes. Gradually stretch inhales and exhales, and session lengths based on each family member's abilities. My friend Vicki Zakrzewski, from the Greater Good Science Center, told me that "the exhale should be twice as long as the inhale to activate the vagus nerve and create a relaxation response," so make that the ultimate goal.[44]

Step 4: Make Mindfulness a Family Ritual

Find ways to do breathing exercises a few times a day—like before leaving home, in the carpool, at dinner, or bedtime—so it becomes a ritual. Short, repeated practices work best to get you into a habit, so think: *Brief times, many times*. Read also *10 Mindful Minutes*, by Goldie Hawn; or *Calming Your Anxious Brain*, by Jeffrey Brantley and Jon Kabat-Zinn.

AGE-BY-AGE STRATEGIES

I learned one of the wisest ways to teach self-regulation from a high school junior at Taiwan's Taipei American School. He was a stellar student, star athlete, and student body officer, but he also had great humor and a caring heart: the epitome of the "all-around, balanced kid" that I fear is on today's endangered species list. You couldn't help but be impressed with his achievements and optimistic outlook, but something bothered me.

"Most teens with half as much going on aren't as upbeat as you, so why aren't you stressed out?" I asked.

He laughed. "It's my parents," he answered.

"Your parents? Please tell me more."

"Most of my friends feel pressured to get high grades and accepted into good colleges, so stress is hitting them hard," he said. "My parents knew that high school would be tough, so they gave me little doses of hard stuff when I was young. And they never rescued me like other parents do but showed me how to calm down. They helped me learn I can handle tough stuff, so I don't get overwhelmed like my friends."

His parents were not only wise, but they also used what I call the Baby Step Model to help their son learn to manage emotions and handle life. It's also the best way to help kids learn self-regulation: just practice managing emotions in small, baby steps.

Symbols designate the recommended age and suitability for activity: L = Little Ones: Toddlers and Preschoolers; S = School-age; T = Tweens and Older; A = All Ages

- **Rate the feeling.** Encouraging kids to rate the intensity of their emotion increases self-awareness. So when your child notices a strong feeling, say: "Name it." ("I feel sad . . . mad . . . scared.") Then on a scale of 1 to 10, ask him to rate the emotion's strength, with 1 being the mildest ("A soft cloud drifting by") and 10 the most intense ("A volcano exploding"). Find a way for your child to share his emotions, so you can empathize and then help him self-regulate. **A**

- **Show how to breathe deeply.** Many kids inhale too quickly, so the breathing doesn't help them calm down. Try these tips to help your family activate the relaxation response. **A**

  ▷ **Buddy Breathing.** Sit back-to-back with your child with his arms and your arms intertwined at the elbows, and breathe together. Your child tries to feel your slow breaths and adjust his breathing to match yours, while you match yours to his.

  ▷ **Belly Buddies.** The child lies flat on his back, places a small, smooth stone or stuffed animal on his tummy, and feels it slowly go up and down with each breath.

  ▷ **Candles and flowers.** Say: "Pretend you are smelling a flower, and then slowly blowing out a birthday candle." The image helps kids visualize "breathing in" (inhaling) and "breathing out" (exhaling).

  ▷ **Cotton ball puffs.** Sit facing your child with your palms up and fingertips touching. Put a cotton ball on your palm and then practice gently blowing so the ball shifts back and forth between her palms and your palms without dropping.

  ▷ **Bubble blowing.** Blow soap bubbles with a young child "without them popping." Then practice blowing "imaginary bubbles" with deep breaths to "slowly blow worries away."

- **Teach a self-regulation strategy.** Stress stimulates some kids while paralyzing others, but every child benefits from learning self-regulation skills. Once your child can recognize his stress signs, teach him a cool-down strategy to use the instant his body sign kicks in. **A**

  ▷ **Imagine a calm place.** For instance: the beach, his bed, Grandpa's backyard, a tree house. The child closes his eyes and visualizes the spot while breathing slowly.

  ▷ **Self-talk.** Teach a positive message your child can say to himself in stressful situations, like: "Stop and calm down," "Stay in

control," "I can handle this." Suggest a few phrases, have your
child choose one she feels most comfortable saying, and then
help her rehearse it a few times each day until it becomes automatic.

▷ **"1 + 3 + 10."** As soon as you feel stress, tell yourself: "Stop
and be calm." That's 1. Now take three deep, slow breaths from
your tummy. That's 3. Then count slowly to ten inside your
head and focus on each number as you exhale. That's 10. Put
them all together and you have 1 + 3 + 10.

- **Make a Calm-Down Jar.** Glitter jars are a fun way for kids to soothe
themselves, and are easy to make. Into a Mason jar, pour 1 cup of
hot water and 2 tablespoons of glitter glue or a bottle of clear glue,
and then whisk. Add some fine glitter ("fairy dust") until there is a
layer of glitter on the bottom, from one-half to three-quarters of an
inch deep. Fill the jar with water plus a bit more of chunkier glitter
(or sequins, beads, or small plastic jewels), leaving about one inch
of room at the top. Add a drop of food coloring and screw the lid
on tightly. As your child shakes and watches the glitter swirl slowly
to the bottom, he practices breathing slowly as his stress "magi-
cally fades."[45] You might have your child make a Calm-Down Jar
for someone who might appreciate it. **L, S**

- **Breathe kind thoughts!** Once your child learns Belly Breathing (see page 111), you can teach breathing variations that boost
mindfulness and compassion. **A**

▷ **Try Gratitude Breathing.** Take a deep breath and count "one"
as you exhale and say something you're grateful for. ("I'm
grateful for my family.") Take another breath, count "two,"
and as you exhale, say another thing you're grateful for. ("I'm
grateful for my health," or "I'm thankful for my puppy.") Keep
breathing, counting, exhaling, and telling yourself things
you're grateful for until you get to five, and then start at one
with either repeating your gratitude list or adding new ideas.

▷ **Think about helpers.** Think about people who are helpful to you (even if you don't know them well, like the school nurse or bus driver). Then think how they help you while you do Belly Breathing.[46]

▷ **Breathe kind wishes.** Close your eyes and think of a person you want to send kind wishes to, people who have been especially kind to you. Then silently repeat phrases like "May he have a good day," "I hope she is happy," "May they be safe" while doing your Belly Breathing.

• **Learn yoga.** Teen girls from New York told me that yoga keeps their stress in check. Yoga also increases awareness of breathing, thoughts, and body movements, and it helps work off stress and tension. Find an age-appropriate yoga DVD and do yoga with your child, seek classes in your area, or start a mother-daughter (or mother-son, dad-daughter) yoga group. **S, T**

• **Try an app.** Download an app to help your child practice self-regulation. *Young children:* Inner Peace for Kids. *School age:* Super Stretch Yoga. *Tweens and teens:* Smiling Mind, Stop, Breathe & Think, or Take a Break! **A**

• **Get educated.** Keep informed about scientific discoveries that are revolutionizing the way we parent. A few: *Brainstorm*, by Daniel J. Siegel; *NurtureShock*, by Po Bronson and Ashley Merryman; *The Marshmallow Test*, by Walter Mischel; *Focus*, by Daniel Goleman; or *The Emotional Life of Your Brain*, by Richard Davidson. **T**

THE TOP FIVE THINGS TO KNOW ABOUT CULTIVATING SELF-REGULATION

1. Kids must learn to control their emotions before they can recognize others' feelings.

2. The more kids are aware of their stress signs, the better they are at self-regulation.

3. Deep breathing with a long, slow exhale creates a quick calming effect.

4. The best way to teach your child self-regulation is by modeling self-regulation yourself.

5. Your home is the optimum place for your child to learn to manage his emotions. Reinforce his efforts so he can get into the habit of calming himself on his own.

ONE LAST THING

I was observing a special education class in Oregon and noticed long pieces of rug yarn tied to students' chairs. One child caught me looking at his yarn filled with knots.

"It's for calming down, so I can get along with kids," he whispered. "My teacher says that I'll get better if I practice, so every time I do my belly breaths, I tie a knot," he explained. "It's like making muscles. You gotta work at it, you know."

The boy proudly showed off his ten knots and admitted he had a ways to go, but those deep breaths were helping.

His teacher told me that the boy had a kind heart, but his "short fuse" was hindering his relationships and empathy. The deep-breathing strategy was improving both qualities, and he'd even made a friend.

The child was lucky to have such an empathetic teacher who understood his needs and helped him manage anger. Self-regulation habits can be learned through practice and can even rewire our children's brains and help them develop the Empathy Advantage. But as this child would remind us: "You gotta work at it, you know."

CHAPTER 6

Empathetic Children Practice Kindness

Developing and Exercising Compassion Every Day

Kindness is contagious, needs just a small spark to ignite, and spreads quickly. I discovered those lessons while communicating with a group of students and their counselor over the course of a school year. Their goal was to create a kinder school climate, but the steps they took to succeed should be required reading for parents and teachers alike. The teens proved that practicing simple, regular kind acts nurtures empathy, alters behavior, changes a culture, and transforms lives. They showed me how anyone can start a "kindness revolution."

It was October, and four girls from a Delaware high school were sharing their concerns to school counselor Su Chafin and two teachers, Cami Morgan and Daikiri Villa. "The girls were really disturbed at the lack of compassion among students and couldn't understand why some could be so cruel," Chafin told me. "So the three of us blurted: 'If you do a million acts of kindness by the end of the school year, we'll shave our heads'—never dreaming they'd take us up on our offer!"[1]

The women's off-the-cuff remarks launched a yearlong crusade at Milford High School that the girls named Students for a Million Acts of Kindness. The group convinced their friends and staff to help, four schools joined, and their kindness crusade began.

Ideas of kind deeds kids could do were posted around the school. They ranged from simple acts—such as writing a note; opening a door; complimenting; smiling; or helping someone with homework—to lengthier deeds, like participating in a group beach cleanup, volunteering at a nursing home, or organizing a canned food drive. A website was created to track each deed. The tally was announced by Chafin riding a big tricycle through the cafeteria and holding a student-made sign that revealed the weekly number. Fun!

Within a month, the students' sign now tallied 10,000 acts, and their movement spread. More kids joined the crusade. Other schools throughout the state as well as in New Jersey and Pennsylvania wanted to build kindness, too.

By December, the staff saw a change: kids were nicer, the school was more positive, and students were pressuring each other to be kind. "If one kid said something negative, five kids stepped in to stop it," Chafin said. Kindness was becoming the new norm.

Students felt the difference, too. "It seems like a happier environment than what it was," said freshman Chaz Schmitt.[2] "People are trying harder to be kind and more willing to be nice," said senior Hannah Knechel.[3]

By February, the "kindness contagious factor" had taken hold. "They're 'catching' kindness by watching others be kind, and it's motivating them to pass it on," Su Chafin told me. And she affectionately nicknamed the students "Generation K"—the K for kindness. It fit!

In April, Milford High had clearly caught Kindness Fever. The students' sign read: "700,000 Acts of Kindness." That month I interviewed twenty-five students via Skype to get their perspectives. They, too, were elated with their campaign. "We're getting caught up in something we believe in," a teen said. "Kids are united in trying to reach a million acts of kindness and stop the bullying," one girl told me.

By May, the students were closing in on their goal: 800,000 kind deeds completed! The school year would close in four weeks, but the kindness momentum continued. "Kids will never back down from a challenge," said Knechel. "Bet kids that they can't do something, and be sure they will try."[4] "Try" was an understatement—the students were now unstoppable.

At the last school week, the final kindness tally was announced with fanfare in the auditorium at a school-wide assembly. Milford students had reached 1,069,116 kind deeds—seventy thousand more acts than planned, and some women shaved their heads while the Gen K students and the town cheered. A group of compassionate teens showed the world that "pay it forward" is more than a celebrated movie title—it's also a proven psychological principle that changes lives.

LEARNING TO PRACTICE KINDNESS

Milford High's achievement was extraordinary. But understanding *why* the teens succeeded is crucial so we can increase caring behavior in our own children. There are three key takeaways:

- First, kindness is strengthened by seeing, hearing, and practicing kindness. Milford students experienced so many kind deeds that the new norm of "be kind" became contagious and something they all wanted to be part of.

- Second, the Milford teens proved that kind acts don't have to cost a dime, take much time, or require any particular talent. In fact, the easier the task, the more willing kids are to practice kindness.

- Finally, kids must have ample opportunities and encouragement to practice kindness. The momentum of Milford's kindness campaign continued building throughout the year because the students continued doing simple, regular kind acts, and other kids saw or experienced them and wanted to do the same.

Those three lessons can help create our own mini Kindness Revolutions in our families, schools, and communities.

Being kind is what helps children tune in to other people's feelings and needs, trust more, step out of their own skins to understand others, and become more "We," less "Me" oriented. Each kind act nudges kids to notice others ("I see how you feel"), care ("I'm concerned about you"), empathize ("I feel with you"), and help and comfort ("Let me ease your pain"). Each time children practice kindness they are also filling in the empathy gap, so they are also more likely to *act* prosocially. Helping children develop empathy is far easier than we may suspect. Encouraging children to smile, nod, say hello, and hold a door can be what jump-starts them toward sharing the feelings of another. Aesop, the Greek storyteller, said it best: "No act of kindness, no matter how small, is ever wasted." Our job is to ensure that children take those words to heart.

Kindness is often considered just a warm and fuzzy skill, but science shows surprising benefits to being nice, including boosting health, reducing anxiety, enhancing self-esteem, increasing gratitude, and even elevating happiness.[5] In fact, study after study shows that a simple act of kindness also activates empathy, and that's why it's one of the nine essential empathy habits that we'll be learning about in this book. The more kids practice kindness—that is, without expecting gold stars, trophies, or monetary rewards—the likelier they'll develop the skills to succeed in work and in life and acquire the Empathy Advantage. And just as with the other tools we discuss in this book, kindness is a habit that can be cultivated in children. Read on to learn how.

WHAT'S SO HARD ABOUT TEACHING KINDNESS?

If there is one commonality in the exclusive club called Parenting, it's that we love our children dearly and will do everything to help them achieve their dreams. But many parents subscribe to the modern myth that boosting achievement and self-esteem is the exclusive formula to success and happiness (despite evidence that this approach is unfounded and even counterproductive). What's more, a troubling trend shows we are deprioritizing kindness in our child-rearing efforts to concentrate more on helping kids earn those grades, trophies, and test scores. And it's further reason for the rise of the Selfie Syndrome, the dip in youth empathy, the widening of the empathy gap, and a call for us to align our parenting with science.

The Bay Area communities in Northern California are in prestigious zip codes close to Stanford University, Apple, and Google. Residents are well educated, and their offspring are clearly privileged. (Though as we discussed earlier, data also shows that privileged kids are experiencing depression, anxiety disorders, and substance abuse at rates higher than those of any other socioeconomic group of young people in this country.[6]) I was speaking to several schools about how to raise less stressed, more caring kids in an ultracompetitive culture. The irony was that every parent group I spoke to that week was feeling the hyper-focus on achievement, self-esteem, and happiness. Children's empathy, kindness, and character were put on the back burner. I also spoke with many principals that week, all of whom shared concerns about the overemphasis on performance and its impact on children.

The principal of one school was also aware that high test scores and exemplary grades were the chief ways her students gained parental accolades. So she planned a switch. At the next school assembly, the staff would honor students who demonstrated not only school success but also kindness. That day each deserving child was called to the stage and acknowledged for their kind acts.

"Danny was kind because he stuck up for his friend."

"Sara was kind because she phoned Kelly every night to tell her to get well."

"Joshua was kind because he shared his lunch with his classmate."

And so on. The staff felt this new emphasis on character was the exact message students needed. What they weren't prepared for was the deluge of angry parent calls.

"My son is devastated because he didn't get a Kindness Award," a parent said. "He's worked so hard to win the achievement certificate. Switching gears isn't fair!"

"What does kindness have to do with achievement?" another mom yelled. "You're supposed to prepare kids to succeed—not to be nice!"

And this: "If you told us you were giving kindness awards, I would have taught my daughter to be kind so she could have won!"

I didn't see many "Proud Parent of a Kind Kid" bumper stickers in this community. "Achievement and Success" were clearly trumping "Kindness and Character." But the parents' sentiments aren't limited to the Bay Area: kindness is taking a dent across the United States, and data proves it.

A Meeting at Harvard

In June of 2014, I met with an impressive group of professionals at the invitation of Richard Weissbourd from Harvard's Graduate School of Education at their Making Caring Common initiative. Invitees included researchers from Committee for Children, the National School Climate Center, Rutgers University, Character.org, the Greater Good Science Center at Berkeley and others. Harvard was releasing a survey of 10,000 diverse middle and high school students from across the nation as to which values were most important to them.[7] Results were concerning, to say the least. Eighty percent of the students chose "high achievement or happiness" as their top priority and said that the most important task assigned to them by their parents is "to succeed." Only 20 percent of the students picked "caring for others." What's more, those who gave caring low priority tended to also score low on a scale for empathy.

But where they were learning those priorities was the red flag: *Four out of five of teens said their parents cared more about achievement or happiness than caring.* Kids were also three times as likely to agree as to disagree with the statement "My parents are prouder if I get good grades in my class than if I'm a caring community member in class and school."

The headlines were clear: "Today's Kids Value Achievement over Caring" because they believed their parents did, too. Every adult in that room was stunned. But there was also a conundrum: 96 percent of the surveyed parents said they *do* want to raise caring children and that they *do* believe that the development of moral character is "very important, if not essential." Maybe so, but the "Be kind!" message is being lost in translation on the kiddos. Two favorite kid quotes sum up the mismatch:

"Dad says 'being kind' matters, but he really wants me to win—whatever it takes."

"Mom tells me I should be nice, but she's a lot more excited when I make honor roll than Citizen of the Month."

Parenting styles may change, but there's one thing we can count on: kids will always be "gifted" in spotting hypocrisy—especially when parents deal it out. The Harvard results should be our wake-up call: if we are serious about raising a kindhearted, caring generation, then our expectation must be a lot clearer to our kids. And understanding how kindness benefits children and gives them an advantage for success and happiness might be just the motivator needed to change our own ways.

WHAT SCIENCE SAYS:
HOW KINDNESS BENEFITS CHILDREN

The Houston sixth graders planned the surprise for days and couldn't wait to see the five-year-olds' reactions. Since September, each older student (the "Big Buddy") helped a kindergartener (the "Little Buddy") with reading and writing. It was almost Christmas and the Big Buddies wanted to do something special for their young friends. So they asked the kindergarten teacher to have her students write to Santa. The older students would answer the letters pretending to be St. Nick, but with a twist. Before delivering the letters, the sixth graders would have cafeteria workers store them in freezers to look like they came straight from the North Pole.

Two days later, the sixth graders lined up to watch the principal hand envelopes now covered with icicles to the five-year-olds. The Little Buddies were screaming with excitement: "The letter really is from Santa!!!"

"Mine has snow on it from Santa's house!" But the best response came from the sixth graders: they were ecstatic. "We surprised them!" "Can you believe how happy they are?" "What are we going to do next?"

The "kind givers" were more elated than the five-year-old receivers. Like the Milford teens, the sixth graders had caught the contagious feature of kindness and learned the joy of doing for others. A simple act of kindness had opened their hearts, and proved the latest science. Kindness is like a boomerang: send it out, and it comes right back to you so you want to send it back again.

Want Unselfish Kids? Help Them Practice Kindness

We hear that kindness is contagious, but now there's proof. James Fowler, of UC San Diego, and Nicholas Christakis, at Harvard, provided the first laboratory evidence that prosocial behaviors really can spread from person to person to person. It happens because when people benefit from receiving a kind, cooperative, or unselfish gesture, they generally "pay it forward" by helping others not originally involved. How it works is that one person's kind deed spreads first to three people, and then to the nine people that those three people later interact with, and then to still more people in the future. The result is "each person in a network can influence dozens or even hundreds of people, some of whom he or she does not know and has not met."[8] It's a kindness cascade!

But participating in a Kind It Forward campaign also can alter a child's character and produce a lasting effect. "You don't go back to being your old selfish self," Fowler explained.[9] Practicing kindness is an empathy-building and UnSelfie-stretching experience! And that's exactly what happened to the Milford teens and the Houston sixth graders. Doing kind acts changed their character and helped the students focus on others. "Giving kindness is now my passion," several Milford students told me.

Want Happier Kids? Help Them Practice Kindness

Of course, we hope our kids succeed, but we also want them to be happy. A Google search of "raising happy kids" reaps almost 46 million hits— seems a lot of parents these days are searching for answers, and for good reason. More than two-thirds of adults say they are "extremely concerned" about the well-being of children, and their concern cuts across gender, ethnicity, age, and political affiliation." [10] But we may be turning to the wrong sources to boost our kids' happiness quotients. Helping children practice kindness elevates not only their empathy but also their happiness levels, and what's more, it's proven.

To discover what works to maximize kindness *and* happiness, University of California–Riverside psychologist Sonja Lyubomirsky conducted a series of groundbreaking studies. Two groups of students were asked to carry out five random acts of kindness of their choice per week for six weeks. Acts could be simple to fairly big ones and could be anything from buying a Big Mac for a homeless person, helping a younger sibling with schoolwork, and writing a thank-you to a teacher, or visiting a nursing home, doing someone's chores, or working at a shelter. One group was to perform the five kind acts anytime throughout the week. The other group was to do the five acts on one single day (for example, every Tuesday). Then once a week for six weeks both groups turned in their "kindness reports" describing their deeds. The results surprised even Lyubomirsky. Those who did all five kind acts in one day gained the biggest happiness boost at the end of the six-week study period." [11] And a main reason that being kind made participants happier is that "it led them to recognize how much the recipients appreciated their kind acts," Lyubomirsky explains. "They perceived gratitude in those they helped." [12]

But perhaps the psychologist's most crucial finding had nothing to do with happiness: the habit can change children's self-image and behavior. "When you commit acts of kindness, you may begin to view yourself as an altruistic and compassionate person," Lyubomirsky says. That finding matches a long-held psychology tenet: our behavior usually matches our self-image. If a child sees herself as kind, she is more likely to act kindly. Kindness jump-starts a cascade of effects not only for the receiver, but also for the giver.

Want Popular Kids? Help Them Practice Kindness

What parent doesn't want their child to have friends and be popular? University of British Columbia and the University of California–Riverside[13] researchers found an unanticipated result: doing nice deeds can elevate both kindness and happiness *as well as* help kids gain friends. Here's how:

Hundreds of nine- to eleven-year-olds in Vancouver, Canada, tried a four-week experiment at school. The students were placed randomly into two groups, and for thirty days each child did an experiment. One group performed three weekly acts of kindness—like sharing their lunch, vacuuming, or giving Mom a hug if she seemed stressed. The other group visited three pleasant places each week—such as the playground, the baseball field, or a grandparent's house. And both groups kept track of their kind deeds or pleasant visits on class surveys.

At the end of the month, researchers retested the students. And no surprise: all the children were happier. But there was an unexpected result: Students who performed the kind deeds also gained friends during that month-long experiment. Far more classmates said they "wanted to be in school activities or spend time" with kids who were the kind givers than with those who had visited the pleasant places. Practicing kindness also boosts kids' popularity. Kids enjoy being with kindhearted peers.

Want Kinder Kids? Help Them Practice Kindness

A snapshot from science shows promising findings on how to help kids thrive and reap the Empathy Advantage: practicing kindness increases children's prosocial behaviors as well as their happiness, self-esteem, gratitude, popularity, health, *and* resilience. But perhaps most important: when our kids practice kindness, they discover the joys of giving, feel the gratitude from others, see themselves as more compassionate, and step briefly into the shoes of another. And the doorway to empathy opens and the empathy gap decreases!

HOW TO CULTIVATE KINDNESS IN CHILDREN

The question is simple, but it's stumped over half a million parents. I call it the Family Reunion Test, and I ask every parenting group I speak to, so let's see how you do:

> Pretend it's twenty-five years from now and you're at a family reunion eavesdropping on your now-grown kids discussing their childhoods. How are they describing your typical behavior? And what do they remember as "the most important messages" you told them as kids?

No matter where I speak, I get the same reaction: stunned silence and a strong dose of guilt. Parents suddenly realize that their emphasis is on performance and that their kids are receiving the "Achievement Above All" message.

If there's any consolation, their response is the same everywhere. After all, we've become a test-obsessed, competitive world where grades, rank, and scores are the end-all benchmark for success (and assumed happiness). So our kids' schedules are crammed with academic tutoring, study drills, homework sessions, and spelling bee practices. Then comes violin lessons, soccer practices, and debate clubs—and whatever else— to give our kids an "Ivy League edge." Our typical, everyday parent-kid inquiries become predictable: "What did you learn?" and "What grade did you get?" Queries about kindness and empathy—"What nice thing did you do for someone today?" or "How would you feel if you were the new kid?"—are sadly scarce since the topics just don't match our agendas, financial investments, or the "big picture" priorities for our children's lives.

In all fairness, our lives are hurried and harried. It's tough enough getting through everything on our own schedules, let alone pausing to examine what our kids might be "catching" from us. But those unscripted family moments do add up. Our around-the-clock behavior is the template our kids use to learn—or dismiss—the value of kindness and caring for others.

The truth is our kids *are* watching and *are* copying us. Research confirms that children do imitate kind *or* selfish behaviors modeled by adults. Children exposed to altruistic caregivers generally adopt their caring orientation. Adults who talk about the importance of helping others and being kind do influence their children's empathy quotients.[14] We do matter in instilling character in our kids—that is *if* we talk and walk the example we hope they become. Hopefully, our modeling includes kindness.

Kindness is one of the easiest habits to cultivate in kids, and the best way to do so is not with fancy, purchased materials, textbooks, and worksheets, or time-consuming programs. Modeling, expecting, guiding, explaining, and reinforcing are much more effective ways to cultivate this sixth habit. The secret is to make practicing kindness a natural part of your family routines and your behavior so your children see it, copy it, and want to adopt it. Here are ways to weave kindness back into our hurried lives:

- **Model kindness.** Look for simple ways for your child to see *you* extend kindness. There are so many daily opportunities: offering your seat on the bus or train to an elderly person, phoning your friend who is down, asking someone how she is feeling. Just be sure to tell your child how good it made you feel! The more kids witness or experience what it feels like to be a kindness giver, the more likely they will incorporate the trait as part of their character.

- **Expect kindness in others.** Studies find that parents who express their views about unkind behavior and explain why they feel that way tend to have kids who adopt those views.[15] So plainly explain your beliefs again and again: "Unkindness is wrong, it's hurtful, and it will not be tolerated!" It sets a standard for your children's expected conduct and lets them know in no uncertain terms what you value.

- **Value kindness.** It's easy to be caught up in stressing performance and achievement in a test-driven society. Push the Pause button periodically and listen into your dialogue. What proportion of your messages addresses achievement and performance? What about kindness and caring? If you notice an imbalance of one-sided messages, make an intentional effort to tip the scale back to stress kindness a bit more and performance a bit less.

- **Reflect on kindness.** Harvard's Making Caring Common initiative suggests asking more questions that elicit your children's thoughts, feelings, and experiences. So instead of always asking, "What did you learn today?" include "What did you do that you feel good about?" "What's something nice that someone did for you? What's something kind you did?" The simple tweak helps kids start looking for kindness and reflecting upon the virtue.

- **Explain kindness.** Explaining the specific way kindness benefited someone is effective in nurturing kindness.[16] So look for kind behaviors that occur naturally and use them as openings to discuss how they affected the recipient. My TIP strategy helps kids identify how kindness can make a positive impact, and the acronym TIP helps you recall the three parts:

  ▷ **T** = **Tell** who was the kindness recipient.

  ▷ **I** = **Identify** the kind act said or done.

  ▷ **P** = **Point** out how the gesture affected the recipient.

Then look for ways to apply the three parts. Your daughter helps a classmate pick up his spilled homework: "Sara, you were kind to help Jimmy pick up his papers. He was upset, and you made him feel better." Or your son tells kids to stop making fun of his brother. "Kevin, you knew your brother was upset and stood up for him. Did you see how relieved he was? That was kind."

So now, let's get back to the Family Reunion Test. How do you think your children would describe your behavior during the past week or even today? Would the description include kindness? Remember, the kids *are* watching!

EMPATHY BUILDER: THE TWO KIND RULE

Don't think of kindness as a fixed trait that is predetermined by DNA, but more like a muscle that can be strengthened with exercise.[17] Just as practice improves our kids' performance in reading, tennis, cello, and ballet—and whatever else—practice enhances their Empathy Quotient. Stretching kids' kindness muscles is simple, but like any good exercise regime, sticking to a routine that includes regular workouts is crucial for real change.

An easy way to help kids practice kindness is using the Two Kind Rule: "Say or do at least two kind things to people each day." To nurture empathy, the deed must come "straight from the giver's heart" (no fair purchasing), delivered "face-to-face" (at least at the beginning so the giver sees the recipient's response), and delivered without expecting anything in return. Start by encouraging your kids to do two *simple* deeds a day to get them into the routine of practicing kindness. The rule can later be switched to One Big Deed a Week or Three Deeds on Wednesday. Here are five easy ways to do a Family Kindness Workout.

1. **Define kindness.** Make sure your kids understand what kindness means and why it is important. You might say, "Kindness means you care about other people. Kind people think about another person's feelings and never expect anything in return. They just treat other people kindly because they want to help

make someone's life better. And being kind is how I expect you to act. Kindness is something you get better at with practice. Using the Two Kind Rule of saying or doing two kind things each day will help you exercise your kindness muscle."

2. **Generate possibilities!** The more aware kids are of ways to be kind, the more likely they'll use kind behaviors. So brainstorm together easy ways to be kind that don't cost a dime. Post the list on your refrigerator or as a screen saver and keep adding to it to remind your kids of possibilities such as:

- Say hello, smile, or share something.

- Find someone new each day to look in the eye and say "Morning!"

- Help around the house without being asked.

- Open the door for someone.

- Wave and smile to two new people each day.

- Read a book to your brother or sister or anyone.

- Give a compliment to a different person each day for a month.

- Write a thank-you to someone deserving.

- Congratulate or give a high five to a deserving person.

- Shovel snow or rake leaves for an elderly or disabled neighbor.

- Ask someone who looks lonely to eat or play with you.

- Hug your mom or dad.

- Bake cookies and deliver them to someone who needs a smile.

- Give someone a "Have a Good Day" note on a Post-it.

- Drop off old, gently used books to the library or children's hospital.

- Help your younger brother or sister with homework.

3. **Mix it up.** Find fresh ways to help your children stretch their "kindness muscles." A spur-of-the-moment drop-by to a special someone? Picking a flower bouquet and delivering it to an aunt? Drawing a picture to thank a teacher?

4. **Create reminders.** Nothing turns kids off faster than parents "nagging," so help your kids develop their own cue to remember to use the Two Kind Rule, such as posting a reminder on the door, sneaking a note in her backpack, setting an alarm on his cell phone, or having her wear a bracelet or watch.

5. **Keep it up.** Continue helping your child practice kindness on a routine basis until it becomes a habit.

HOW TO HELP KIDS ADOPT THE HABIT OF PRACTICING KINDNESS

- **Walk your talk.** Kids learn kindness best through example, so be more intentional about modeling kindness. Periodically ask yourself, "What have I done today to show my kids I value kindness?" Or "If my child had only my example of kindness to watch, what did he catch?"

- **Surround your child with good examples.** Look beyond your own example to the adults in your child's life: coaches, teachers, babysitters, relatives, and other parents. Are their examples ones that will help or hinder your child from adopting a kindness mind-set? Be picky!

- **Show the impact.** Children who are given the opportunity to help others tend to become more helpful—especially if the effect of their kindness on those they helped was pointed out to them.[18] So describe the impact: "Grandma was so happy when you called to thank her," "Did you see Sarah's smile when you shared your toys?"

- **Pose the right questions.** The right questions help kids recognize the effect kindness has on others as well as on themselves. Make it a routine to help your child reflect on kindness such as at dinner or before bed. Questions might be: "What did the person do when you were kind?" "How do you think he felt?" "How would you feel if you were the person?" "How did you feel when you were being kind to him?" "Do you think he'll 'kind it forward'?"

- **Do a weekly family kindness ritual.** Look for ways to put a little fun into your family deed giving, and if you can create a simple, fun weekly ritual, it's a "win-win." One mom has her kids write "Happy Holiday" notes, attach them to candy canes, and then leave them secretly on neighbors' doorsteps. (She says her kids love hiding behind the shrubs and watching the neighbors' delighted reactions.) Or make Tuesday "Cookie Day" when you and your kids deliver a batch—store bought or homemade—to a different deserving person.

- **Put away your wallet.** One of the simplest ways to enhance kindness is by reinforcing the action as soon as it happens. When you notice your child being kind, let her know how it pleased you: "You always ask Grandma how she's feeling. It makes me so happy knowing how kind you are." Effective praise is specific, genuine, and deserved. But use words—not rewards—to praise.

AGE-BY-AGE STRATEGIES

During one holiday, Jessica and Mark noticed that their three sons had fallen into the "Gimme" trap. "We wanted them to learn that giving is just as fun as receiving," they said. So the parents initiated a new tradition: Secret Kindness Buddies. Each person—including Mom and Dad—pulled a name from a basket and then was to perform a *secret* act of kindness toward the buddy each day during Hanukkah. Deeds may *not* be purchased but must come "straight from the heart."

Any hesitations faded by their first secret act. The kids baked cookies, picked a flower bouquet, restrung a sibling's broken necklace, cleaned a brother's room, and even delivered breakfast in bed to Mom. "They couldn't wait to try to surprise their sibling and watch his reaction," Jessica said. "The best thing was that my boys relearned the joy of giving."

Jessica and Mark aren't alone: many parents want their kids to focus more on kindness, caring, and giving. Here are more ways to start a Kindness Revolution in your home, school, or neighborhood. Make sure to keep the activities fun, varied, and ongoing, and take time to chat about how both recipients and givers were affected. Doing so will build your kids' kindness muscles, help them think more about others and less about themselves, and help them acquire the Empathy Advantage.

Symbols designate the recommended age and suitability for activity: L = Little Ones: Toddlers and Preschoolers; S = School-age; T = Tweens and Older; A = All Ages

- **Start a family Kindness Box.** An old shoebox with a slit cut in the top will do for this simple activity. Just encourage your family to look for others doing kind deeds. Write or draw the deeds and slip them in the box. Then read those notes during your family meal, a Sunday breakfast, or family gathering. It will help everyone start looking for the "good" in one another. **L, S**

- **Create a Kindness Jar.** Usha Balamore, the lower division director at Pennsylvania's Shipley School, has a Kindness Jar (a large plastic see-through container) to help four- and five-year-old students practice kindness. A penny is added to the jar for each kind act, but the honoree is the *kindness recipient*, not the giver. The receiver reports the giver's name and deed: "Larry was kind because he folded up my blanket." Or "Kelly was kind because she hugged me when I fell." The adult then adds a penny to the jar. Focusing on the recipient halts givers from bragging or expecting rewards. When filled, the kids decide where to donate the money. Last year, students chose an orphanage in Uganda to be the recipient. "We're making the world a better place," a kindergartener said proudly.[19] Start a kindness jar at home! **L, S**

- **Catch your kids being kind with pebbles.** Keep a stack of small, smooth stones or other small objects by a basket or container. Family members are to "catch" Mom, Dad, or siblings being kind, compliment the recipient, write their kind person's initial on the pebble with a black marking pen, and add it to the Kindness Basket. At the end of the month—or whenever filled—celebrate your family's kindhearted efforts together at a fun outing. **A**

- **Create a Kindness Centerpiece.** Gather your kids to brainstorm kind deeds to do for anybody. Next, help your kids cut fifteen to twenty-five colored paper shapes about three inches wide. Shapes can vary: hearts for Valentine's Day, pumpkins for Halloween, etc. On each cutout, write a deed and decorate it with glitter, stickers, marking pens, scraps, or whatever. Tape a pipe cleaner to each back and put into a vase. Each morning, invite family members to pull a kindness deed from the vase and then to do that deed for someone that day. Members can share their kindness-giving experience at dinnertime. **L, S**

- **Make a Kindness Wall.** Many schools encourage students to list acts of kindness on Post-its and stick them on a wall. In no time, a collage of kindness covers hallways, sparking kids to "pay it forward." Try the idea at home by posting kids' kind actions on walls, mirrors, or doors, and encourage them to do the same. **A**

- **Make kindness a regular happening!** At Starr Elementary in Fresno, California, Marceen Farsakian's first graders begin each day saying a kindness pledge: "I pledge to myself on this day, to try to be kind in every way. To every person big and small: I will help if they fall."[20] The six-year-olds are encouraged to do ten simple kind acts each month (like hug Mom or read to a younger sibling) and track them in a notebook. The class also does a weekly random act of kindness such as writing nice messages on the playground with sidewalk chalk and making bookmarks with words of kindness to hide inside library books for fellow students to find. They can't wait to do the next random act of kindness. Use the teacher's strategy and find *fun* ways for your kids to practice kindness regularly and maybe create your own family kindness pledge. **A**

- **Teach "bucket filling."** *Have You Filled a Bucket Today?*, by Carol McCloud, is a wonderful children's book with a powerful message: Everyone carries an invisible bucket to hold good thoughts and feelings. When your bucket is filled, you're happy; when empty, you're sad. We all can be "bucket fillers" by practicing kindness. Many schools use the book to teach that message.[21] Each student has a small paper bucket to be filled by classmates with notes: "Thanks for filling my bucket when you asked me to play." Or "You were a bucket filler when you helped me pick up my books." Try the activity at home using small plastic buckets or cups from the dollar store. **L, S**

- **Track kind.** Encourage your child's kindness successes by helping her track her efforts, both small and large. Give each child a small journal in which to describe special deeds. Take a photo of your children's "bucket-filling" moments and preserve them in a family scrapbook. Or use paper chains: each child writes or draws their kind deed and staples it to another chain, and in no time, you'll have a long string of kind deeds hanging. **A**

- **Read or watch movies together that inspire kindness.** For younger kids read: *The Kindness Quilt*, by Nancy Elizabeth Wallace; *Heartprints*, by P. K. Hallinan; or *Kindness Is Cooler*,

Mrs. Ruler, by Margery Cuyler. Older kids can read: *Ordinary Mary's Extraordinary Deed,* by Emily Pearson; or *Kids' Random Acts of Kindness,* by Conari Press. Teens can watch: *Pay It Forward, The Kindness School,* or *Finding Kind* (the latter two available on the Web). (There are more than 150 Kind Club chapters that urge girls to start a movement to be kind. After watching the film *Finding Kind,* girls are asked to write down an action step they want to take to become the change they would like to see, write an apology to someone, and write something nice about another person to leave as a Kind Card on their seat.) **A**

- **Choose a caring cause.** Identifying your child's passion or concern and matching it with a caring cause is a known kindness motivator. A boy's mom survived a cancer battle, so he convinced his soccer team to send daily email greetings on hospital computers to young cancer patients at a local pediatric ward. The patients adored the gesture, but the boys got even more enjoyment from doing the caring deeds. A teen Care Club's passion is knitting, but their love is giving, so they're knitting scarves for the US Navy (the Ships Project in San Diego) and hats for our troops. **A**

THE TOP FIVE THINGS TO KNOW ABOUT PRACTICING KINDNESS

1. Kindness is contagious, needs just a spark to ignite, and spreads quickly.

2. The more kids see, hear, and practice kindness, the more likely they'll adopt it as a habit.

3. Kindness can be strengthened like a muscle, but regular workouts are crucial for it to become habitual.

4. Acts of kindness must be meaningful and varied to reap gains.

5. Kids learn kindness by comforting, helping, caring, sharing, and cooperating, not through hearing lectures or doing worksheets. It should be taught as a verb, not a noun.

ONE LAST THING

Kindness is strengthened by practice but doesn't have to cost a dime, take much time, or require any particular talent. Like any exercise program, regular workouts are required to reap the gains. Doing simple, regular kind acts—holding the door open for someone, helping a classmate with homework, and asking a lonely friend to play, just a few times a week—make our kids not only more caring but also happier. But even more important, those gestures help tune our kids in to others, provide opportunities to step out of their own skins, build caring connections, nurture compassion, open the doors to empathy, and reduce the empathy gap so that kids are more likely to act on their empathetic urges instead of hesitating or even shutting them off.

CHAPTER 7

Empathetic Children Think "Us" Not "Them"

Cultivating Empathy Through Teamwork and Collaboration

School recess is where an "Us" versus "Them" scene can flourish, and it was why I was eager to observe Aldama Elementary School in Los Angeles. The staff had implemented a new kind of recess for their 685 students, based on a program called Playworks. The approach was reducing aggression and bullying while creating a caring culture where kids worked through problems collaboratively, and it all focused on play.

Jaron Williams, the Playworks program manager, escorted me to a typical-looking school play area: jungle gyms, a handball backboard, basketball hoops, four-square courts, and a lot of asphalt.

"Some of these kids have a tough life," Williams said, "so we try to create a safe place and build a positive experience for them."

I saw several houses in the school's low-income neighborhood covered with graffiti. Most local businesses had heavy metal gates locked in front of windows and doors for security. I knew that for many students, the playground might be the only place to experience safe, fun outdoor play.

Each Aldama class receives a forty-five-minute coach-instructed playground lesson two times a month, and class game time was about to begin for fifth graders. "Coach" Lisa Frias, the program coordinator, greeted students.

"What's our agreement for healthy play?" she asked.

"Include everyone, be kind, work together, and have fun!" the students answered.

Williams and Frias work on those core values yearlong to make recess a positive community experience. They're the same values kids need to get along, and these students could recite *and* apply them.

The day's game was 4 Line Basketball, and students counted off in fours so no one was left out. (As a child, I was always chosen last for my poor athletic ability and hated recess, but there was none of that here.) Throughout her lesson, Frias reminded kids to encourage others ("Give your partner a high five." "Say, 'Awesome job!'"), and to use conflict-solving skills: "If you have a problem, rock it out." (Translation: Use Rock, Paper, Scissors to solve a problem.) Coach Frias was teaching social-emotional skills in context—the way kids learn habits best. And, in turn, students were encouraging their teammates: "Nice teamwork!" "Good try!"

"What positives did you see?" asked Frias when the game finished. Kids were quick with answers: "We're including others." "We're having fun." "We're working together." "We're a community!" No arguments there.

I realized I just observed one of the best lessons in collaboration, and it was taught on a playground.

Next, it was time for the third- through sixth-grade recess, and once again, it was a different approach. For one thing, it was organized. Frias and Williams first explained the game choices: Relay; 4 Line Basketball; Tetherball; Handball; and Rock, Paper, Scissors (taught at a previous Class Game Time). Within seconds everyone was playing, no one was left out, and coaches were playing with the kids.

At one point, kids disagreed about a serve, and two boys used Rock, Paper, Scissors to solve it and then resumed their game. Students also used other collaborative tactics taught by coaches: "One mike" (or microphone—only one person speaks at a time), "Step up, step back" (if you're not sharing or playing, "step up"; if you're stepping up too much, "step back" and let somebody have a turn), and "Try it on" (try the activity before you commit to not liking it). I kept wondering: What if every kid—or adult, for that matter—learned those simple collaborative strategies?

But something else was different: a few fourth and fifth graders wore purple T-shirts that signified they were trained junior coaches. These kids played but also helped peers understand game rules, encouraged them to get along, and served as Conflict Resolvers.

"Kids argue, ya know," Jeff, a junior coach, explained, "so we tell them to do Rock, Paper, Scissors. Then their problem is solved, and they go back to playing."

Kacelen told me that those peacemaking strategies help. "Sometimes kids argue, and the junior coaches try to stop it with different Conflict Resolvers," she said. "The kids watch and then try it in the classroom."

Havier, another junior coach, added, "If kids learn to be nice and not hurt each other now, they'll do the same thing when they grow up."

If we'd only listen to kids!

The Playworks play-based approach was started by accident in 1996, when Jill Vialet was conversing with an elementary school principal. The Oakland principal was sharing her frustration over how much time she and her teachers spent dealing with playground conflicts and seeing the same kids in her office every day for fighting. Vialet founded Playworks to transform recess into a positive experience to help kids get along, play safely, and practice conflict resolution. The Bay Area–based organization is currently in 380 low-income schools nationwide and impacting nearly 425,000 American students.

An independent study by Mathematica Policy Research[1] and Stanford University found that schools implementing Playworks have 43 percent less bullying and exclusion. What's more, students demonstrate better behavior and more attention in class than those in schools without the program. All that modeling, community connectedness, adult supervision, and empathy building seem to be working, and the skills students learn on the playground are spilling over into classrooms.[2]

Joseph Peila, a Chicago principal, noticed a change—especially at their school spelling bee held in front of parents, students, and community. In past years, students who misspelled might be upset or cry, and teachers would have to stifle other students from giggling. "But now when a child misses," Peila said, "students clap for the child! Those on stage call out 'That's okay!' 'You'll do better next time!' 'Good try!' And the next child up to spell gives a high five to the student who missed."[3] Peila attributed that "Them" to "Us" transformation to Playworks.

"The idea that play has the power to bring out the best in every kid can't be overlooked," Vialet told me.

She also spoke to me about the untapped power of play as a tool for cultivating empathy as well as a way to help kids learn to care for one another.

"There's a connection when you play with someone that makes empathy possible," Vialet said. "When you don't play, it just perpetuates that sense of otherness—that we are more separate and different from others than we really are. Play is a great door opener for empathy."[4]

LEARNING TO BUILD TEAMWORK

The shortest poem on record is attributed to boxing legend Muhammad Ali, who delivered it at a Harvard graduation address. After urging graduates to go out and change the world, a student suddenly shouted, "Give us a poem!" Ali responded off the cuff with just two words: "Me . . . We!"[5] His concise message illustrates a key premise for nurturing empathy: It is only when we let go of our self-centeredness and feel *with* others that our hearts open. After all, empathy is always a "We" experience.

Working together on common goals can help kids make that crucial shift from "I-Me-Mine" to "We-Ours-Us." Those "us"-type experiences also sensitize children to those who may be different or have conflicting interests, and broadens their social spheres, which allows empathy to blossom. (Roman Krznaric, author of *Empathy: Why It Matters and How to Get It*, says, "Think of it as being in the same boat rather than the same shoes as other people."6) The type of goal or team doesn't matter, but an emotional and meaningful connection is always a straighter path to empathy.

Cooperative, caring relationships can also make our children smarter, happier, and healthier, as well as more prosocial, resilient, *and* empathetic. "Considerable research," Alfie Kohn points out, "has established that cooperation also enhances children's ability to take the points of view of other people."7 Collaboration also has the capacity to "join people who have separate or conflicting interests, who do not feel good about each other, who are unequal, or who simply do not understand one another," says sociologist Richard Sennett.8

But the fact is that many aspects of our contemporary culture and modern parenting styles threaten our kids' ability to care. And in today's digital-driven, hypercompetitive world the need for children to learn to collaborate and experience emotional connectedness has never been greater.

That day on the Aldama playground, I saw how play was indeed a door opener for empathy. I also noticed kids smiling, feeling included, and working out problems. I never heard a whistle, but I did hear a lot of "Good job"s and "Nice try"s, and saw a host of high fives. Students were happy and having fun but also learning to collaborate and care about others. But even more promising was that their blacktop experience seemed to be closing the "Us"-"Them" divide. Mixing up friendship groups in team activities was broadening these children's social circles for empathy to grow.

In our fervent quest to help kids succeed, we may be overlooking that the optimum training grounds for learning empathy and the rules to get along are asphalt, four-square, and sandboxes. Old-fashioned play enriches our children's social, emotional, cognitive, and physical development as well as the potential for empathic experiences and reaping the Empathy Advantage. But the sad truth is that far too many kids are living play-deprived, hypercompetitive childhoods that diminish their chances to learn Rock, Paper, Scissors, "Be fair!", and "Do you want to play?"

WHAT'S SO HARD ABOUT TEACHING TEAMWORK?

I recently spoke in Istanbul, Manila, Cairo, and Miami; a month earlier in Barranquilla, Greenwich, Taipei, and San Diego; and I'm concerned. In every industrialized area I've visited in the past five years—more than thirty countries and counting—I've seen a seismic shift in culture that is reconfiguring childhood and jeopardizing our kids from learning to get along, form healthy relationships, and empathize. It's time for a serious wake-up call.

Good-bye, Playtime

Childhoods a few decades ago were spent bike riding, cloud gazing, and playing outdoors, but growing up has changed dramatically. Between 1981 and 1997, the amount of outdoor "free play" (defined as unstructured and unsupervised) fell by 50 percent.[9] Even 85 percent of mothers agree that their children play outdoors less often than just a generation ago.[10] In those decades that play declined and social networking increased, Peter Gray states that "there has been a measurable rise in childhood anxiety, depression, narcissism and measurable declines in empathy." And the Selfie Syndrome also escalated.[11]

Playing is how kids learn to get along, collaborate, care deeply, solve problems, negotiate, share, communicate, and compromise. Play is also a powerful socializing tool that helps kids appreciate differences, break down barriers, and develop an "Us Not Them" mentality. As Jeremy Rifkin, author of *The Empathic Civilization*, so eloquently stated: "It is difficult to 'imagine' how empathy could develop in the absence of play."[12]

But the absence of play in our children's lives is real. Whether it's due to fear for our children's safety, prioritizing achievement over grass, sandbox, and play dates, relying on digital devices for entertainment instead of Monopoly, tumbling, or four-square, or because we can't "fit it into our schedules," our kids' mental health and empathy quotients are suffering.

Overstructured Existences

There's nothing new about parents wanting their kids to excel, but these days we're in super drive. Part of our push is based on the current academic rat race and "success" criterion measured by rank and résumé, and it makes us worry that our kids won't make the grade. So children's schedules are packed with coding classes, violin practice, academic tutors, etiquette classes, chess, and whatever else we hope might give them "the edge." While some extracurricular activities can be kid confidence builders, stress reducers, and growth promoters, the problem surfaces when "social enrichment" is cut from the lineup or activities are too adult structured. The skills kids need for building caring relationships (like listening, communicating, compromising, negotiating, problem solving) and acquiring the real advantage for success and happiness are learned face-to-face with minimal adult supervision.[13]

A University of Colorado study found that kids who spent too much time in structured extra activities, like academics and sports, were *less* able to use their executive function skills (a broad range of crucial thinking skills like planning, problem solving, and decision making) than children who spent *more* time engaged in free play. In fact, the "*more* time kids spend in structured activities, the *less* able they were to use executive function."[14]

Giving kids a bit more latitude for free time and social interactions may be better for their happiness and empathy quotients as well as their academic performance.[15]

Banning Recess

Remember playing hopscotch, duck-duck-goose, dodge ball, and freeze tag? Many of today's children may never experience them. Forty percent of American schools have either eliminated daily recess or considered doing away with it to find more time to prepare kids for tests.[16] But banning recess is one of the *least* effective ways to boost academic performance.

A review of fifty studies by the Centers for Disease Control and Prevention found that physical activity benefits grades, test scores, and academic achievement, and positively affects children's concentration and classroom behavior.[17] A Stanford study found that high-quality school recess helps students feel *more* engaged, safe, and positive about their school day (and positive climate is linked to a host of favorable student outcomes including achievement).[18] And a report by Kenneth Ginsberg, written for the American Academy of Pediatrics documents that play promotes cognitive growth and intelligence as well as boosts children's social skills and strengthens our parent-child connection.[19]

Yet despite proven benefits, many schools continue axing recess, and there go golden opportunities for kids to practice collaborating, problem solving, and resolving conflicts as well as to reduce stress, make friends, and acquire the Empathy Advantage.

Hypercompetitiveness

Of course, we want our kids to succeed. The danger comes when everything turns into a winner-take-all contest, and that's when *all* kids lose. After all, an "I'm better than you" mentality only widens the "Us" and "Them" chasm, increases the Selfie Syndrome, and diminishes empathy. (Take note: competition *is* a known empathy reducer.[20]) What's more, the belief that "competition is crucial for success" doesn't pan out. In fact, more than eighty original studies refute the claim: "Children who learn cooperatively (compared with those who learn competitively or independently) learn better, feel better about themselves and get along better with each other," writes Alfie Kohn, author of *No Contest: The Case Against Competition*.[21] They also get along better with peers, are more empathetic, and are collaborators.

So how do we strike the balance so our kids can play, learn to collaborate, and still succeed in school? Luckily, science has an answer that might help not only our children but also the grown-ups.

WHAT SCIENCE SAYS: HOW TO TEACH TEAMWORK

Social psychology is concerned with how humans relate and tackles those "human" topics like compassion, hate, aggression, and prejudice. These scientists don't rely on paper-and-pencil tests or brain imagery scans; they watch people directly. Their findings show optimum ways to nurture empathy and create the kinds of environments where kids collaborate and care about one another. As bullying continues to be a serious problem (one in three US students say they have been bullied at school[22]) and racism plagues our nation and college campuses,[23] those answers are paramount.

Moving from "Them" to "Us"

Over fifty years ago, a Turkish social psychologist named Muzafer Sherif[24] conducted an experiment to find how to move people from "Them" to "Us."[25] His motivation began when he was twelve, and Greek soldiers massacred residents of Izmir, Turkey. Muzafer was in line to be murdered when a soldier spared his life. Sherif eventually became an eminent professor at Princeton and Yale (among other universities) and devoted his career to discovering what reduces hostility. On June 1954, he conducted the infamous "Robbers Cave Experiment" and finally found answers.[26]

Sherif invited twenty-two fifth graders (with parents' permission) to attend a summer camp at Robbers Cave State Park outside Oklahoma City.[27] The plan required that all boys be similar in age, demographics, and background as well as "well-adjusted psychologically." None of the boys knew each other prior to camp and assumed they were going off for a fun summer experience. They arrived in separate buses and were split into two groups. Each group was housed together in a separate cabin and knew nothing of the other's existence. (Camp counselors were actually psychology grad students and professors; Sherif disguised himself as a janitor in order to observe the boys without being noticed.)

During the first week, each group explored their new camp, created a team flag, chose their group name (the Eagles or the Rattlers), and developed a strong feeling of "Us." Then they were pitted against each other in camp competitions such as tent pitching, baseball games, and tug-of-war. One group was deliberately given better food, entertainment, and treatment, and, as predicted, animosity grew between them. Physical scuffs broke out, and "jeering, demeaning, exchanges of unflattering words" materialized until neither side wanted anything to do with the other.[28]

Sherif had created the "perfect" study conditions, but now researchers had to figure out how to reduce the animosity. The staff eliminated competitions, offered prizes, and extended joint movies and meals, but friction remained. Finally, Sherif discovered the secret to breaking down barriers: the counselors introduced problems that required the Rattlers and the Eagles to cooperate because their well-being depended on it.

First, there was a drinking water crisis, forcing the thirsty boys to work together to repair the mysteriously broken pipe. When fixed, there was unified rejoicing. Then the camp truck broke (again, on purpose by the staff) after the boys' long hike on a hot day. The only way back to camp was for the groups to fix the truck together. When the engine started, there were collective cheers. Their animosity was fading; the boys even insisted on a group camp photo to recall their great times "together." Sherif had discovered the way for the Rattlers and the Eagles to get along.

"Hostility gives way when groups pull together to achieve overriding goals that are real and compelling to all concerned," Sherif explained.[29]

It's an important finding to remember. *A key to activating empathy is creating the right social dynamics so kids are drawn into the same circle of concern, share an emotional experience, and then learn to care for each other.* Raising kids in a competitive environment not only can increase animosity but also suppress generosity and prosocial behaviors.[30] In fact, hundreds of studies document the harm competition can cause our children's empathy and altruism muscles if kids are pitted against each other.[31] So to discover how to create an atmosphere that encourages kid collaboration, cultivates empathy, *and* increases academic performance, we turn to another famous social psychologist.

The Jigsaw Solution

In 1971, Elliot Aronson was head of the social psychology department at the University of Texas when he received an urgent call from the Austin school superintendent to help defuse an explosive situation. Riots had broken out following the recent desegregation orders that placed white, black, and Hispanic youngsters together in classrooms for the first time, which created a hostile atmosphere. Aronson developed what he called the Jigsaw Classroom, and it worked not only to reduce the racial friction and the "Us"-"Them" divide but also to help bitter kids learn to care about each other.

Aronson divided fourth, fifth, and sixth graders into small, racially mixed teams to work on a joint lesson such as a historical event like the Battle of Gettysburg or a scientific principle such as the earth's orbit. As in a jigsaw puzzle, each student was responsible for learning one piece of the subject and then teaching it to team members. Collaboration was essential because their grade depended on one another's knowledge and contribution.

At first, students resented working together, but after a few weeks of collaborating, they began to like each other, until finally "them" became "us." "Prejudice, measured by a psychological test, declined, and students of different races were even playing together at recess." [32] As in Sherif's Robbers Cave experiment, Aronson's approach required students to collaborate on a common goal.

Since 1971, thousands of classrooms have used jigsaw learning and found similar success including improved test performance, reduced absenteeism, and greater liking for school. [33] The approach also helps students develop critical collaborative skills such as teamwork, decision making, communicating, and managing emotions. But something even more significant transpires in these classrooms: it is sharpening students' empathy quotients. [34]

"If kids spend just one hour a day working in groups," Aronson said, "they develop empathy for people they would otherwise have had nothing to do with because of their appearance." [35]

One of Aronson's proudest moments was receiving a letter from a boy who was involved in a jigsaw classroom years earlier. He recalled how his fifth-grade classmates treated him as an outsider and remembered their cruel, hostile treatment. Of Mexican American descent, he had spoken with a heavy accent, came from the "poorer" neighborhood, and was always one of "them." But the jigsaw experience changed everything. His group slowly started to help Carlos because students had to depend on his piece of the puzzle. "I began to realize that I wasn't really that stupid. And the kids I thought were cruel and hostile became my friends," he wrote. His stress faded, his confidence bloomed, and his performance excelled. "And today," Carlos told Aronson, "I got a letter admitting me to the Harvard Law School."[36]

"Getting to know you" is the first step to turning "Them" to "Us" and "Me" to "We." The more kids share with others, the more they grow to identify with each other, and the more indifference or even hostility wanes, leaving room for empathy to grow.

"Someone can tell you over and over that the short, fat kid with pimples is really sweet," said Aronson. "But there's no substitute for being in a small group with that kid and seeing that he's warm, funny, and clever."[37]

Sherif and Aronson showed us that it's in those collaborative-type experiences that children can learn to understand others' feelings and needs, and empathy has a chance to blossom. And the best news is there are dozens of ways we can incorporate those findings in our homes, schools, and communities and enrich our children's lives so they learn this seventh essential habit of empathy.

HOW TO CULTIVATE COLLABORATION IN CHILDREN

In writing this book, I discovered many powerful ways schools promote collaboration and empathy. One of the most inspiring is at Maury Elementary in Washington, DC, which holds a school-wide morning meeting once a month. The principal, Carolyne Albert-Garvey, facilitates the session as 330 elementary students sit in one giant circle in their multipurpose room. They greet one another, share positive school happenings, acknowledge student "empathy leaders," encourage each other, and practice social skills.[38] That collaborative experience also helps Maury students feel part of a caring learning community. Albert-Garvey is creating an environment that social scientists say promotes empathy.

When I taught, I'd always start my own mornings with a "class meeting." We'd begin with students saying something kind to the person sitting next to them, then discuss our schedule, and finally share any special news or concerns. I wanted to create a forum where my students would feel connected, notice others' needs, and learn collaborative skills like communication, perspective taking, and problem solving.

I never realized how powerful those meetings were until one day I came upon an unexpected sight: my class was sitting in a circle deeply engaged in a discussion. One classmate was crying while others comforted her: Christie had been bullied at recess, and my students called an emergency meeting to help.

I watched them empathize, discuss a serious issue, listen respectfully, and then work together to solve their classmate's problem. They agreed to take turns being with her at recess so she would never be alone. It was one of my proudest teaching moments: those morning meetings had built a feeling of "us" that mobilized my students to help their classmate.

Family meetings, class meetings, and Maury's school-wide meetings are great ways for kids to support one another and understand different perspectives while discussing problems in a loving environment. Meetings are also a place to polish important social-emotional skills like listening, encouraging, collaborating, perspective taking, and posing good questions. Such habits are acquired with practice—there are no shortcuts. It's up to us to provide our kids with the training grounds to learn them whether at home, in a classroom or at school.

8 TIPS FOR EFFECTIVE FAMILY, CLASS, AND SCHOOL-WIDE MEETINGS

1. **Be flexible with your agenda.** Topics are endless: what happened last week, upcoming plans, electronic time, allowances, sibling conflicts, something wonderful class or family members did for one another, voicing concerns. Set aside a suggestion box so as problems come up, members can include them to the upcoming agenda. And if you hear complaints, just say, "Add it to the agenda, and we'll discuss it at the meeting."

2. **Hold regular meetings.** Most families and teachers hold meetings once a week lasting ten to thirty minutes, depending on kids' ages. Find a time that's convenient for everyone, then post a reminder and mandate attendance.

3. **Rotate roles.** Assign roles that can be rotated weekly so kids can be active participants: a chairperson to stick to the agenda, a timekeeper to start and stop meetings, a parliamentarian to ensure rules are followed, a planner to post the meeting, and a secretary to take notes. Keep a Meeting Journal to record decisions, review previous notes, and serve as a wonderful family or class memory.

4. **Keep communication open.** Set clear rules so that each member's opinion is considered equally, everyone has airtime, and judgments are off limits. Use "I Messages" to help members understand each other's feelings and needs: "I feel sad when . . ." or "I get upset when . . ." And teach kids to paraphrase what they heard: "You said . . ." "You think . . ." "You feel . . ." "I think I just heard you say . . ."

5. **Give compliments.** Some families start each meeting by acknowledging members' efforts during the week or taking turns giving a compliment to each person. Post a sentence frame

until your kids get the idea: "I really appreciated when you . . ." "You did a great job this week when . . ." or "Thanks for . . ."

6. **Determine decision making.** Use consensus to decide solutions and then keep the conversation open until everyone agrees with a decision (or at least agrees it's okay to disagree). Decisions made during the meeting must be kept at least until the following meeting, where they can be changed.

7. **Resolve issues fairly.** Use brainstorming to solve problems. Name the problem, jot down all ideas (no judgments!), and keep ideas coming until you've exhausted possibilities. Then discuss the pros and cons of each. Give each member a chance to air his opinion, and then decide on solutions that are useful and respectful to all.

8. **Keep it upbeat.** You might share the funniest or best things that happened that week. End on a fun note: serve cookies, play Monopoly, do an interactive game, or give one big group hug.

EMPATHY BUILDER: TAKING A STAND TO SOLVE PROBLEMS COLLABORATIVELY

Collaborators work through problems together so that everyone is satisfied, and the act of collaborating stretches empathy through shared challenges and triumphs. Use the following steps to help your child learn the habit of solving social conflicts peacefully while also considering the other person's feelings and needs. Each letter in the acronym STAND represents one of the five steps in problem solving. It is often easier to teach one skill at a time until kids can put all five skills together to "Take a STAND."

Step 1. S = Stop, look, and listen to feelings. The first step to solving problems is to stay calm. Once in control, you can begin to figure out why you're upset and then find an answer to your problem. "Take a slow, deep breath to stay cool or walk away until calm." "Ask yourself: 'How do I feel?'" "Tune in to the person. How does she look?"

Step 2. T = _T_ake _T_urns _T_elling the problem. Each child takes a turn sharing his or her feelings about the problem with these rules: "Listen respectfully. No interrupting. Try to feel what it's like to be in the other kid's shoes." Sharing feelings using "I" not "you" helps kids stay focused on the problem without putting the other down. Sameer: "I'm ticked because I never get a turn." Kevin: "Well, I'm mad. I want to use the controller, too."

Each child then puts into words what the other person said. Sameer: "So, you're upset because you think you don't get a turn." Kevin: "And you feel the same way and think I don't let you choose."

Step 3. A = List _A_lternatives. Brainstorm options to find fair solutions. "No put-downs, and try to come up with ideas that work for both sides." Setting an oven timer for a few minutes can be a gold mine for younger kids or those with shorter attention spans. Stretch the brainstorm time depending on the children's age and problem-solving skills. Sameer: "We could pick straws to see who goes first." Kevin: "Maybe we could make a rule that the guest always chooses." Sameer: "We could rotate so everyone gets a turn."

Step 4. N = _N_arrow choices. Narrow options to a few choices by eliminating choices that aren't safe, someone isn't comfortable with, are not possible, or go against the house or school rules. Sameer: "Let's not do the rule that a guest always chooses because we may be on the playground and not in our houses." Kevin: "We may not have straws with us either."

Step 5. D = _D_ecide the best choice. Now choose the best solution from the remaining choices that everyone can agree to. Once you decide, shake on your agreement and stick to it. Sameer: "So the only one that's left is rotating turns. We just need to remember who chose last. Is that okay with you?" Kevin: "Yep, let's shake on it."

HOW TO HELP KIDS THINK "US" NOT "THEM"

Dr. Seuss's classic story *The Sneetches* is about birdlike creatures that look exactly alike except some have stars on their bellies, and some don't. Those little stars create an "Us" versus "Them" division. The Star-Belly Sneetches are the Selfies: they think they're better, they always brag, and they look down upon the Plain-Belly Sneetches. And the Plain-Belly Sneetches are depressed for being excluded from associating with their star-bellied counterparts. Finally, both sides realize that whether they have a star belly or not, they are really the same. Dr. Seuss teaches children the perfect empathy lesson: differences in appearance shouldn't divide us; after all, we are all "Us."

1. **Say "We."** Self-absorption diminishes empathy, so intentionally switch your pronouns (when appropriate) from "Them" to "Us" and "Me" to "We" when talking with your kids. "What should *we* do?" "Which would be better for *us*?" "Let's take a '*We*' vote, to find out what *we* choose." Subtle pronoun changes can help kids realize that life should revolve around "Us" and "We" not "Me" and "I."

2. **Broaden horizons.** Encourage your child to have contact with individuals of different races, cultures, ages, genders, abilities, and beliefs in school, after school, or at summer camp. Make sure you display an openness that is positive to diversity so that your kids model how you respect differences.

3. **Look for similarities.** Help your child look for what he has in common with others, not how he is different. Your child: "They have dark skin." Answer: "But they go to our church and play

guitar like you." Your child: "They're different." Answer: "There's lots of ways you're different from others, so let's think how they're like you. You both play soccer. What else?"

4. **Stress "Like me."** Expand the notion of the above activity to help your child consider common fears, dreams, feelings, worries, and joys that your child shares with others. "Yes, he comes from a different nation, but when he's left out, how does he feel?" "Yes, he speaks a different language, but what worries do you think he has that are the same as yours?" "She is in the lower math class, but she seemed to be angry at missing the bus just like you would be." Continue to widen your child's views about others to help her see that she shares more commonalities than differences with others.

5. **Teach "Reality check!"** An important part of stopping stereotypes that destroy empathy is helping kids listen for sweeping categorical statements they or another person might make, such as: "They *never* . . ." or "They *always* . . ."[39] What follows often increases the "Us" versus "Them" divide. So suppose a family member makes a sweeping statement. Another member gently says: "Reality check!" Child: "Asian kids always get good grades." Parent: "Reality check! Is that true for *every* Asian kid?" Child: "None of Grandpa's friends will hear me." Sister: "Reality check! You know a lot of elderly people who hear just fine." Child: "Girls make bad leaders." Dad: "Reality check! Let's name a few girls on your student council who are great leaders!"

A recent Harvard study by Richard Weissbourd of nearly 20,000 students from diverse middle schools and high schools across the United States found that students were least likely to support giving more power to the student council when it was led by white girls and most likely to support giving this power when it was led by white boys. Our girls' leadership capacities are being eroded by the biases they hold and confront in others. It's time to help them (and us) take a reality check![40]

6. Use diverse literature. Less than 8 percent of children's books published in 2012 addressed people of color.[41] So expose your child to literature that features positive images of all cultures, ages, abilities, and genders. Younger kids: *Bringing Asha Home*, by Uma Krishnaswami (India); *Grandfather's Journey*, by Allen Say (Japan); *How My Family Came to Be: Daddy, Papa and Me*, by Andrew Aldrich (African American boy adopted by white, gay couple); *The Girl Who Loved Wild Horses*, by Paul Goble (Native American). Older kids: *Children of the River*, by Linda Crew (Cambodia); *Dear Mrs. Parks*, by Rosa Parks (African American); *The Invisible Thread*, by Yoshiko Uchida (Japan); *Night*, by Elie Wiesel (Jews).

AGE-BY-AGE STRATEGIES

When our youngest son was in the eighth grade, his social studies teacher, Jo Anne Gill, assigned a project sponsored by the Constitutional Rights Foundation called National History Day. More than 600,000 students worldwide compete individually or in teams in the yearly event that requires extensive research on a historically significant topic.

My son, Zach, and his teammates, Duncan MacEwan and Tim Keane, were intrigued about Japanese American internment camps. President Franklin D. Roosevelt ordered the incarceration of over 120,000 Japanese living in the United States following Pearl Harbor. "But most were American citizens," the boys said. "How could we do that to our citizens?" And the team aimed to find out.

The boys found a woman to interview who had been interned as a child. I still remember how patiently Cherry Ishimatsu described her experience to three thirteen-year-old white kids who didn't have a clue. But she used perspective taking to help the boys understand her history, and it was powerful.

"How would you feel if you were given hours to pack only what you could carry in a suitcase and taken to a camp with barbed wire all around?" she asked. "What would you think if your mom and dad lost their home, business, or farm? Can you imagine how you'd feel if armed guards at the camp watched you around the clock with orders to shoot if you tried to escape?"

At one point, I had one of those rare parenting moments when you see your child and his friends grasp something profound: they understood the effect of discrimination through the eyes of someone who had experienced it. At the end of two hours, the boys thanked Cherry profusely.

And so began a collaborative venture among the boys that would produce an unimaginable outcome. They divided up their research like in an Aronson jigsaw lesson, but with one common goal: to tell the Japanese American internment story to others. They dug deeper, interviewed more internees, and the more they learned, the more irate they became.

At that point, their fathers decided to help them "live the event," and drove the boys five hours to the Manzanar War Relocation Center—the place where Cherry was detained—to spend the night. They saw where the sentry guard posts once stood years earlier, walked over the cement foundations where the internees were housed, felt the desolation, and (at least for that one night) grasped why the internees said they felt lonely, frustrated, and afraid. They felt Cherry's pain. It was as though a fire had been lit in these kids, and the flames never seemed to go out. Their class project turned into a personal crusade to let the world know about the injustice dealt to "their friends."

I watched in amazement over the next few months as their team won the school, district, and county competitions, and cheered when they won first place in California. When they won first place in the nation at the University of Maryland, I just cried.

My son and his teammates had learned far more than history: their experience taught them about collaboration and compassion and about injustice and racism. But the boys weren't the only ones who gained an education: I learned that sharing oral histories is a powerful tool for unlocking empathy.

I'm firmly convinced that the best way to erase destructive prejudices is through meaningful experiences that expose children to differences and break down barriers until "Them" becomes "Us." And it all starts with empathy.

Symbols designate the recommended age and suitability for activity: L = Little Ones: Toddlers and Preschoolers; S = School-age; T = Tweens and Older; A = All Ages

- **Cut one activity!** A survey found that 80 percent of kids say they wish they had more free time; 41 percent admit feeling stressed most of the time because they have too much to do.[42] Check your kid's calendar: is there one extra activity that can be cut to free up time to connect with peers and practice collaborating? **A**

- **Learn one new thing.** Encourage your children to learn "one new thing" about someone each day. The habit requires kids to listen deeper, ask questions, and focus more on one another and less on themselves. The acronym FACT helps children recall four simple "conversation starters" that can start dialogues, make new friends, strengthen relationships, and build empathy. Why not also encourage your kids to share their "people discoveries" at dinner, practice good ol' face-to-face communication, and use one new conversation starter with your family each night?

  ▷ **F = F**avorites: A food, sport, team, movie, TV show, book, or place to go ("What's your favorite baseball team?")

  ▷ **A = A**ctivities: An enjoyable pastime or interest ("What do you like to do for fun on Saturday?")

  ▷ **C = C**ontacts: A favorite teacher, coach, friend, teammate, or common connection ("Who was on your team last year?")

  ▷ **T = T**alents: A special skill, interest, sport, or instrument ("Do you play an instrument?")

  Once a relationship opens, kids can ask deeper questions about a person's hopes, dreams, worries, opinions, personal challenges, or memories. **S, T**

- **Praise the camaraderie, not the win.** While you can congratulate your child's successes, don't forget to praise actions that show compassion, teamwork, and encouraging others: "Nice pass to Samantha." "I love how you listened to your classmates' opinions." Also, explain how an intense competitive drive turns kids off. "You won, but how did your team feel when you fought every call?" "You are a great drummer, but watch your band's reaction when you say you're a 'musical genius.'" **A**

- **Start youth service groups.** Why not encourage your kids (and friends) to start a Care Club in their friendship group, neighborhood, school, scout troop, faith group, or community organization? They can brainstorm ways to make their mark on the world together—collecting toys for homeless kids, baking treats for a senior home, becoming pen pals with pediatric hospital patients, making care packages for soldiers—and then choose what ignites their passion. Check out Kids Care Clubs that were established to inspire a spirit of volunteering in children at the fabulous organization called generationOn. **S, T**

- **Mix up the social scene.** Mix It Up at Lunch Day is a national campaign launched by Teaching Tolerance that encourages students to cross social boundaries and meet new friends. One day of each school year students move out of their comfort zones and connect with someone new over lunch. The many schools that extend the event to occur monthly or weekly are discovering that students are diversifying their friendships and that doing so helps reduce bullying. Find ways for your kids to "mix up" their own social scene so they can broaden their perspectives. See also Rachel's Challenge as a powerful program to bring to your school. **S, T**

- **Hold neighborhood movie nights.** Movies can be a great way to discuss the power of collaborating as well as to elevate kids' empathy. So why not show flicks to kid groups? Some neighborhoods hold summer "movies under the stars" in neighbors' yards. Hang a sheet, spread blankets, and show the film via your DVD. Younger kids: *An American Tale, Miracle at Midnight, Perfect Harmony, Finding Nemo, March of the Penguins*. Older kids: *Glory, Remember the Titans, Hoosiers, Au Revoir Les Enfants, The Blue and the Gray, Apollo 13, Paper Clips*. **A**

- **Use cooperative games.** Teach your kids and friends team-building games to stress collaboration, not competition. Resources include: *Cooperative Games and Sports: Joyful Activities for Everyone*, by Terry Orlick; *Everyone Wins! Cooperative Games and Activities*, by Josette and Sambhava Luvmour; and *Great Group Games: 175 Boredom-Busting, Zero-Prep Team Builders for All Ages*, by Susan Ragsdale and Ann Saylor. **A**

- **Stress encouraging others.** Good collaborators are team players, so teach encouraging comments that your kids can say to support others and inspire collaboration. "Let's keep going." "Nice one!" "This is good!" "Keep it up!" "We're doing great!" "What a team!" **A**

- **Teach decision makers and deal breakers.** Teach Rock, Paper, Scissors to help your child resolve questions like "Who goes first?" "Was the ball outside?" "What should we play?" and other issues that can derail cooperation. Show the three hand shapes: Rock: a closed fist; Paper: a flat, open hand; Scissors: a fist with the index and middle fingers extended to form a *V*. Then, while saying "Rock, Paper, Scissors," each child simultaneously extends his hand toward their opponent and reveals one hand shape. "Rock crushes Scissors," "Paper covers Rock," "Scissors cut Paper," and the decision is made! If kids throw the same shape, they try again. Sometimes, the game can be "best two out of three." **A**

- **Practice how to disagree respectfully.** Disagreeing is bound to be part of any group, so teach kids how to disagree respectfully to keep communication open. Explain: "You have the right to disagree. If you do, be calm and tell us your view. You could say: 'I disagree because . . .' 'That's one idea, here's another . . .' 'I have a different view because . . .' 'There's another way to look at it . . .' 'Have you thought about it this way . . . ?' 'Did you consider . . . ?' Then listen to everyone's ideas. Be ready to change or stick to your opinion, but remain respectful." **A**

- **Do family projects.** Find ways for your family to work together on projects such as arranging a picnic, planting a garden, doing service, planning a trip, or even spring-cleaning. Go through the steps so kids experience the process of collaborating, such as putting on a family garage sale. Divide tasks from making sale signs, finding old games and books to sell, labeling and pricing each item, and arranging them on your lawn. Older kids can help younger kids assume "cash register" duties, and unsold items can be donated to a charity chosen in a family vote. **A**

THE TOP FIVE THINGS TO KNOW ABOUT CULTIVATING COLLABORATION

1. Skills kids need to work together—like encouraging, resolving conflicts, shaking hands, and problem solving—are like muscles: if you don't use them, you lose them.

2. The more opportunities kids have to connect and collaborate, the more likely they are to think "We" not "Me."

3. Exposing children to differences and providing collaborative opportunities to learn about others can cultivate empathy and help them gain the Empathy Advantage.

4. Family meetings as well as class meetings help kids practice social-emotional skills and understand perspectives.

5. The best ways to learn relationship skills are by watching, doing, and repeating.

ONE LAST THING

When my oldest son was nine, his teacher arranged for his class to sing at a nursing home during the holidays. Students practiced for weeks, but my son was hesitant because he hadn't had many experiences with the elderly. Once we talked about what he could expect, his concerns eased, and by the time he came home, his fears were gone. In fact, he couldn't wait to visit his "new friends" again.

"They're just like us, Mom," he said. "They like music and get lonely when their family doesn't visit, too. A bunch of kids want to go back. Can you take us?" The experience stretched my son and his friends to see his new, older friends in terms of "us" and no longer "them."

Exposing children to differences and providing collaborative opportunities to learn about others is one more path to cultivating empathy and increasing the Empathy Advantage. It's also another way to produce a generation of children who care deeply about others and want to make a difference in their world.

PART THREE

LIVING EMPATHY

Sow a thought and you reap an act; sow an act and you reap a habit; sow a habit and you reap a character; sow a character and you reap a destiny.

—Charles Reade

CHAPTER 8

Empathetic Children Stick Their Necks Out

Promoting Moral Courage

Bullying is a widespread concern, and parents everywhere want solutions. Fifty states have established anti-bullying policies, and hundreds of anti-bullying curriculums are rolling off the presses for use in classrooms for all ages. But in our quest to stop peer cruelty, we may be overlooking the most effective anti-bullying strategy: mobilizing the empathy of bystanders to care for each other. Bullying is reduced dramatically when kids who witness peer cruelty stand up for the victim, and this is the next stage of empathy. In part 1, we learned how to help our kids develop empathy. In part 2, we learned how to help them practice it. But part 3 contains the most important habits of all: how to help our children live with empathy every day of their lives.

Dateline was familiar with my work, and the producers there asked me to help film an episode about bystanders. NBC News television journalist and anchor Kate Snow was the on-air correspondent, and I was the parenting expert. And so began an elaborate ruse: child actors were hired to play the bully, victim, or henchman; producers sent out a bogus casting call for a "tween reality show"; and dozens of middle school–aged kids showed up for what they believed was their chance for fame (parents were told the real context only after arriving with their kids).

Each mini-bullying experiment was composed of six kids: three actors portraying three roles—a bully, a victim, and a henchman—and three unsuspecting young tweens who waited in a room (with no adults) for their "audition." Then on cue, hidden cameras rolled and the young actors played their roles for a few minutes: the "bully" tormenting the "victim," the "henchman" supporting the "bully," and the "victim" acting increasingly distressed. Each parent (watching via monitors from another room) was confident that their child would help, but most were wrong. We taped all day, and not one child intervened.

Then the final group of "auditioners" walked in, and one father shared his concerns. "I always tell Lucy that I expect her to help others," he told me. "I hope Lucy steps in; it's big in our family."

The dad's words are a prime reason why some kids are morally courageous: their parents expect social responsibility, and this was the first parent who voiced moral expectations for his child. Most told me that their child would not step in because "winning the audition" was more important. That message said volumes.

Then the cameras rolled and the actors assumed their parts, but this time something was different: one child clearly did *not* approve of "the bully's" antics from the get-go. She was also far more tuned in to "the victim" than other kids had been: her "emotional radar" was fully extended. As the taunting intensified—as the actor was instructed—she moved closer to ensure that the boy was okay and tried to get the others to intervene. Realizing their passivity, she stepped between the two actors as a diversion. And when "the victim" seemed distressed, she went to code red. Within three minutes, this girl had had enough: the boy's pain was now her pain. She told "the bully" in no uncertain terms to "stop," that his behavior was "not cool," and then she comforted "the victim." All the while she was calm, courageous, and just plain glorious. And that bold and humane child was Lucy.

Well, her dad was ecstatic and could no longer contain himself: "She stepped in!" he exclaimed. "Oh, how I love that kid! She stepped in!" Hearing a dad's pride about his child's humanity is far too rare.

Producers in the control room cheered, cameramen brushed away tears, and the rest of us stood in awe: we'd witnessed a morally coura-geous child. And when Kate Snow finally explained to the kids that the bullying was all a hoax, Lucy broke down and cried.

"Oh, I'm so glad this was fake!" she sobbed. "I felt so bad for him. I couldn't stand to see him hurting."

Every adult knew we'd witnessed something magical, but they also wondered why this child intervened when no other did.

"Empathy," I told them. "You saw the power of empathy."

Lucy's empathy compelled her to help, but moral courage pushed her to act. It was impossible for this girl to *not* speak out: she felt that boy's pain.

LEARNING TO EXERCISE MORAL COURAGE

Moral courage is a special inner strength that motivates children to act on their empathic urges and help others despite the consequences. It's not always easy: sometimes there are risks, and it may not rate as "cool" to other kids, but these children stick their necks out and stand up for justice and compassion. It's all because moral courage pushes kids from just feeling someone's pain to helping, comforting, and speaking out for those in need. These children are Upstanders—the empathic elite—and they stand up for others because they know deep down it's the right and caring thing to do.

And why would we want our child to be morally courageous? Oh, let me count the ways. A bold child is more likely to withstand nega-tive peer pressure, say no to temptations that counter your family's val-ues, and fight the good fight. But moral courage also plays a surprising role in predicting success and happiness and giving kids the Empathy Advantage. This essential habit boosts kids' resilience, confidence, and willpower as well as their learning, performance, and school engage-ment.[1] It also stretches children's risk-taking muscles and their creativity (which has taken a disturbing dip in American kids; the correlation to lifetime creative accomplishment is more than three times stronger for childhood creativity than childhood IQ).[2] These kids might be the ones to improve the human condition.

This chapter teaches habits of moral courage that children will need especially in our complex and uncertain world. In a culture hyped with greed, selfishness, and fallen integrity, it behooves us to raise our children to have personal valor. Morally courageous children are the true UnSelfies: quiet, unsung heroes who don't expect accolades and trophies, but who act on their concern for others out of moral beliefs. And, oh, how the world needs them.

WHY ARE KIDS BYSTANDERS RATHER THAN UPSTANDERS?

Fresh insight about the roles witnesses play in bullying has generated a major educational shift in how to stop it. When bystanders step in on behalf of bullied peers, bullying stops more than 57 percent of the time and within 10 seconds,[3] yet in most cases only 19 percent of bystanders get involved.[4]

Why don't they help? To find out, I asked the best source: kids. I've interviewed more than five hundred children in remarkably different areas of the globe including Armenia, Nicaragua, Taiwan, Mexico, Rwanda, Canada, Colombia, Germany, Italy, on our overseas US Army bases, and across the United States. Bullying concerns children everywhere, and the reasons they don't intervene are similar regardless of region, culture, or demographics. It's time we listen to kids.

Powerlessness. *"I didn't know how to make it stop."* Most kids tell me they would step in, "but nobody tells us what to do." A feeling of powerlessness or lack of training restrains kids' courage, but can be overridden *if* they learn *how* to respond. Kids witness 85 percent of bullying incidents, usually when adults aren't present. We must teach them how.

The Upstander Solution: The Empathy Builder section on pages 181–82 provides seven Upstander skills so kids know how to intervene safely.

Offer your child a range of options depending on the situation and practice those your child feels most comfortable with using until they become habits.

Vague expectations. *"I wasn't sure if I should help."* Kids don't want to make things worse, be embarrassed, or get themselves (or others) in trouble. But if they are clear about expectations, know that adults will support them, and understand what bullying is, they are more likely to help.

The Upstander Solution: Review the school bullying policy, so your child understands the staff's and your expectations. Teach the definition of bullying using the acronym CAP:

- **C** = Bullying is repeated *cruel* behavior.

- **A** = Bullying is never *accidental*: the child who is bullying is intentionally causing another kid verbal, emotional, and/or physical pain.

- **P** = Bullying is a *power* imbalance: the target cannot hold their own and needs help.

Peer pressure. *"I don't want to be a snitch and lose my friends."* Friends play a big part in our children's lives, and losing social status is a huge kid concern.

The Upstander Solution: Kids are more apt to report bullying anonymously *and* if adults take them seriously. Find out if your child's school has a confidential phone hotline, website, or report boxes, and review them with your child. Several activities in this chapter help kids recognize that the vast majority of peers are against bullying. Enlist those ideas to help your child and his friends switch peer norms so it's "cool to be kind."

The diffusion of responsibility. *"Somebody else will help."* Bystanders are less likely and slower to intervene if others are present because they assume that someone else will step in, so no one does.

The Upstander Solution: The new wave of bullying prevention teaches kids how easy it is to succumb to bystanding. A set of studies found that students attending social psychology lectures about the bystander effect were less susceptible to those influences.[5] Discuss the diffusion of responsibility and situational awareness skills in age-appropriate terms with your child. (See "Teach S.O.S. Safety Smarts" on pages 187–88.) Watch documentaries about the bystander effect like Philip Zimbardo's famous *The Stanford Prison Experiment*, and review the Good Samaritan study (described on pages 176 and 177) with your teen. Zimbardo now advocates that we teach children situational awareness skills to prepare them for social pressures so they are more likely to step in.

Empathy overarousal. *"I felt too bad to help."* There's no doubt that bullying can cause severe emotional harm to the bullied, but witnesses also suffer severe psychological and physiological stress.[6] Lucy on the *Dateline* segment became visibly distraught, believing that the victim was hurting, and her reaction is typical with highly empathetic kids. Not to help a victim can cause guilt (*"I should have helped"*); fear (*"I could be next"*); and empathic overarousal (*"It felt like I was bullied"*). It's why adults must be educated about bullying and another reason children must learn self-regulation strategies (discussed in chapter 5) so they can cope, keep their empathy channels open, and fill in the empathy gap so they act on their empathic urges.

The Upstander Solution: Review "How to Help Kids Stay in Control and Find Moral Courage in Crucial Moments," on page 182, which teaches four crucial skills to help kids reduce fear, guilt, and compassion fatigue. Stress: "If you don't feel comfortable helping on the spot, you can help later." (See also "Use Your HEART" on page 186 for more strategies in the Age-by-Age Strategies section starting on page 184.)

Weak adult support. *"My mom didn't believe me."* Many kids admitted they didn't tell an adult about a bullying incident "because she didn't believe me." Some said the adult downplayed the severity: "The teacher said it wasn't a big deal." Others worried that it might make things worse and that they'd be targeted next. Fear of retaliation is a huge concern.

The Upstander Solution: Helping children find courage to help in a risky situation is possible *only* if they trust adults. That is why it's crucial for adults to understand the devastating impact bullying has on children. Listen and believe your children so they will come to you and remind them that you will support them.

Bullying hurts children everywhere. Children in every spot of the globe are concerned about peer cruelty. Colombian kids: "Do other kids in the world hurt like us?" Texas tweens: "Ask teachers to watch the halls so we feel safer." British teens: "There's so much bullying that we can't think." California children: "No one listens to us, and we're hurting. Thanks for listening."

The first step to building courage is to listen, support, and believe our children so they know that we care. Listen!

WHAT SCIENCE SAYS: WHY DO SOME INTERVENE WHILE OTHERS DON'T?

"Why do some care so much that they take the risk to help, while others walk on?" The question has kept me up nights. I've seen firsthand how a lack of empathy is a catalyst to humanity's darker side. I studied genocide in Rwanda, and visited death camps in Auschwitz and Dachau. I stood on Blind Street (yes, a real street) in Cape Town, where whites turned their blind eyes to their black neighbors during apartheid. Some do walk away.

I've experienced the antithesis of empathy and know what's at stake for our children's future if empathy and moral courage wither and the empathy gap widens. But now science is discovering what frees and shackles the traits of humanity, and those findings are crucial as we parent our next generation.

Why Don't We Help?

Psychology professors John Darley and Bibb Latané decided to study this very question, and they conducted a series of well-known social psychology experiments. They set up faux emergencies in subways, hotel rooms, street corners, and in laboratories with dozens of unaware participants, and then watched how long it took them to help (if they did). Sometimes the subject was alone with the "confederate" who feigned the need for help; sometimes the subject was in the presence of others.

In one experiment, smoke entered a room as unsuspecting subjects filled out questionnaires. In another, a confederate appeared to have a life-threatening seizure and pleaded for assistance. Or they thought they heard a "lady in distress" moaning about her hurt leg (actually a tape recording that simulated a fall and moan). So who helps?

The Bystander Effect

Darley and Latané discovered that empathy is tethered to situations. One is called the "diffusion of responsibility": the *more* witnesses involved in an "emergency," the *less* people feel responsible to intervene and the *slower* they help.[7] We don't step in because we figure someone else will. The social dynamic changes if the victim is a friend, and then 95 percent of us intervene within the first three minutes. Even briefly meeting "the victim" prior to an emergency increases the speed of our stepping in.

Bystanders may also misinterpret what is happening or incorrectly assume that others accept what is happening (a phenomenon called "pluralistic ignorance"). Or they deny the seriousness of the situation, misread the victim's concerns, or fear they could make things worse by responding. But even those who didn't intervene showed genuine concern and were often nervous and trembling. Their empathy for the victim's suffering was often aroused, but they didn't help *because they didn't know what to do* (a major reason for the empathy gap).

Darley also did another experiment with psychologist Daniel Batson. This time seminary students were recruited and asked to walk to a chapel and give a talk about the parable of the Good Samaritan. On the way, they encountered a man slumped and moaning for help (as instructed by Darley and Batson). Whether or not the seminarians responded depended largely if they were late to the talk—even if they were to deliver a speech about altruism![8] About two-thirds of the students who thought they had plenty of time stopped to help, but only 10 percent of the students who thought they were late did so.

Kids also tell me they sometimes don't help because "we don't want to get in trouble for being late." So be clear that helping someone is *always* more important than getting a late slip, and that you will back your child up if he is reprimanded for tardiness.

The Bystander Effect Also Impacts Kids

The bystander effect isn't exclusive to adults: the latest science shows that it influences young children. Researchers from the Max Planck Institutes in Germany recruited 60 five-year-olds for an experiment. In one room were three children: two were part of the study and instructed what to do; the third child was the subject. The children thought they were going to color a picture. Then a woman experimenter "accidentally" spills water on her table, tries to stop it, and groans. "I need something to wipe it up," she says, while glancing at paper towels placed conveniently nearby. The woman displays more distress, and if no child helped, she asks, "Could somebody hand me the paper towels there?"

How do you think your child would respond? Keep in mind, the experimenters ruled out shyness as a condition. The study found that five-year-olds are less likely to help when other children are available.[9] The diffusion of responsibility affects young children also.

Why Some Children Are Bold

For decades, Ervin Staub, author of *The Psychology of Good and Evil*, has studied extensively why some hurt and others help. He now helps schools develop anti-bystander curriculums to encourage children to intervene against bullying. His research shows a disturbing downward spiral in children's heroism, and this should be another wake-up call.

Staub's experiment has a young woman playing with two children in a school and then telling them she's leaving for a bit, exiting, and closing the door. The children then hear a loud crash followed by a child crying from what they assume is the playroom next door.

About half of the time, at least one of the five-year-olds runs next door to help and fully 90 percent of second graders go for help. But then children's courage begins to slide. By fourth grade, 40 percent help, while just 30 percent of sixth graders respond to the child's cries.[10] To fight the "courage dip," Staub is adamant that we must keep encouraging our kids to be socially responsible to help others and strengthen their inner hero from an earlier age.[11] That advice also applies to decreasing the empathy gap so kids are more likely to act on their compassionate urges.

Staub also found that kindergarteners and first graders are more likely to respond to another's distress when paired. Younger kids share their concerns with each other ("I'm scared. Are you?" "Do you think we should help?"), and that strategy helps them stay calmer and be *more* likely to help another. Teens are more apt to keep their fears to themselves and are *less* likely to intervene. So encourage your kids in troubling situations to "tell your worries to a friend."

The Science Lessons

Though moral courage can be nurtured, some factors (like the diffusion of responsibility) may rein in our children's "helping muscles." John Darley, the psychologist who identified the bystander effect, shares the silver lining: "If given the proper tools and primed to respond positively to a crisis, most of us have the ability to transcend our identities as bystanders."[12] And that hopeful outlook also applies to our kids.

HOW TO CULTIVATE MORAL COURAGE IN CHILDREN

Kelly Lyons and her five-year-old son, Rocky, were driving home after visiting friends.[13] Rocky was asleep as Kelly steered down a twisting two-lane Alabama country road when their pickup truck hit a pothole, flipped, and rolled down a twenty-foot ravine. Rocky was miraculously unhurt, but Kelly was seriously injured and pinned against the door.

Fearing the truck might explode, Kelly told her son to run for safety. He started up the hill as his mom told him but then stopped midtrack and scrambled back to help. His mom was losing consciousness, but somehow the kindergartener found strength to pull Kelly from the crushed vehicle and then helped her inch herself slowly up the steep slope. At times Kelly's pain was so excruciating that she wanted to quit, but Rocky wouldn't hear of it and never left her side.

To inspire his mom to not give up, Rocky reminded her "to think about the little train that climbed the steep mountain" from his favorite book, *The Little Engine That Could*. He kept repeating his own version of the story's refrain: "You can do it, you can do it, YOU CAN DO IT!" and never stopped coaxing his mom as they crawled up that steep 45-degree slope.

When they finally reached the top, Rocky hailed a driver to take them to the hospital. The doctor said Kelly's injuries were among the worst he'd ever seen, and he credited the young child's can-do spirit for saving her life. Rocky's courage made the national news, but the kindergartener insisted he didn't do anything special. "I just did what anyone would have done."[14]

Helping Kids Find Their Inner Hero

Not every child would respond to such a challenging situation with such courage and confidence, but science contends that Rocky's heroics were nurtured by parenting. Here are five ways to stretch your child's moral courage.

1. **Expect social responsibility.** Lucy's father instilled in her that he expected her to care. Rocky's dad told him: "Take care of Mama" whenever he wasn't there.[15] Kids are more likely to help if they believe that their parents and friends expect them to support those in need. A vast majority of Holocaust rescuers said

that their parents expected them to care for others, and that sense of responsibility was imparted in their childhoods.[16]

2. **Set an example.** Let your child see you stand up for what you believe in and step out of your comfort zone to tackle a simple fear of heights and ride that cable car. Kids who watch their parents stick out their necks to help others are more likely to do the same.

3. **Offer heroes.** Kids need heroes to inspire their courage, so find one that appeals to your child. They can be found in real life, like Gandhi, Mother Teresa, Abraham Lincoln, and Nelson Mandela, or in fiction: Matilda, Huck Finn, Dorothy Gale, Harry Potter, The Little Engine That Could (Rocky's hero), or Aunt Harriet and the nice kid next door.

4. **Stop rescuing.** Always solving your child's problems strengthens her dependence on others for rescue. If you're "overhelping," start building your child's confidence by putting him in the driver's seat. He—not you—tells his coach he can't make practice. He—without assistance—apologizes to his pal. She—not you—tells Grandma her worries about spending the night. Moral courage is possible only if kids believe in their capabilities and have opportunities to prove it to themselves.

5. **Try small-scale courage.** Facing any fear takes courage, so encourage your child's efforts no matter the size. Instead of picking her daughter up, Krista Hoffmann helped her three-year-old find courage to cross a small bridge by empowering her. "Be brave, Clara," Krista said. "You can do it." Clara continued repeating to herself "Be brave, Clara!" and learned something when she crossed it: "I'm brave, Mommy! I'm brave!" Kids learn courage by doing and in small steps.

EMPATHY BUILDER:
HOW TO STANDUP FOR OTHERS

Mobilizing children's moral courage to be Upstanders may be our best hope to stop peer cruelty. Kid interventions cut bullying by more than half the time and within 10 seconds,[17] but they *must* learn how to step in or get help. Here are seven Upstander strategies I've taught hundreds of kids over the years and were featured on the *Dateline* special "The Perils of Parenting" with Kate Snow. Focus on one at a time, until it becomes a habit and your child can use all seven strategies to STANDUP for others.

- **S = Seek Support.** Turn to another bystander and try to create an ally to help you by saying "That's mean!" "He shouldn't do that." Or ask for support: "Are you with me?" "Come on, let's help!"

- **T = Tell a Trusted Adult.** Break the snitch code by teaching the difference between "reporting" (stopping someone *from* being hurt) versus "tattling" (getting someone *in* trouble). "If someone could get hurt, find an adult or dial 911 to get help."

- **A = Assist the Victim.** If others see you helping, they're more likely to join you. You could stand closer to the victim. Ask: "Do you need help?" Empathize: "I know how you feel." Offer assistance: "I'll take you to the office." "Let's get out of here." You could also support the victim *after* the incident. "What he did was mean." "You didn't deserve that."

- **N = Negate with a Positive View.** Upstanders can stop rumors or counter degrading comments with a positive perspective. "My experience was . . ." "She was in my class and I saw . . ." "I was there and never heard that." "I've known her awhile and know a different story."

- **D = Design a Detour.** Upstanders can drain a bully's power by reducing the audience, so try to get others to leave. "You coming?" "What are you all doing here?" "Let's go!" If you can't get others to exit, walk away. If you stay, you're fueling the cruelty.

- **U = Use a Distraction.** A distraction can disperse a group, let the victim get away, and may get the bully to move on. A few Upstander distraction possibilities are: A question: "Don't you know you'll get suspended?" A diversion: "Why aren't you at the volleyball game?" A false excuse: "A teacher is coming!" An interruption: "Did you watch the basketball game last night?"

- **P = Pause and Rethink.** An Upstander's comment can make bystanders pause to consider consequences. Kids are also more likely to intervene if they know *why* it's wrong. "Let's just cool down." "You'll get suspended." "He'll get hurt." "How would you feel if they said that about you?"

HOW TO HELP KIDS STAY IN CONTROL AND FIND MORAL COURAGE IN CRUCIAL MOMENTS

One of my most rewarding experiences was training mental health counselors on US Army installations to help our military kids cope during their parents' deployments. While there, several commanders shared with me the new training for Navy SEALs, the most elite force in our services. The revised technique is designed by neuroscientists and changes the way SEALs' brains react to fear so they stay in control in the midst of chaos.

The four strategies are so simple, and I realized they could be taught to kids and have since revamped my counselor trainings to include them. These tools will strengthen your child's resilience, help him find moral courage in crucial moments, and keep empathy open since fear can shut it down. They also reduce the empathy gap so kids are more likely to act on their empathic urges and step in or speak out to help.

Skill 1: Positive Self-talk

SEALs are taught to tell themselves positive words to override the brain's fear response, so help your child develop a phrase to stay calm and build moral courage. A few could be: "I'm calm and in control," "I'll be okay," "I'm brave," "I can do this," or even Rocky Lyons's "I think I can" that he used to save his mom's life. Then make the phrase easy for your child to remember. Young kids could hang it on the wall or in a frame next to their bed. Teens might tape it to their mirror or upload it as a screen saver.

Skill 2: Mental Rehearsal

Mental rehearsal (or "visualization") is reviewing an activity in your mind repeatedly so that when the real situation happens, your body has a less stressful response. Michael Phelps, the Olympian, mentally rehearsed every possible scenario in a swim race, so when water flooded his goggles at the Beijing Olympic Games, he didn't panic. He had repeatedly visualized exactly how many hand movements he needed to reach the final wall, and won another gold medal. "I can visualize the worst race, the worst circumstances," Phelps said. "That's what I do to prepare myself for what might happen . . . You have to have a plan."[18]

Help your child develop a plan to reduce a concern like getting on the wrong bus, and then help him review it frequently in his mind: "I wake up, eat breakfast, and walk to the bus stop, and take the bus number I wrote inside my shoe."

Skill 3: Chunk It

In a stressful situation, emotions go into panic mode, so it's hard to think. Navy SEALs are taught to set goals in extremely short chunks, so in stressful situations they think of just getting through the next step . . . then the next . . . to bring calmness to their chaos. But they must visualize something positive in the *very* near future.

Suppose your child worries he won't make it through the baseball game. He sets a goal to get through the first inning, and when successful, he thinks of getting through the second . . . and third. If your son worries he won't survive the first day of school, he visualizes just making it through recess, then lunch, then home.

Skill 4: Deep Breathing

The fastest way to reduce stress is deep breathing, because it gets oxygen to your brain and creates an instant relaxation response. So teach your child that the second he feels stressed to breathe in for two counts, hold for three counts, breathe out four counts, and then start again (call it 2-3-4 Breathing).[19] For younger kids, name it Dragon Breathing: "Take a deep breath and blow out your worries so they go far away, like a dragon's breath." Watch the movie *Pete's Dragon* with your child as you're reviewing the strategy.

AGE-BY-AGE STRATEGIES

The path to moral courage often starts with empathy. And "feeling with another" is what inspired two boys to send a silent message of support to a bullied classmate, never realizing that their gesture would impact the world.

It was the first school day at Central Kings Rural High School in Nova Scotia when a ninth grader walked in wearing a pink polo shirt. He was bullied mercilessly by a group of twelfth-grade boys who called him "fag" and let him know in no uncertain terms that "he'd be sorry" if he ever wore pink again.

When twelfth graders Travis Price and David Shepherd heard what happened, they were outraged and wanted to do something. So they pooled their money and bought seventy-five pink women's tank tops— every pink shirt they could find—at a discount store. Then they got on social media and encouraged their classmates to support this boy by wearing pink the next day. Their plan was not to confront the bullies directly but to let them know that other kids didn't approve and were standing together in a "sea of pink."

Travis shared his plan with his parents, who endorsed it but insisted that the school be notified. Travis made the call and was warned that if a fight broke out over the incident, he could be disciplined. And now came their moral courage dilemma.

"I knew what it felt like to be bullied, and what it's like to not want to go to school. I wanted to show this kid that he was not alone," Travis told me. "We had a choice, and our choice was to stand up for this kid regardless of the consequences." [20]

Empathy and moral courage won, and Price and Shepherd's "sea of pink" campaign began.

The boys had no idea how many of the 1,000 students would join them, but when the bullied thirteen-year-old walked into school the next day, hundreds of his classmates were wearing pink—many covered from head to toe. Nobody needed to say a thing; everyone knew that the flood of pink meant they were united in their support for him, and the bullying stopped.

But their pink campaign didn't go unnoticed. The national news picked up the story, and it went viral. Kids around the world wanted to wear pink and stand up to peer cruelty as well. Pink shirts have become an international symbol against bullying, and once a year more than six million people in more than a dozen countries hold Pink Shirt Day and wear pink. And it started with the empathy and moral courage of two boys who wanted to help a troubled classmate.

Here are ways to help kids find moral courage and stand up for each other.

**Symbols designate the recommended age and suitability for
activity: L = Little Ones: Toddlers and Preschoolers; S = School-age;
T = Tweens and Older; A = All Ages**

- **Make Courage Chains.** St. Dominic's Elementary School in
  Alberta teaches a monthly courage theme. Teachers read books
  (*Courage*, by Bernard Waber; *Brave Irene*, by William Steig;
  Wringer, by Jerry Spinelli), and kids learn courage affirmations:
  "I am willing to try new things." "I listen to my heart." "I have the
  courage to do the right thing." Students also are encouraged to do
  daily courageous deeds like introducing themselves to someone
  new, inviting a new classmate to play, or standing up for another.
  Successes are listed on paper strips stapled together to form courage chains. I saw chains wrapping hallways, and many students
  proudly shared their deeds. Help your kids understand the meaning of courage and find their inner hero. **L, S**

- **Use your HEART.** "Empathy overarousal" is a challenge for many
  children who become distressed watching others treated unfairly
  and expands the empathy gap. If they don't help, they can suffer
  from guilt or shut down their empathy as a way to cope or dim
  their own pain. So teach: "It's never too late to show a friend you
  care" with ways to comfort someone at the scene . . . or later. **A**

  - ▷ **H = Help.** Run for first aid. Call others to help. Pick up what's
    broken.

  - ▷ **E = Empathize.** "He did that to me and I was scared." "I know
    how you feel."

  - ▷ **A = Assist.** "Do you need help?" "I'll find a teacher." "I'll walk
    you to the office."

  - ▷ **R = Reassure.** "It happens to other kids." "I'm still your friend."
    "Teachers will help."

  - ▷ **T = Tell how you feel.** "You didn't deserve that." "I'm so sorry."
    "I know it's not true."

- **Dispel the "Superman Myth."** Many kids assume they need to look like the Incredible Hulk to be courageous. Dispel that myth by sharing stories of people who changed the world with their quiet, nonphysical courageous acts. A

  ▷ *Pee Wee Reese:* Jackie Robinson, the first black Major League Baseball player, was heckled because of his skin color. At one game, Pee Wee Reese, his white teammate, walked over, put his arm around Robinson, and stopped the jeering crowd with his quiet gesture of courage and compassion. "He didn't say a word," Robinson said, "but he looked over at the chaps who were yelling at me and just stared."[21] Read your child Peter Golenbock's *Teammates* about that stirring moment that changed baseball history.

  ▷ *Mahatma Gandhi:* The leader of nonviolent civil disobedience was painfully shy as a boy and "could not bear to talk to anybody," so he ran home after school every day.[22]

  ▷ *Rosa Parks:* The African American civil rights activist who refused to give up her seat to white passengers was described as "soft-spoken . . . timid and shy."[23]

  ▷ *Captain Chesley Sullenberger:* The pilot who landed the crippled US Airways plane deemed himself shy and more comfortable in a cockpit than with people.[24]

- **Teach S.O.S. Safety Smarts.** Philip Zimbardo, author of *The Lucifer Effect*, believes that courageous individuals can pick up on cues that suggest someone might be in trouble—or headed that way. And those habits are trainable. Zimbardo now offers a "heroes" curriculum to help children learn situational awareness and boost their courage in tough times. Here are three Safety Smarts skills to help kids avert danger and decide if it's safer to step in or wiser to get help. **S, T**

  ▷ **S = Safety first.** "Could someone get hurt? Do I need an adult?" If the risk is too great or if someone could hurt, get help! It's *always* better to be safe than sorry.

▷ **O = Assess Options.** "Do I have the skills, options, and resources to handle this?" Think things through and choose what's best for you and the situation.

▷ **S = Use your Sense detector.** "What does my gut tell me?" Go with what you feel deep down is right and what your first instincts tell you. Your gut is usually right.

- **Start a book club.** A Washington middle school principal, worried about the school's mean-girl scene, started a book club. The principal and the upper-grade girls met once a week to read Rachel Simmons's *Odd Girl Out* and then held conversations like: "How do you feel about bullying?" "Have you experienced it?" "What do you hope your friend does if you were bullied?" Those chats changed the norms as the girls realized their peers were against bullying and wanted their friends to defend them. Why not start a book club with your child's friends and parents? **A**

- **Hold movie nights.** Two Miami moms worried that "cruel" was the new "cool" at the middle school, so they initiated parent-kid movie nights. One Saturday a month, the parents *and* kids watched films including *Mean Girls*, *Billy Elliot*, *Bully*, and *Cyberbully*, and then discussed how kids can stick up for each other. Those talks helped switch the social scene so kids now think it's cool to be kind. **A**

- **Read about Upstanders!** Here are a few favorites about kids who stick their necks out for others. Younger kids: *Hooway for Wodney Wat*, by Helen Lester; *Nobody Knew What to Do*, by Becky Ray McCain; *The Juice Box Bully*, by Maria Dismondy and Bob Sornson. Older kids: *The Bully Blockers Club*, by Teresa Bateman; *Say Something*, by Peggy Moss; *Number the Stars*, by Lois Lowry. Teens: *Bystander*, by James Preller; *The Forgotten Hero of My Lai: The Hugh Thompson Story*, by Trent Angers; *Stand Up for Yourself and Your Friends*, by Patti Kelley Criswell. **A**

- **Start family courage rituals.** A father of three learning-disabled children knew his sons would face difficulties and wanted to help them find courage. So he read them *Knots on a Counting Rope*, by Bill Martin Jr., about a young blind boy who faces enormous obstacles (his "dark mountains") but finds strength not to let them get in his way. Then he gave each son a small rope. "There will be trying times, but courage will help you not give up," he said. "Every time you cross a dark mountain, tie a knot as your knot of courage." He taught his sons to be brave "one step at a time" and helped them handle life. Start a family courage ritual to empower your children to face setbacks. A

THE TOP FIVE THINGS TO KNOW ABOUT CULTIVATING MORAL COURAGE

1. Kids discover their inner hero from the right parenting style, experiences, and training.

2. Modeling, encouraging, expecting, and acknowledging a child's moral courage helps instill it.

3. Upstanders are kids who unselfishly help others without expecting anything in return.

4. A child's temperament and physical strength don't determine moral courage: almost every child can be taught how to stand up and speak up to help others.

5. The seeds of moral courage must be nurtured in every developmental stage.

ONE LAST THING

A favorite movie about courage is *We Bought a Zoo*. One scene is especially powerful: the teen son admits to his dad that he is crazy about a girl, but unless he musters the courage to tell her that, their relationship is over. His dad's advice is priceless: "You know, sometimes all you need is twenty seconds of insane courage—just literally twenty seconds of just embarrassing bravery, and I promise you that something great will come of it." [25]

The truth is sometimes kids just need gentle nudges to step out of their comfort zones and discover their inner strength. Our job is to help our children find their "twenty seconds of *safe* courage" so they can do the right thing when their empathy and moral identities urge them to step in and help. And moral courage can be trained, and the empathy gap can be reduced.

CHAPTER 9

Empathetic Children Want to Make a Difference

Growing Changemakers and Altruistic Leaders

It was a cold December night and eleven-year-old Trevor Ferrell was watching a television report about Philadelphia's street people struggling to survive. He lived in a five-bedroom home in the suburbs and couldn't believe people were sleeping in the streets. He was taught in school that poverty occurred only in countries like India but not America, so he begged his parents to drive him downtown so he could see for himself.

Janet and Frank Ferrell realized that if they wanted their kids to care, not going would send the wrong message. So Trevor grabbed his special pillow and a yellow blanket, and they drove twelve miles to downtown Philadelphia. The boy spotted a homeless man crumpled on the sidewalk and couldn't believe he was lying on a grating. He got out of the car with his dad close behind and knelt down.

"Sir, here's a blanket for you," Trevor said and handed it to the man along with his pillow.

The man stared in disbelief, and then his face lit up with one of the biggest smiles Trevor had ever seen, and he said, "Thank you."

"When we were driving away, I looked back, and he looked more comfortable," Trevor recalled. "It gave me a good feeling inside. I felt like I had accomplished something." [1]

The sixth grader had experienced an empathetic breakthrough: a rare, spontaneous "elevating" event when for a brief moment "two hearts connect" and feel with each other. Science says it is a key factor in reducing the empathy gap, activating empathy and increasing the likelihood of acting with compassion and courage. The following day Trevor pleaded with his parents to let him return. And he delivered two more blankets and discovered that many more people needed food and comfort. Trevor didn't know anyone's name, so he decided to create nicknames for those he met to create a more personal connection. Empathy!

And the very next night Trevor and his dad once again drove back to give his mom's old coat, every extra blanket in the house, and dozens of homemade peanut-butter sandwiches to anyone in need.

"People aren't always what they seem to be," he later said. "They might look mean to you, but when you go over to them, they're good, they're nice."[2]

While other sixth graders were doing their homework or watching television, Trevor's life was changing dramatically, as were his perspectives about homeless people: they may live and look differently, but they have the same feelings and needs as he did.

The trips continued, and Trevor began posting flyers around town asking for more blankets and warm clothes. Donations slowly poured in, and volunteers stepped up to help. And the young boy could not stop his campaign. He was seeing that he was making a difference. "I'm going to keep doing this as long as I can," he said. "It's real easy to do. Anybody can do it."[3] Trevor was becoming a Changemaker: someone who recognizes a social problem and is committed to create a solution. And—as do many Changemakers—he began to inspire others to lend a hand.

Two years later, the thirteen-year-old was spearheading a 250-person operation that brought food and blankets to the homeless. President Ronald Reagan introduced him to millions during his State of the Union address and described Trevor and those like him as "heroes of our hearts . . . the living spirit of brotherly love."[4]

Trevor's Campaign has served more than three million meals to Philadelphia's homeless.[5] And it all started when the eleven-year-old just happened to hear about a concept beyond his imagination: people were hungry, cold, and sleeping on streets, and he had to do something to help.

LEARNING TO MAKE A DIFFERENCE

The instant that Trevor gave his pillow and saw the look of gratitude on the man's face was the "transformational moment" that would alter this child's life: two strangers emotionally in sync. Empathy generally lies at the core of such moments and is often activated by a deep personal connection. Such experiences are never planned and are usually brief, but they deeply stir the heart. Whether a gentle whip or a seismic jolt, the event forces the child to see things in a new perspective. I call it an "empathetic breakthrough": the heart opens with fresh understanding about a person (or group) that was once "the other" and "Me" turns to "We": "He (she, they) may be homeless (destitute, a different race, religion, culture, gender, age, ability), but he (she, they) needs comfort and support just like me."

That new awareness is what helps kids recognize that someone is hurting, needs comfort, or is treated unjustly. The awareness that "something is not right" is what motivates their empathy to make things right, to push boundaries, fight challenges, and not waver until the wrong is righted. These children become Changemakers and are the people who will make the world better. They usually have an unexpected experience that stirs their heart and a caring adult to help support their caring commitment, but their quest to make a difference all started with empathy.

Changemakers are kids who don't stand back when they see a problem, but instead step in to make a difference. Here are a few altruistic kids who are making the world a better place:

> Dylan Siegel, age six, knew he had to help when his best friend, Jonah Pournazarian, was diagnosed with an incurable liver disorder, and so he wrote *Chocolate Bar*. His book has

raised more than $1 million that has resulted in new gene-therapy treatments.[6]

When nine-year-old Rachel Wheeler learned that Haitian kids eat mud cookies and live in cardboard houses because they're so poor, she vowed to make a difference. "You can't just sit around and think about doing it," Rachel said. "You got to actually get out there and do it." And she did by running bake sales, selling homemade potholders, and asking for donations. In just three years, her fund-raising efforts surpassed $250,000, enough to erect twenty-seven concrete two-room homes in a neighborhood in Haiti now dubbed Rachel's Village.[7]

When Yash Gupta broke his glasses and couldn't see, he started thinking about the millions of kids who can't afford corrective eyewear. So the fourteen-year-old created Sight Learning and began collecting used eyeglasses from optometrists. He has donated more than 9,500 pairs to kids in Haiti, Honduras, India, and Mexico. "Kids are passionate and can make a difference," Yash says. "It's just a matter of finding out what you care about and focusing on that."[8]

Altruistic children are the ultimate UnSelfies: they feel another's pain or recognize a social problem and are driven to find solutions to help. And they do so not for accolades, trophies, rewards, or to "look good" on college applications, but because they are driven by the passion of their hearts. Such is the power of empathy!

There are proven physical and mental health benefits to stretching children's "helping muscles." Giving—not receiving—is what makes kids happier, healthier, less stressed,[9] and feel better about themselves.[10] A fifty-year study of 10,000 Wisconsin teens found that those who volunteered regularly and cited altruism "as important" lived longer.[11] University of British Columbia researchers discovered that toddlers just shy of their second birthdays are happier giving treats to other toddlers than receiving them.[12] But there's another plus to instilling a helping habit: it increases the odds that kids will use their empathy muscles in unjust situations and make a difference, bridging the empathy gap.

Every child has the potential to become such a Changemaker *if* we provide the right experiences and proven parenting strategies. This final chapter is about how we can parent a generation of caring kids to become altruistic leaders who will build a more empathetic world. We can equip them with the skills that prepare them to make a difference, in large ways and small, because deep in their hearts they know it's the right thing to do. They are our best hope for a humane world, and it all starts with empathy.

WHAT'S SO HARD ABOUT HELPING KIDS BECOME CHANGEMAKERS?

Our children are wired for goodness, but culture and parenting can help or hinder their potential to become empathetic leaders and Changemakers. Here are three obstacles that can limit a child's empathic gifts and altruistic leadership potential.

Fame-Driven "Heroes"

Today's kids admire celebrities and fame, and those values can jeopardize their empathetic potential. After all, most celebrities are all about flaunting *their* status, *their* fame, and *their* brand, and that "Me" not "We" emphasis can increase children's self-centeredness *and* decrease their concern for others.

The "I just want to be famous" kid trend was first noticed in a 2007 UCLA study. In every previous year, a "to be famous" aspiration ranked near the bottom of a sixteen-item value list. During the same period, youth narcissism continued to increase, while empathy spiraled downward.[13]

Just two decades ago, kids said they hoped to spend their careers in a helping profession such as teacher, firefighter, or doctor.[14] A preteen's top three occupational choices today are "sports star, pop star, or actor."[15] It's probably no coincidence that "fame" is also the top value communicated to tweens on popular TV.[16] The wrong examples can distort our kids' worldview as to what values matter, and "fame" appears as their clear winner over "compassion, integrity, and character." In fact, 60 percent of college students even admit that a celebrity influenced their beliefs, attitudes, and personal values.[17]

Philip Zimbardo, founder of the Heroic Imagination Project, describes this parenting challenge: "One of the problems with our culture is that we've replaced heroes with celebrities. We worship people who haven't done anything. It's time to get back to focusing on what matters, because we need real heroes more than ever."[18] And for our kids to become Changemakers, they need examples of selfless, compassionate leaders to emulate.

A Materialistic World

While our kids want to be famous, they are also growing up in a me-absorbed society that values possessions, appearance, and consumption over compassion, charity, and generosity. The overarching emphasis is all about how *I* look, the brands *I* tout, the possessions *I* own, and those materialistic values do affect children. Eighty-one percent of young adults now name "getting rich" as their generation's most or second-most important life goal,"[19] and that points to yet another challenge for nurturing empathy.

Of course, we don't want our kids to be poor, but science finds there is a surprising advantage to growing up in a less materialistic environment. Research shows that the more money we have, the *less* we care about others' feelings and the *more* self-focused we become.[20] Wealth actually *decreases* our feelings of compassion for others. In fact, people of lower economic status are more helpful and generous than individuals of higher economic status.[21] And why? When you're part of an environment where you're vulnerable, "you solve problems by turning to others."[22] The more money or possessions we have, the less need we have for others, and we rely on ourselves.

Paying attention to others strengthens our empathy muscles and social connections. In a materialistic world, kids often turn their focus from people's feelings and needs to what others own, wear, and look like. So those inside character-building qualities like gratitude, charity, and compassion take a lower rung on the ladder of life priorities.

But do all those possessions that we give our kids really make them happier? "No!" is the unanimous answer from science. Unhappy kids are found to be *more* materialistic than kids who are happy and content with their lives.[23] And a preoccupation with possessions is associated with *decreased* happiness as well as *increased* anxiety.[24] Giving to others actually makes our children happier than spending on themselves, and increases the likelihood that they'll give again and again.[25] So the next time your kids are begging for something, I suggest putting your wallet away and encouraging them to do a good deed for another. While the ploy probably won't work the first few times, with consistency your children will get the message that "Who you are is more important than what you own."

An "Overhelping" Parenting Style

Nationwide surveys of our college-age set show troubling trends for those raised by Tiger Parents. While their teen cubs bear exemplary résumés and grades, far too many college students suffer from weak inner strength that threatens their mental health, confidence, and empathic capabilities.

- College freshmen with helicopter parents are *less* open to new ideas and actions, and *more* anxious and dependent than "students who were given responsibility and not constantly monitored by their parents."[26]

- Intrusive parenting is linked to problematic development because "it limits opportunities for kids to practice and develop important skills needed for becoming self-reliant adults."[27]

- Students with "hovering" or "helicopter" parents score lower on measures of psychological well-being and are more likely to be medicated for anxiety or depression.[28] (And 95 percent of college counseling center directors surveyed said the number of students with significant psychological problems is a growing campus concern.[29])

Always "*ing*-ing" for kids (solving, doing, rescuing) makes it tough for them to learn crucial skills like coping, decision making, problem solving, and empathizing that are crucial for changemaking. All that "doing" also sends a disturbing message to our kids: "I'll help because you can't do it alone." Instead of boosting confidence, our micromanaging lowers our children's self-esteem and reduces their moral courage to step in or speak up to help. It's also why overprotective parenting can be disastrous at producing empathetic leaders.

Shielding kids also reduces their opportunities to practice handling stress and adversity. The truth is that empathizing isn't always easy—it's distressing to feel another's pain and suffering. Lacking confidence and coping skills can make kids turn down their empathic feelings instead of comforting one another. It's why we must start stepping back so our kids can begin marching forward to make their mark in the world.

What Will It Take for Parents to Counter a Toxic Culture?

Despite a materialistic, fame-driven, "helicoptering" culture, we can nurture empathetic leaders, but that must start by raising our children from the inside out. An empathetic kid is one who recognizes "Who I am is more important than what I look like or own. I care about others." Those beliefs are the makings of future Changemakers, and odds are that their parents intentionally instilled a "You" not "Me" message in their childhoods.

WHAT SCIENCE SAYS:
HOW TO RAISE A CHANGEMAKER

For years, the predominant view has been that babies' mental capabilities are nothing more than "little blank slates." But the dawn of baby science revealed that a whole lot more is going on inside than we ever dreamed possible. Some of the most fascinating studies are taking place at the Infant Cognition Center at Yale University under the direction of Karen Wynn,[30] who designed special puppet shows just for wee ones' nanosecond attention spans. Results turned our notions about infants' capabilities upside down: they clearly prefer kindhearted "good guys."

In the first puppet show, a baby watched a red wooden character with large glued-on eyes attempt to climb a steep hill two times and then fail. (Imagine the theme of *The Little Engine That Could* presented in eighteen seconds using three geometric, colored blocks instead of train engines.) On the third attempt, the "climber" is either aided by a "helper" pushing the engine from behind or a "hinderer" pushing it down.[31] (The "helper" or "hinderer" is either a yellow triangle or blue square.) Then a tray with the wooden-block characters representing the helper and hinderer are presented to the baby, and almost every six- and ten-month-old infant reaches for the "helper." The verdict is clear: babies like the good guys!

In another experiment, babies watch three furry puppets appear onstage, and then the puppet show begins. One of the furry creatures struggles to open a box, and the "nice" puppet comes to the rescue and helps him open it.

Then the scene repeats itself, but this time a different puppet pops in and slams the box shut. So do babies prefer the kinder puppet or the meaner puppet? To find out, an assistant offers the baby the "naughty" and the "nice" puppets. Once again, over three-quarters of the infants don't hesitate: they choose the kinder helper and show an aversion to the bad guy. Their choices are based on how one puppet treats the other![32] Though not yet crawling, talking, or walking—and still in diapers— babies show a clear preference for Good Samaritans.

By their second birthday, toddlers try to make others feel better and even exert kindheartedness to help strangers complete a difficult task. Researchers Felix Warneken and Michael Tomasello developed clever experiments in which an adult acts as if he needs help, and then watched how eighteen-month-olds respond.[33] (For instance, the adult tries to hang towels on a clothesline, "accidentally" drops a clothespin, and then pretends to have trouble reaching it.) Toddlers helped if the experimenter's facial and body gestures looked as though he needed assistance.[34] What's more, even fourteen-month-olds crawled over to pick up the object—even when the researchers made no explicit request for help. The children simply saw that the experimenter needed help and wanted to lend a hand.

Where Did the Good Samaritan Go?

Toddlers comfort, help, and act kindly at surprisingly early ages. They clearly prefer Good Samaritans and do so without expecting a reward or even a high five from Mom or Dad! But by five years of age, our kids' caring nature is already slipping: one report shows that 20 percent of kindergarteners are now engaging in mean-spirited, bullying-like behaviors.

Tween and teens aren't even placing "helping others" on the tops of their priority lists. A Harvard survey of thousands of teens by Making Caring Common found that a large majority "ranked personal success—achievement and happiness—over concern for others."[35] Those findings are dismal if our hope is to raise empathetic, just leaders.

So what happened in a brief three-year span to cause one in five young children to begin losing their partiality toward "nice guys"? Science shows that though our children have a Good Samaritan instinct, their helping muscles must be exercised continually or they'll lose their power. We just might be taking our children's "natural-born helping" trait for granted, and that is a loss for developing kids who care.

HOW TO CULTIVATE A
CHANGEMAKING MIND-SET IN CHILDREN

Here's a quiz: Does your child believe that empathy is something you're born with or a skill that can be developed? What about you? The answer has a surprising impact on whether children become Changemakers, because their empathetic mind-set is a big factor in determining whether they switch on the dimmer switch on their empathy and whether they step in or out to help. Alfie Kohn, author of *The Brighter Side of Human Nature*, explains: "Encouragement to think of oneself as a generous person—an appeal not to self-interest but to genuine altruism—seems to be the most reliable way to promote helping and caring over the long haul and in different situations."[36]

A study by psychologists Carol Dweck, Karina Schumann, and Jamil Zaki found that people who believe that empathy can be developed extend more effort to understand and share the feelings of another than those who think that empathy is a fixed trait that can't be improved.[37] They also found that when people learn that empathy can be enhanced, they are more likely to empathize with those whose races differ from their own.

We tend to empathize with those "like us." Changing the way your kid thinks about empathy so he believes the core trait of humanity can be improved will help him feel with others "not like me." That finding has potential for reducing bullying, racial dissension, and hatred as well as shaping children into compassionate, altruistic leaders who make their mark in the world.

Step 1: Teach the growth mind-set model. Tell your child: "Empathy can be increased with practice just like your muscles increase with exercise. Learning to be kind is like learning to play cello, baseball, or chess: the more you practice, the better you'll be at understanding another's thoughts and feelings."

Step 2: Emphasize effort. Emphasize the *process* ("You are really making an effort to help others. Look how happy your kindness made Grandma feel"), not the end *product* ("You delivered fifty blankets today!"). The subtle switch stresses that empathy can be expanded. Stress how your child's effort is expanding her empathic skills: "Your ability to read people's emotions is improving, so keep working at it." "Practicing deep breathing is helping you stay in control."

Step 3: Encourage practice. "Children who view themselves as altruistic are likely to assist in the future," says Nancy Eisenberg, a leading empathy authority, "because people generally want to behave in ways that are consistent with their self-image."[38] So provide ways for your kids to *see* themselves as altruistic.

- Keep a box handy so they can donate their gently used toys to a shelter.

- Encourage giving a portion of their allowance or tooth fairy money to a charity.

- Suggest "No-present birthdays" (gifts are donated to needy kids).

- Find ways to assist others (walking Grandma's dog or helping the elderly neighbor).

- And keep reminding them: "Practicing empathy is how to become more empathetic."

Step 4: Recap the impact. Dr. Ervin Staub found that children who are given the opportunity to help others tend to become more helpful, *especially if the impact of their helpful actions is pointed out*. It nudges kids to develop a growth mind-set about empathy. So encourage your child to reflect on her servicing experiences: "What did the person do when you helped? How do you think he felt? How did you feel? Is lending a hand easier than it used to be?" And remind your kids that they are kind people, and their caring efforts are making a difference.

EMPATHY BUILDER: HOW TO FACE
SOMEONE TO SHOW YOU CARE

Kaila D. is not yet four, but the San Diego preschooler already has the makings of a Changemaker. When I banged my toe at a party, the three-year-old was the first to my side. I watched her size things up, look carefully at my "injury," and then empathize. Her face switched from inquisitiveness to concern, and then she looked up with the biggest eyes, and said, "I sorry 'bout your toe. You need Band-Aid for your owie? I help you."

Kaila may have missed a few words, but her message was clearly empathetic. Her parents were raising her to care and had taught her *how* to help even at a young age. Children may recognize another's pain, but their empathy can wane if they don't know what to do. Changemakers—regardless of age—see obstacles and find caring solutions, and they are raised to care by their parents.

Teach your kids these steps so they can FACE someone who needs help and show they care, closing the empathy gap.

1. **F = Feelings.** Read the person's feelings. Does the person look upset, sad, angry, frustrated? If so, maybe she can use help. If unsure, ask the person how they are feeling, to clarify: "Are you sad?" "You look upset." "Is everything okay?"

2. **A = Analyze.** What is the problem? What is causing the person distress? Analyze the situation. "Is the person hurt?" "Does the person look like she needs or wants help?" "Do I feel comfortable giving this person help?"

3. **C = Care.** If you feel comfortable (and the person looks like she wants help), offer it. "What can I do?" "Can I help?" "Do you need a Band-Aid?" "Should I get the teacher?" If the person looks like she needs to be alone, honor it. You can always comfort and support a person at a later time that may be more appropriate.

4. **E = Empathize.** Let the person know you're concerned. "I'm sorry." "I hope you feel better." "That happened to me." "I know how you feel." "I'll be back if you need me."

HOW TO HELP KIDS BECOME CHANGEMAKERS

Amanda Perlyn was in the first grade in the 1990s when she learned that her teacher's daughter was dying of cancer. Amanda wanted to help, but she knew that baking cookies wasn't enough. So the child convinced her family to make holiday ornaments as a fund-raiser, and the Perlyn family from Boca Raton became hooked on helping.

"We always focused on education and values, but seeing how helping others affected our six-year-old made us refocus our parenting," Amanda's mother, Marilyn, told me. "We decided that helping was going to be a year-round priority in all our children's lives."

The parents sat down with their three kids to discuss ways they could learn to give. Everyone had to pick a need important to them, and Marilyn and Don would support them. And that was the start of how each child began a Changemaker.

At twelve, Eric started Stepp'n Up which provided free shoes to underprivileged children. His project began as a donation from his bar mitzvah money, which he used to buy shoes for six brothers in a needy family. He has since collected and delivered more than 20,000 pairs of new shoes for children in need donated by local stores and shoemakers.

At fifteen, Chad learned that a girl needed dental work that her family couldn't afford, so he wrote letters to five hundred dentists and got her help. Chad later started Doc-Adopt, which matches poor or neglected children with local physicians who give free medical care. Now a plastic surgeon, Chad continues to donate his time and medical expertise to helping children in third-world countries, and he recently received the prestigious Compassionate Doctor recognition. Of the nation's 870,000 physicians, only 3 percent were accorded the honor in 2012.

Amanda launched To Have and to Hug when she was thinking about how much she loved stuffed animals. "When it makes me feel that good," she said, "imagine how good it would make another kid feel." The nine-year-old started giving new stuffed animals to children in shelters, foster homes, and hospitals, and has distributed hundreds of toys.

Over the years, the Perlyn kids have received many awards and even appeared on *Oprah*. And their helping legacy continues: each child— now grown—remains active with their Changemaker projects that have each helped thousands of children.

"People don't realize it's so easy to make a difference," Chad said.[39] Nor do most parents.

1. **Find a cause that concerns *your* child.** The most successful Changemakers are determined to achieve a goal that is deeply meaningful to them.[40] You might start by volunteering together at different local organizations and then note the issues that excite your child. Does he prefer working alone or with others? Outdoors or inside? With younger kids or older kids? Match the cause with your child's passion, interest, and style.

2. **Think of possibilities.** Once you identify a concern, help your child brainstorm ways to make a difference. Narrow down ideas to those that are realistic and that she wants to commit to doing. It's great to think big but suggest she start small. So instead of building a new shelter, she might send emails asking neighbors to donate coats.

3. **Plan it.** The more your child thinks through his plan, the greater the success. Help him list required resources and people. If he needs toy donations, encourage him to make flyers and post them. If he wants to start a letter campaign, help him find the addresses. Stress that he *must* tell you his plans and never go anywhere unfamiliar without an adult.

4. **Start locally.** There are big problems across the ocean, but also in your community. Consider volunteering together at a local food bank, pediatric hospital, or soup kitchen, or help your child initiate a food drive and then distribute the donations together.

5. **Encourage "direct contact."** Empathy is best activated face-to-face, and Marilyn Perlyn suggests selecting projects that put your child in direct contact with the recipient. It could be bringing toys to the children's shelter or delivering books to a senior citizens' home. Trevor Ferrell's life was changed when he gave his pillow to a homeless man and saw the look of gratitude on the man's face.

6. **Keep going!** A one-time-only service project is usually not enough to instill an empathic mind-set. So Marilyn suggests that you help your child choose a project that can be repeated: weekly, monthly, or yearly so your child develops a habit of helping.

AGE-BY-AGE STRATEGIES

Twelve-year-old Craig Kielburger's empathetic breakthrough happened at breakfast when a news headline jarred him: "Battled Child Labor Boy, 12, Murdered." Iqbal Masih's mother had sold him into slavery at four; he was chained to a weaving loom fourteen hours a day for six years to make carpets. The Pakistani boy suffered countless beatings until he was finally freed and became a prominent voice against child labor. And then Iqbal was murdered while riding home on a bicycle with two friends.

"I thought slavery was something out of the past, that it had been abolished," Craig said. "What kind of parent would sell their child into slavery? Who would chain a child to a carpet loom?"[41]

Shock or disbelief about a view that doesn't fit the child's perspective is often the beginning of changemaking. Craig couldn't understand why no one was helping these children, and he discovered that kids even younger than Iqbal are forced to work as slaves.

One day Craig asked his teacher if he could speak to his classmates. He passed out copies of the article about Iqbal and statistics about child laborers. Then he asked for volunteers to help him fight for children's rights. Eleven classmates raised their hands, and Free the Children was born. Craig led the cause, and his home became headquarters, with his parents' blessings.

"About ten of us started doing small things to help," Craig said. "It wasn't anything dramatic. We passed around a couple of petitions to political leaders and heads of corporations. Then a few of us gave speeches in schools and to religious and community groups, and it just began to snowball from there." [42]

Free the Children is now the world's largest network of children helping children. More than 2.3 million young people are involved in forty-five countries, where they have built hundreds of schools for over 50,000 needy kids, funded largely by their birthday money, laying bricks on volunteer trips.

In 2006, Craig was awarded the World's Children's Prize for the Rights of the Child, considered the child's version of the Nobel Prize. Free the Children has been nominated three times for the Nobel Peace Prize. Craig Kielburger and his brother, Marc, continue working full time to change the lives of children, [43] all because he read about a child slave his age and couldn't stand back.

Changemaking often starts with empathy when an unexpected experience stirs a child's heart and pushes her to do something that sometimes turns out to be remarkable for society. Here are kids who had such extraordinary moments on ordinary days, and whose inspiring efforts can teach us how to help our children become difference makers.

Symbols designate the recommended age and suitability for activity: L = Little Ones: Toddlers and Preschoolers; S = School-age; T = Tweens and Older; A = All Age

- **Find your child's passion.** Match your child's interests with a "giving project."

  Ryan Traynor was eleven when he volunteered at the library. Reading to his young listeners opened his heart. "I got really attached to these kids, and I saw how much books meant to them," he said. It was also the first time the Bay Area boy realized that many didn't have books, so he left boxes for donations in his backyard. In six months, Ryan distributed more than 25,000 books to children, and now teens from seven schools help as well.[44]

  The best service projects are meaningful to the child, not ones that look good on résumés. Take your child's lead whether it's volunteering at the Special Olympics, playing Chutes and Ladders with kids at a shelter, or planting vegetables to give to a soup kitchen. Kids don't have to leave their backyard to make a difference and can lead other like-minded peers. S, T

- **Start with one.** Every Changemaker I interviewed said that their motivation to help started face-to-face. (Trevor Ferrell met *one* homeless man; Craig Kielburger saw *one* child slave's photo). Paul Slovic, from the University of Oregon, discovered that our brains are more likely to empathize with *one* needy person, not multitudes who are suffering.[45] "As the numbers grow," Slovic explains, "we sort of lose the emotional connection to the people who are in need," and we may feel "nothing I can do will make a difference . . . it's really about self-efficacy."[46] And the less a child feels confident in his changemaking abilities, the less likely his empathy and moral courage will be activated.

  Cayden Taipalus was in the school cafeteria line when the student in front of him was denied a hot meal because he didn't have enough funds in his account. The third grader from Michigan felt that boy's pain and wanted to make sure no other classmate faced such humiliation. Cayden started collecting empty bottles and asking friends for donations to pay off outstanding balances for kids on free and reduced lunches. Word spread about his Pay It Forward: No Kid Goes Hungry campaign, and more than $20,000 poured in within two weeks through generous donations of children, adult, and business donors—enough for kids in Cayden's school and county.[47]

Help your child realize that he can make a difference by helping one individual: tutoring a child, reading to an elderly person, or just saying regular friendly hellos to the inbound neighbor. **A**

- **Use the news.** Help your child become aware of world concerns to increase global consciousness and recognize that problems are everywhere.

   "Our father always read the paper spread out flat on the breakfast table, drawing us into his daily routine and all that was going on in the world," Craig Kielburger explained. "Usually we picked one article as a point of discussion and spent five to ten minutes talking about it. Our parents would then take the discussion one step further by encouraging us to think about possible solutions and actions."[48]

   When an issue (bullying, racism, poverty, human trafficking, etc.) captivates your kid, help him develop an action plan to help solve it. **S, T**

- **Prepare kids for dissension.** Changemakers need to practice standing up for their views, so as not to waver if others try to dissuade them.

   Vivienne Harr was eight when she saw a photograph of two young Nepalese boys who were child slaves. "We have to do something," she told her father,[49] so she set up a lemonade stand and asked customers every day to "give what's in their hearts" because "It's a 'giveness' not a business." In six months, Vivienne raised more than $100,000 for antislavery organizations but admits it wasn't always easy. "You can't worry about what other people think or let people get you down," she said. "It takes courage."[50]

Prepare your child for possible naysayers by rehearsing "comeback lines" ("I disagree, this is what I believe because . . ." "That's your view, here's mine . . ."). Practice helps strengthen kids' views and the ability to find their voices so they can speak out for others. **S, T**

- **Share stories about Changemakers.** Elevating experiences are contagious, so when kids see other children making a difference, they often want to help.

  Christian Bucks, a second grader from Pennsylvania, felt for classmates who didn't have friends and thought a playground Buddy Bench would be a solution. A lonely child could sit and signal classmates that he wanted someone to talk to, and kids could invite him to play.[51] Christian shared his changemaking idea with his principal, and a bench was added to the playground. The local paper posted a picture that went viral. Hundreds of students worldwide asked for a bench at their school to help peers make friends.

  Share news of kids' changemaking efforts on Kidsareheroes .com, generationOn.org/kids-care-clubs, VolunteerNation.org, Dosomething.org, or the My Hero Project to inspire your children to make a difference. **A**

- **Utilize positive social media.** Social media is often equated with the darker side of human nature, but some teens are using it for changemaking.

  Kevin Curwick got tired of seeing peers bullied, so the Minneapolis teen created an anonymous account—@OsseoNice Things—to tweet kind comments and let kids know someone cared. "I didn't know how people would react or if I would be bullied myself, but I just couldn't stand back," Kevin told me. "I had to support these kids."

Classmates began copying Kevin's strategy of posting kind tweets about peers. Then a news station published the story, and Kevin's "nice campaign" went viral. Teens from as far as Croatia, South Korea, and Australia started "nice" accounts to stop online bullying. Best yet, cyberbullies lost their power because kids stopped following their mean-spirited posts.[52]

Social networking may be a way to encourage introverted kids to lead, and efforts can be anonymous. Not until a newspaper printed Kevin's name did students learn who sent those tweets! S, T

- **Watch for desensitization.** Changemaking isn't always easy, especially with tough issues like homelessness, child slavery, and cyberbullying. Protect your child from being overly aroused about another's pain, which can cause people to be less helpful to those in need and increase the empathy gap. Teach your child ways to cope with emotional distress with these ABCs of stress management. "You have to take care of yourself, so you can help others."

  ▷ **A = Aware.** Teach your child to tune in to *his* feelings. "What am I feeling?" "What do I need?" You may need to help him learn to create some distance or be involved with a less intense project at first. Self-management is crucial for empathy, especially for kids who are easily overaroused with other's needs.

  ▷ **B = Breathe.** Focusing on deep, slow breaths can reduce stress. Review "Mindful Breathing" exercises in chapter 5.

  ▷ **C = Calm.** Find what helps your child decompress: exercising, being with others, watching funny movies, praying, sticking to structure. Find a healthy stress-reducing ritual! Even better, practice it as a family. **S, T**

- **Stretch boundaries.** Visiting homeless people transformed Trevor Ferrell's life. "We heard in school about poor people in Ethiopia, in India, but not about poor people in America," Trevor said. "That's why I was so drawn to it."[53]

  Expand your child's comfort zone to include "different" experiences—at a soup kitchen, with the elderly, or with homeless children—so he can empathize with those "not like him." Such encounters can be especially powerful for self-absorbed kids who need a nudge to see a world beyond "me." Find ways to help your child be comfortable with *all* people. Such heart-stretching experiences not only enrich children's lives but also expand their empathy so they want to become compassionate leaders who make a difference. **A**

THE TOP FIVE THINGS TO KNOW ABOUT RAISING CHANGEMAKERS

1. Stretching your kids' "helping muscles" must be ongoing, so make "helping others" a routine part of their childhood.

2. A child who sees herself as altruistic is more likely to help others, because children act in ways that match their self-image. Help your child see herself as a helper.

3. Kids who are given regular opportunities to help and comfort others tend to become more helpful and compassionate.

4. People who believe that empathy has the potential to grow are more likely to exert effort to empathize when it is needed most.[54] Help your child recognize that empathy can be improved with practice and help him develop an empathetic growth mind-set

so he knows that traits like empathy, caring, kindness, and courage can be developed.

5. Kids tend to empathize with people they're close to, so expand
   your child's Circle of Familiarity to include those of different
   backgrounds and experiences.

ONE LAST THING

Nine-year-old Nate Dreyfus from Stillwater, Minnesota, saw something
on a cold day that stirred him. "There was this man," he said. "He got
out of his car, took off his jacket, and gave it to a man on the street. I felt
really good inside that he did that, so I wanted to start doing something
like that." With his family's help, Nate distributed boxes in his neighborhood and collected seventy-nine coats that he delivered to families in
shelters. "It's just really heartwarming," Nate said.[55]

Scientists would say that Nate's heartwarming glow is a "helper's
high," and once you catch a "giving fever," you want to help more and
more. There's even a biological basis: the hormone serotonin is secreted
in the body to create that warm, elevating feeling.

In our quest to help our children find "happiness and success," we
may be overlooking the real brass ring. Encouraging children to help
others gives them immense joy and opens their hearts. But doing for
others also lets kids see themselves as Changemakers: people who make
positive differences and inspire others to follow.

And it all starts with empathy, and planting those seeds is what nurtures that crucial Empathy Advantage your child needs for success, happiness, and leading a meaningful life.

EPILOGUE

The Empathy Advantage

The Seven Most Creative Ways to Give Children the Edge They Need to Succeed

In writing and researching *UnSelfie*, I flew the world, spoke with hundreds of researchers, conducted focus groups with more than five hundred children, and visited dozens of schools. I witnessed countless ways to cultivate empathy, but the most effective were always real, meaningful, and matched a child's needs. Here are a few of the most creative ways adults around the world are making a difference in cultivating children's empathy, creating an UnSelfie world and giving them the Empathy Advantage.

1. Be Friendly

Empathy is *always* a "We" affair. A simple, overlooked way to increase empathy is by making the culture friendlier. Just being with people in a friendly setting can increase your empathy toward them and make you want to be kinder. The small South Pacific island of Vanuatu exemplifies that social premise. It's called "the Friendliest Place on Earth" and after visiting their island, I can see why. Everywhere residents greeted you with a sincere hello and a smile and seemed genuinely interested in you.

Their friendliness was contagious, so you responded right back with a hello and a smile to a stranger. When I asked Vanuatu residents why they were so friendly, their answer was simple: "Because everyone else is." Friendliness makes you tune in, observe emotional cues, be more receptive to others' feelings and needs, and instead of walking by, you smile and acknowledge a person's existence right back. But you don't have to move your family to the South Pacific to gain that "friendly effect." Just intentionally take friendliness up a notch in your home, school, and neighborhood; here are a few ways.

Moms at Greens Farms Academy in Connecticut started a kindness club where they meet weekly with their children to practice manners and friendliness together. A Bremerton, Washington, middle school started a student club called Friendly Greeters to welcome peers each morning at the front door. My first-grade teacher greeted us every day with an "H and H" (we chose a hug or a handshake from her, and then passed it on to a peer). These strategies are simple but they became an ongoing routine, and in a short while, the culture became friendlier because everyone was copying friendliness.

At the base of any empathetic moment is human connection. In today's hyper-individualistic, plugged-in culture, we need to find ways to create friendlier, caring cultures to help our children see with the eyes of another, listen with the ears of another, and feel with the heart of another.

2. Break Down Barriers

Martin Hoffman, a leading empathy authority, points out that we are more likely to empathize with people in our immediate circles or care about those "like us." Expanding our children's familiarity circles to those "not like them" opens the path to empathy, and nowhere have I discovered a more creative way to break down barriers than in Kabul.

Skateistan was started in 2007 as an initiative to create educational and empowerment opportunities for Afghanistan's youth, using skateboarding as a hook. Most participants are kids with the greatest social needs: working children, illiterate children, those from low-income families, and disabled youth and girls, who still face countless barriers. And 40 percent of Skateistan participants are girls—quite remarkable since women are banned from riding bicycles, associating with boys, or receiving an education. But 1,500 girls attend the skating school three days a week and skate in the afternoon through war-torn regions right alongside boys.[1]

Noah Abrams, a prominent photographer whose work has appeared in the *New York Times, Rolling Stone,* and *Vanity Fair,* had just returned from Kabul, where he had captured the skateboarding images on film. He described the extraordinary scene to me: Afghan girls skating with unstoppable courage as they hurled themselves forward, bounced right back up from tumbling down, and in many cases outskated the boys.

"Watching the girls skate side by side with the boys and considered as 'equal'—at least on skateboards—was unforgettable," Abrams said. "You hope that the boys remember those moments—that these girls were better than them, and treat them differently when they grow up."[2]

Among the constant tension between Israelis and Palestinians, a preschool in Jaffa, Israel, is determined to teach young Arab and Jewish children about living together peacefully. The Hand in Hand school "aims to respond to growing Jewish-Arab segregation and violence with mutual respect and open dialogue. 'Psychologically, this is the only place where we feel that my children, and my neighbor's children, are secure,' said Hani Chamy, an Arab parent of two girls."[3] The idea is revolutionary but many parents are recognizing that the school may be the best way to show children that it is possible to "be together, while still different, and learn about each other."

My experience at Seeds of Peace, where Israeli and Palestinian as well as Afghan and Pakistani teens attend summer camp in Maine, convinced me that the best hope we have for peace among war-torn areas is with children. More than 5,000 teens have graduated from the camp and more than half are now leaders in their countries, one in five of whom are working in the coexistence movement, according to studies.[4] They have become Changemakers.

We must expose our children to diversity and expand their circles of familiarity at an earlier age. Empathy has limits: we care most about those who are like us, which increases the empathy gap. Find opportunities to enlarge your child's circles of caring.

3. Give Kids a Voice

Today's kids are growing up in a hyper-connected world and admit they'd rather text than talk. But empathy is driven by face-to-face connection, and it's why we must keep the art of conversation alive. A daily tradition at the ancient Sera Monastery in Tibet holds a key. Every weekday afternoon monks gather in the courtyard built in 1419 to hold hour-long debates to grasp Buddhist philosophy. The session involves a Defender, who sits and gives answers to the Challenger, who stands and asks questions. Monks use their entire bodies; each time they make a point, there are vigorous claps and dramatic hand slaps, and then pauses to consider their next argument carefully, all in a spirit of camaraderie and fun. No notes or books are allowed: debaters must depend on memorized points of doctrine and their understanding of the topic and ask nonstop questions. I watched the debates with reporters from all over the world and though I didn't understand a word, I knew I was observing a critical piece to cultivating empathy: "voice" practice. The monks created a daily ritual in which they practiced verbalizing their opinions face-to-face and hearing others' ideas and feelings.

Empathy wanes without moral courage and moral identity. That's why children must understand what they stand for and practice using their voices so they can speak out for others. Those monks practiced asserting themselves and describing their beliefs daily.

At Seeds of Peace International Camp, teens experienced daily dialogue sessions to help them grasp each other's perspectives. "Stop and Listen" signs were nailed on trees to encourage campers to stop and talk. (And I kept thinking that suggestion should be posted on every playground as well as in every home as a reminder for us all.)

KIPP Public Charter Schools teach SLANT (which stands for Sit up,

Listen, Ask questions, Nod, and Track the speaker with your eyes), and the skill is posted on classroom walls and practiced daily.

Family meetings or dinner discussions where kids learn to share their opinions, hear others, and disagree respectfully are crucial experiences for our digital natives. Common Sense Media has issued their report that finds teens age thirteen to eighteen now spend almost *nine hours a day— that's longer than they usually sleep—on "entertainment media"* (checking social media, music, gaming, or online videos). Tweens' (aged ten to twelve) media diet is about six hours a day. *But one third of infants are now using devices such as smartphones or tablets.*[5] We must not let conversation become a forgotten skill in today's plugged-in world. Face-to-face communication is crucial for activating empathy. So set unplugged times for your children to tune in to real people around them, practice face-to-face communication and voice, and hear the views and feelings of others.

4. Play Chess and Unplugged Games

The cognitive part of empathy is the ability to understand another's thoughts and feelings—to step into their shoes. One of the interesting perspective-taking lessons I observed was in a school in Yerevan where elementary school kids were taught to play chess. Armenia is the first country in the world to make chess compulsory for every student starting at six years of age. Armenia's rationale is to use chess to boost their children's character and leadership. So I watched these young Armenian students walk into their mandatory class, greet their chess teacher, sit face-to-face with their same-age opponent, and for the next hour engage in a one-on-one chess match. And they do so once a week. Studies show that the 1,500-year-old game is associated with greater "cognitive abilities, coping and problem-solving capacity, and socio-affective development of children,"[6] as well as increasing creativity, concentration, and improved reading and math scores. But as I watched two first graders named Narek and Arman, I recognized that chess is also a powerful way to cultivate empathy's cognitive side. They played face-to-face, imagined their opponent's next plays, tuned in to emotional cues

("Does he look confident, hesitant, or anxious about that move?"), and predicted "if-then" scenarios ("If he moves that piece, then . . ."). Narek and Arman were learning essential perspective-taking skills, but also having fun and building relationships.

Look for ways to help your kids predict another's view, like card or board games ("What do you think Dad's next move will be?"), theater, role-playing, dress up, or any other such strategy that helps them to step into another's shoes.

5. Create Parent Support Networks

When it comes to nurturing empathy, a parent will always be their children's most important influencer. But how do we help parents recognize the importance of empathy building?

Ashoka, the largest world network of social entrepreneurs, recognizing the critical place of empathy, created Parenting Changemakers, which targets parents of children aged four to sixteen. Parents form a community of like-minded people who develop ways to help their children master empathy, problem solving, leadership, and teamwork skills. The parent-led group meet in what they call Wisdom Circles to share stories of children who have done extraordinary things for society, and become inspired to raise their children as empathetic Changemakers. There is now a parent-led group with low-income Hispanic families in Texas and another in Georgetown Day School to build community between new and existing parents. Ashoka has also created a Changemaker Schools Network of leading schools worldwide that prioritize empathy and changemaking as student outcomes and serve as models to cultivate them.

Chrissy Garton recently participated in a five-week Parenting Changemakers conversation with moms and dads of children from toddler to young adult. "It was refreshing; a remarkably different parenting conversation than I have ever had," she said. "Rather than discussing black-and-white do's and don'ts, the premise of the entire dialogue centered on the type of world our children are being raised in—and the type of skills they will need to succeed."[7]

Conversations about raising children well, especially in our fast-paced, digital-driven, changing world, can inspire us to think about our parenting and how to align it with empathy building. Here are a few topics to initiate parent group discussions, or just ones to hold with your parent partner:

- What skills will our children need to succeed in the global economy when jobs of tomorrow don't exist today?

- What should parents be doing to prepare kids for a world of rapid change?

- How do we help children develop healthy relationships with peers, especially when face-to-face contact is breaking down and the internet is meaner?

- What ways can we broaden our children's views about those of different backgrounds and celebrate diversity?

- How do we cultivate empathy in a culture whose only metrics of success are achievement and performance?

- How do we help children understand racism and injustice happening in the world?

- What types of meaningful service projects can we offer our kids?

- How do we create empathy in those teachable parent-child moments?

Creating parent-led groups to discuss ways to cultivate empathy is one approach, but there are other creative ways.

Some parents form monthly book clubs where they read and discuss selections such as *Generation Me, Born for Love,* or even *UnSelfie,* and how to apply that information to child-rearing. Empathy playgroups have begun with moms and dads meeting weekly with their younger children at each other's homes and focusing on a different empathy-building skill like Calm Down, Dragon Breathing, and the Two Kind Rule to teach their kids together. Parents with teens have initiated service project groups where they build a house together for Habitat for Humanity during school vacations.

Parenting is difficult and often lonely, but is the most important role of our lives. Finding ways to connect with other parents who want to raise empathetic children can be enormously helpful. Be creative and form your own network of like-minded parents who can support each other.

6. Build Caring Relationships

I've witnessed many human moments when a child feels deeply with another. It is always powerful, but among the most memorable was in an impoverished Chicago school. The lesson was on the Civil War, and the middle school students were enthralled as their teacher role-played George Meade and Robert E. Lee at the Battle of Gettysburg, and then had his students take the perspective of each general. Dismissal was in minutes, but students had one final assignment. "Time for Spotlight," the teacher said. Students quickly moved their desks into a circle, plopped a chair in the center, and a child's name was called from a list. Carla jumped up, took the seat, and for one minute I watched a group of tweens show their ability to care. Each student shared a legitimate reason why Carla was a good person by stating sincere, genuine comments—not an easy feat for an age known for awkwardness. Their teacher was not only brilliant in schooling students in history but also in how to care. Carla thanked her peers, and there was time for one more Spotlight participant.

Jeremy's name was called, and my blood pressure skyrocketed. This kid was troubled—clenched fists, taut body, dark circles under his eyes—but he took the seat, and I started praying that the kids would sense his angst. And they didn't let me down. Not only did his peers read his pain, several mirrored his posture: they were feeling anxious with him and aligned their words to help him. Their comments were genuine, but softer and so caring: "We like having you in our class, Jeremy." "You always show up." "Thanks for helping me pick up my books last week."

Within thirty seconds, I saw a physical change in this child. He opened his fists, sat up a little straighter, and even had a wee bit of a smile. And when it was over, the moment of moments came: Jeremy stood up, hugged his teacher, and whispered, "I want you to know how much this class means to me." And then he quietly added, "This class means more to me than my family."

Well, I couldn't hold back the tears, and the girls next to me noticed my pain and began comforting me. One patted my hand, and the second gave me Kleenex, while the third explained the situation.

"Jeremy has a tough life—you should see what he has to go home to," she said. "You know, this classroom really is the only place he feels safe."

And the other girl leaned in and added, "It's okay, we all know what he's going through, so we help him feel cared about because we feel his pain with him."

Empathy opens when children are in places where they feel safe, accepted, and heard. And warm relationships are the incubator of caring—it's why parents who have warm, close relationships with their children are more likely to raise empathetic kids. And why classrooms and schools with positive climates have less bullying and students who feel less marginalized. We can and must work harder to create caring climates in our homes, schools, neighborhoods, and organizations.

Social psychologist Susan Pinker points out in her book *The Village Effect,* that social ties are *strongest in communities where there is an average of about 150 people.* In fact, Oxford evolutionary psychologist Robin Dunbar poses 150 as the maximum number of meaningful relationships that the human brain can manage.[8] As our "villages" break down and mobility, technology, and urbanization increase, it's even more important that we intentionally build caring communities for our children so they reap the Empathy Advantage, and there are so many ways to do so.

- Provide opportunities like Spotlight, class meetings, or team-building activities for kids to get to know each other.

- If you have a new group of children, start activities with ice-breakers to help them feel less anxious, or use minglers to help get them to know each other.

- Break up cliques with Mix-It-Up lunches so students eat with new peers or use cooperative learning strategies or jigsaw lessons to work with different classmates.

- Try approaches such as Rachel's Challenge, formed in memory of Rachel Scott, the first victim of the Columbine High School tragedy in 1999. The school-wide experience nurtures a culture of kindness where students are more likely to help one another in bullying incidents because they've learned to trust and respect one another.

- Use family dinners or together times as opportunities to listen and learn about each other.

"Sometimes adults forget that little things matter a lot to help us care. All kids need to feel safe and cared about and want to belong," a teen from the Seeds of Peace camp told me. "Just give us a chance to get to know each other, give us time, and we won't let you down."

7. Don't Give Up On a Child

The seeds of empathy are planted in our parent-child relationships, where our babies first learn trust, attachment, empathy, and love. Bruce D. Perry, renowned child psychiatrist and author of *Born for Love*, explains: "Babies don't learn to care and connect without specific early experiences."[9] Parents are the roots of their children's empathy quotients, and regardless of zip code, parents also share one common wish: a happy, loving family. But in some cases, our relationships with our children can be so strained they even shut down. Sometimes what we fail to do is empathize with our children and try to see things from their side or get into their shoes and understand their concerns, their fears, and their hurts.

One mom described tough times she had with her son. She and her husband had gone through a difficult divorce, and her teen blamed her for their breakup and refused to talk to her. So she decided to write a short little note to her son every day and leave it on his pillow at night: wishing him luck on his game, telling him she missed talking to him, hoping he'd had a good day, but always ending with 'I love you always, Mom.'"

The mom continued writing the notes for weeks, and her son never said anything about them until one day she was late for work, couldn't find the garage remote, and the only place she hadn't looked was her son's bedroom. She frantically searched his room, and that's when she saw an old cigar box hidden under his bed. She was certain she'd open the box and find drug paraphernalia, but when the mom finally got the courage to open that lid she almost died.

Inside that box was every note she'd ever written her son. When she showed him the box later that day he turned completely white. And then the strangest thing happened: her son started crying. All that time he thought he was the one who caused their divorce and blamed himself for their marital problems.

"I'm so glad I wrote those notes to my son," she said. "But now I think back, I can see all the signs I missed. He wasn't mad at me, just hurt and scared and ashamed. I only wished I would have tried to imagine how my son was feeling."

Empathy works both ways: it can give our children a huge proven advantage for success, but it also can strengthen our bonds with our children. Find a way to keep your relationship strong so you stay connected with your children. And never forget to use these same nine essential empathy habits to help you understand your children so you can parent more effectively.

Empathy is the root of humanity and the foundation that helps our children become good, caring people. But the Empathy Advantage also gives them a huge edge at happiness and success. Empathy has never been more crucial, but the ability to understand others' feelings and needs can be nurtured. It's up to adults not to let the kids down.

ACKNOWLEDGMENTS

There's a wonderful Chinese proverb that says, "A child's life is like a piece of paper on which every passerby leaves a mark." I've been enormously blessed because I've had so many people leave such significant marks on my own life, and each has helped shape my writing and the scope of my work. I express heartfelt gratitude to:

Joelle Delbourgo, my agent extraordinaire, who from the moment I shared this book project was passionate about guiding it to fruition. Thank you for your tenacity, patience, and friendship. I know this book would never have turned from idea to print without your steadfast push and support.

Michelle Howry, my editor, for her wholehearted belief and commitment to this project, wise editorial guidance, and superb insights through every possible step. Every suggestion was gold; every edit was right-on! It has been a joy and an honor to work together.

The seeds for this book were initiated as I sat on a bench in the middle of the Killing Fields in Cambodia. I was struck with a sense of absolute despair for our children's world, and then I came upon the research of a few who offered hope and guided me in another direction: how to raise goodness. Appreciation to Anne Colby, William Damon, Eva Fogelman, Samuel Oliner, and Ervin Staub for their extraordinary work in uncovering the seeds of humanity. And to those who contributed enormously to my thinking about empathy and developing caring communities for children: Daniel Batson, Jack Canfield, Tamar Chansky, Richard Davidson, Nancy Eisenberg, Maurice Elias, Bruce Feiler, Mary Gordon, Michael Gurian, Martin Hoffman, Harvey Karp, Dacher Keltner, Madeline Levine, Bruce Perry, Darrell Scott, Daniel Siegel, Laurence

Steinberg, and Jean Twenge. Your work has been a godsend to youth everywhere.

Special gratitude goes to a few who served as my mentors through a very intense research and writing process: Edward DeRoche, Thomas Lickona, Richard Weissbourd, and Philip Zimbardo. Words cannot describe my gratitude. I only hope I've done your work justice.

Appreciation to Michele Fey Smith from the American Program Bureau, for always being at the other end of an email to keep me laughing and for booking fabulous speaking venues for *UnSelfie*.

Thank you to a group of fabulous empathetic writers and friends who willingly gave not only their expertise and research but always were there to cheer me on. From proposal to print, Sue Scheff (#MBWY), Trudy Ludwig, Marilyn Price-Mitchell, and Barbara Turvett were there to lift me up, hold my hand, and keep me writing. Huge thanks also to Usha Balamore, Carrie Goldman, Sameer Hinduja, Katie Hurley, Jessica Lahey, Amy McCready, Justin Patchin, Marilyn Perlyn, Shannon Service, Theresa Payton, Rachel Simmons, and Rosalind Wiseman for being such supportive pals.

Appreciation to Jim Dunn, Akasha Forcella, Terry Gill, Jaynie Neveras, Judith Patrick, Sue Stroud, Jerry Stroud, and Sandi Young for your friendship. Huge gratitude to my "Big Bear Sanity Savers," who got me through an intense summer of writing: Leticia Danneberg, Cheryl Fey, Kay Giudry, Zoryana Pace, Bridget Holder (and Dave, Bob, Doug, Vince, and Terry). I know, I owe you. Last but not least, to Giulia Damico and the One Laptop per Child folks who let me experience the power of empathy at Kigali and changed my life: Thank you!

I'm indebted to the countless educators and innovators who shared their empathy-building strategies and expertise: Joey Katona, words aren't adequate to describe my gratitude—you are my Changemaker! Noah Abrams, your images of Afghan children altered my views about empathy; Amy Smit of the Ray Center at Drake University, thanks for going above and beyond with your research updates; and Vicki Zakrzewski, Greater Good, your expertise and willingness to help were so appreciated.

Special gratitude to those who took time to share their extraordinary empathy-building endeavors: Playworks: Jill Vialet and Jaron Williams; Maury Elementary: Carolyne E. Albert-Garvey and Vanessa Ford; Milford High School: Su Chafin, Cami Morgan, and Daikiri Villa; Redondo Beach Unified School District: Aaron Benton, Jennifer Bell, and Dr. Tanaz Farzad; Epiphany Prep Charter School: Sarah Raskin, Stacey Rawson, and Mayra Reyes; Healthy Heroes Alliance, Shakti Warriors: Lane JaBaay; Committee for Children: Joan Duffell; San Jacinto School District: Cathy Blythe; Rachel's Challenge, Darrell Scott; Parent's Circle, Yitzhak Frankenthal; Carol Lloyd, Great Schools; Jenna Druck Center, Ken Druck; Harvard's Making Caring Common: Jennifer Kahn; Seeds of Peace: Leslie Adelson Lewin, Bobbie Gottschalk, Daniel Noah Moses, Dindy Weinstein, Madeleine Pryor, Eric Kapenga, Tarek Maassarani, Laura Perrault; Roots of Empathy, Mary Gordon and Amanda Roberts; US Army, Child, Youth and School Services; Pentagon: Judi Patrick and DoDEA principal, Debbie Parks; generationOn: Kathy Saulitis; Shipley School: Usha Balamore and Lucy McDermott; Florida School for the Deaf and Blind: Dr. Jeanne Prickett and Karen Kolkedy; The Hero Construction Company: Matt Langdon; VolunTEEN Nation: Simone Bernstein; Character.org, Anne Bryant, Joan Duffell, David Keller, Linda McKay, Arthur Schwartz and Rebecca Sipos; Character Education Partnership, Philippines; Mann Rentoy; Southridge School, Manila: Luden Prudencio Salamat; Taipei American School, Catriona Moran and Megan Pettigrew; and to the hundreds of educators, counselors, parents of the US Army Europe Region, thank you for your service, sacrifice, hospitality, and humanity!

To the countless teachers and administrators who allowed me the privilege of conducting student focus groups so I could hear the voices of children. Your names are too many, so I list your countries: Canada, China, Colombia, Egypt, England, Germany, Korea, Malaysia, Mexico, New Zealand, Nicaragua, the Philippines, Rwanda, Taiwan, Turkey, and the United States.

To the folks at NBC who produced the segments that helped spin my head into new directions about empathy: Kerry Byrnes, Jamie Farnsworth, Rainy Farrell, Kathie Lee Gifford, Debbie Kosofsky, Lynn Keller, Dana Haller, Hoda Kotb, Joanne LaMarca, Michelle Leone, Patricia Luchsinger, Natalie Morales, Meredith Reise, Stephanie Siegel, Kate Snow, Marc Victor: thank you!

To the youth who are making a difference, thank you for sharing your stories: Kevin Curwick, Travis Price, Megan Felt, the kids of Milford High School, and Simone Bernstein of VolunTEEN Nation.

Last but not least, to my family, who have left the largest and most enduring mark in my life: you are my rock. To my husband and best friend, Craig, for his unending support, encouragement, and love through every phase of this book and my life; to my fabulous, fun new daughters-in-law, Kristie Borba and Erin Malone (yahoo!), and to my wonderful, glorious sons, Jason, Adam, and Zach. You are the ones who helped me recognize that our true parenting role is to produce a generation who will better their world. You have. And you make me so proud.

NOTES

Introduction: The Hidden Advantage of Empathy and Why It Matters for Our Children

1. Juliana Schroeder and Jane L. Risen, "Peace Through Friendship," *New York Times*, August 22, 2014, http://www.nytimes.com/2014/08/24/opinion/sunday/peace-through -friendship.html. Juliana Schroeder and Jane L. Risen, "Befriending the Enemy: Out-group Friendship Longitudinally Predicts Intergroup Attitudes in a Coexistence Program for Israelis and Palestinians," *Group Processes & Intergroup Relations*, July 28, 2014, http:// gpi.sagepub.com/content/early/2014/07/25/1368430214542257.abstract.

2. Quote based on author's personal interview with Leslie Lewin, June 3, 2015, New York City, Seeds of Peace office.

3. Quote from Barbara Gottschalk, cited by John Wallace, *The Enemy Has a Face* (Washington, DC: United States Institute of Peace Press, 2000), p. 2.

4. Maia Szalavitz and Bruce Perry, *Born for Love: Why Empathy Is Essential—and Endangered* (New York: William Morrow, 2010), p. 12.

5. Corinne Segan, "Viewpoint from the West Bank: 'We Are All Humans,'" *PBS NewsHour Extra*, August 26, 2014, http://www.pbs.org/newshour/extra/student_voices/viewpoint -from-the-west-bank-we-are-all-humans/.

6. J. Block-Lerner, C. Adair, J. C. Plumb, D. L. Rhatigan, and S. M. Orsillo, "The Case for Mindfulness-Based Approaches in the Cultivation of Empathy: Does Nonjudgmental, Present-Moment Awareness Increase Capacity for Perspective-Taking and Empathic Concern?," *Journal of Marital and Family Therapy* 33, no. 4 (October 2007): 501–16. Myriam Mongrain, Jacqueline M. Chin, and Leah B. Shapira, "Practicing Compassion Increases Happiness and Self-Esteem," *Journal of Happiness Studies* 12, no. 6 (December 2011): 963–81.

7. Mary Gordon, "Roots of Empathy Program," *Journal of Happiness Studies* 12, no. 6 (December 2011): 963–81. Reduces racism: Gordon Allport, *The Nature of Prejudice* (New York: Perseus Books, 1979), p. 434, and Andrew R. Todd, Galen V. Bodenhausen, Jennifer A. Richeson, and Adam D. Galinsky, "Perspective Taking Combats Automatic Expressions of Racial Bias," *Journal of Personality and Social Psychology* 100, no. 6 (June 2011): 1027–42. Samuel P. Oliner and Pearl M. Oliner, *The Altruistic Personality: Rescuers of Jews in Nazi Europe* (New York: Touchstone, 1992); Eva Fogelman, *Conscience and Courage: Rescuers of Jews During the Holocaust* (New York: Random House, 2011).

8. Mary Gordon, "Roots of Empathy," *Journal of Happiness Studies*.

9. PRWeb.com Newswire, "New Research from Momentous Institute Shows Empathy Predicts Academic Performance," *Digital Journal*, October 13, 2014, http://www.digitaljour nal.com/pr/2252070.

10. Saga Briggs, "How Empathy Affects Learning, and How to Cultivate It in Your Students," *informED,* November 1, 2014, http://www.opencolleges.edu/au/informed/features/empa thy-and-learning/, accessed Nov. 23, 2014.

11. Daniel Goleman, "What Makes a Leader?" *Harvard Business Review OnPoint,* Summer 2014, pp. 24–33.

12. Kathy A. Stepien and Amy Baernstein, "Educating for Empathy," *Journal of General Internal Medicine* 21, no. 5 (May 2006): 524–30.

13. Jean M. Twenge, W. Keith Campbell, and Brittany Gentile, "Increases in Individualistic Words and Phrases in American Books, 1960–2008," *PLoS ONE* 7, no. 7 (2012): e40181, doi: 10.1371/journal.pone.0040181.

14. J. Twenge and J. Foster, "Mapping the Scale of the Narcissism Epidemic: Increases in Narcissim 2002–2007 within Ethnic Groups," *Journal of Research in Personality* 42, no. 6 (2008): 1619–22. J. Twenge, S. Konrath, J. Foster, W. K. Campbell, and B. Bushman, "Egos Inflating over Time: A Cross-Temporal Meta-Analysis of the Narcissistic Personality Inventory, 2008," *Journal of Personality* 76, no. 4 (August 2008): 875–901.

15. S. Konrath, "The Empathy Paradox: Increasing Disconnection in the Age of Increasing Connection," in *Handbook of Research on Technoself: Identity in a Technological Society,* Rocci Luppicini, ed. (Hershey, PA: IGI Global, 2012): 204–28.

16. College students 40 percent lower in empathy than counterparts 30 years ago: Research led by Sara H. Konrath of University of Michigan at Ann Arbor involved seventy-two studies of college students collected over the past thirty years and was published online in *Personality and Social Psychology Review.* "Empathy: College Students Don't Have as Much as They Used To, Study Finds," *ScienceDaily,* May 29, 2010.

17. Rashmi Shetgiri, Hua Lin, and Glenn Flores, "Is There a Bullying Epidemic? Trends in Risk and Protective Factors for Bullying in the US," E-PAS20110825.5, May 1, 2011. Survey based on a nationally representative, random-digit-dial phone survey sample of parents of children ten to seventeen years old. "Ever" bullying was defined as "rarely/sometimes /usually/always" and "frequent" bullying as "sometimes/usually/always." Results analyzed 2003–2007 trends in bullying and found that 23 percent of children ever bullied in 2003, and 35 percent ever bullied in 2007, a 52 percent increase and almost one in six (15 percent) children frequently bullied in 2007. http://www.abstracts2views.com/pas/view .php?nu=PAS11L1_965. Wes Hosking, "Bullying Behavior Starting in Children as Young as Three," *Herald Sun,* August 5, 2014, http://www.heraldsun.com.au/news/bullying -behaviour-starting-in-children-as-young-as-age-three/story-fni0fiyv-1227014497015.

18. Survey: McAfee results from its 2014 "Teens and the Screen Study: Exploring Online Privacy, Social Networking and Cyberbullying," which examines the online behavior and social networking habits of preteens and teens.

19. Sameer Hinduja and Justin W. Patchin, "Bullying, Cyberbullying and Suicide," *Archives of Suicide Research* 14, no. 3 (2010): 206–21. The survey involved approximately 2,000 randomly selected middle-schoolers from the most populous school districts in the United States. Cyberbullying victims were almost twice as likely to have attempted suicide compared to youth who had not experienced cyberbullying. With respect to bullying, all forms were significantly associated with increases in suicidal ideation among sample respondents. It also appears that bullying and cyberbullying *victimization* was a stronger predictor of suicidal thoughts and behaviors than was bullying and cyberbullying *offending.*

20. Six in ten American adults identified "as a very serious problem" young people's failure to learn fundamental moral values, including honesty, respect, and responsibility for others: major survey by the organization Public Agenda, "Americans Deeply Troubled About

Nation's Youth; Even Young Children Described by Majority in Negative Terms," press release, June 26, 1997, http://www.publicagenda.org.

21. Justin McCarthy, "Majority in US Still Say Moral Values Getting Worse," *Gallup*, June 2, 2015, http://www.gallup.com/poll/183467/majority-say-moral-values-getting -worse.aspx.

22. International Center for Academic Integrity, "The Academic Integrity Policy," http://www .academicintegrity.org/icai/assets/policy-and-hearing-information_.pdf, accessed January 4, 2016.

23. S. Thoma and M. Bebeau, "Moral Judgment Competency Is Declining Over Time: Evidence from 20 Years of Defining Issues Test Data," paper presented at the American Educational Research Association, 2008.

24. K. R. Merikangas et al., "Lifetime Prevalence of Mental Disorders in U.S. Adolescents: Results from the National Comorbidity Survey Replication—Adolescent Supplement (NCS-A)," *Journal of the American Academy of Child & Adolescent Psychiatry* 49, no. 10 (October 2010): 980–89.

25. Melissa Healy, "Mental Illness in Youth: A Common Struggle," *Los Angeles Times*, May 19, 2013, p. 16A.

26. American Psychological Association, "American Psychological Association Survey Shows Teen Stress Rivals That of Adults," February 11, 2014, http://www.apa.org/news/press /releases/2014/02/teen-stress.aspx.

Chapter 1: Empathetic Children Can Recognize Feelings

1. Christy Gibb, "Fighting Childhood Aggression," www.changemakers.net, p. 16.

2. Kimberly A. Schonert-Reichl, Veronica Smith, Anat Zaidman-Zait, and Cyle Hertzman, "Promoting Children's Prosocial Behaviors in School: Impact of the 'Roots of Empathy' Program on the Social and Emotion Competence of School-Aged Children," *School Mental Health* 4 (2011): 1–21, http://cemh.lbpsb.qc.ca/professionals/RootsofEmpathy.pdf.

3. Personal interview of Mary Gordon by the author in Washington, DC: October 31, 2014.

4. Mary Gordon quote: Mary Gordon, *Roots of Empathy: Changing the World Child by Child* (New York: The Experiment, 2009), p. xi.

5. Personal interview of Kayne by author at Maury Elementary School, Washington, DC: October 30, 2014.

6. W. F. Arsenio, S. Cooperman, and A. Lover, "Affective Predictors of Preschoolers' Aggression and Peer Acceptance: Direct and Indirect Effects," *Developmental Psychology* 36, (2000): 438–48. C. Izard, S. Fine, D. Schultz, A. Mostow, B. Ackerman, and E. Youngstrom, "Emotion Knowledge as a Predictor of Social Behavior and Academic Competence in Children at Risk," *Psychological Science* 12, no. 4 (January 2001): 18–23. S. A. Denham, M. McKinley, E. A. Couchoud, and R. Holt, "Emotional and Behavioral Predictors of Preschool Peer Ratings," *Child Development* 61, no. 4 (August 1990): 1145–52.

7. Daniel Goleman, *Emotional Intelligence: Why It Can Matter More Than IQ* (New York: Bantam Books, 1995), p. 97.

8. John Gottman, *The Heart of Parenting: How to Raise an Emotionally Intelligent Child* (New York: Simon & Schuster, 1997), p. 25.

9. Victoria J. Rideout, Ulla G. Foehr, and Donald F. Roberts, "Generation M2: Media in the Lives of 8- to 18-Year-olds," Menlo Park, CA: Kaiser Family Foundation, January 2010.

10. Greg Toppo, "Techie Tykes: Kids Going Mobile at Much Earlier Age," *USA Today*, November 2, 2015, 3B.

11. Four point six figure from the Nielsen report cited by Vicki Glembocki, "How to Raise a People Person," *Parents*, January 2015, pp. 50–53.

12. "Not All Screen Time Is a No-No for Infants," *Time*, October 26, 2015, p. 18.

13. Stephanie Goldberg, "Many Teens Send 100-Plus Texts a Day, Survey Says," *CNNTech*, April 21, 2010, http://www.cnn.com/2010/TECH/04/20/teens.text.messaging, accessed Dec. 6, 2010.

14. Poll from the USC Annenberg Center for the Digital Future: "Family Time Decreasing with Internet Use," 2009, http://www.digitalcenter.org/pdf/cdf_family_time.pdf, accessed August 8, 2009.

15. J. Dunn, J. Brown, C. Slomkowski, C. Tesla, and L. M. Youngblade, "Young Children's Understanding of Other People's Feelings and Beliefs: Individual Differences and Their Antecedents," *Child Development* 62, no. 6 (1991): 1352–66. Ana Aznar and Harriet R. Tenenbaum, "Gender and Age Differences in Parent-Child Emotion Talk," *British Journal of Developmental Psychology* 33, no. 1 (2014): 148–55.

16. S. Adams, J. Kuebli, P. A. Boyle, and R. Fivush, "Gender Differences in Parent-Child Conversations About Past Emotions: A Longitudinal Investigation," *Sex Roles* 33, no. 5 (1995): 309–23. A. R. Eisenberg, "Emotion Talk Among Mexican American and Anglo American Mothers and Children from Two Social Classes," *Merrill-Palmer Quarterly* 45, no. 2 (1999): 267–84. R. Fivush, "Exploring Sex Differences in the Emotional Content of Mother-Child Conversations About the Past," *Sex Roles* 20, no. 11 (1989): 675–91.

17. C. A. Cervantes and M. A. Callanan, "Labels and Explanations in Mother-Child Emotion Talk: Age and Gender Differentiation," *Developmental Psychology* 34, no. 1 (1998): 88–98.

18. William Pollack, *Real Boys* (New York: Henry Holt and Co., 1998), p. 346.

19. S. Adams, J. Kuebli, P. A. Boyle, and R. Fivush, "Gender Differences in Parent-Child Conversations About Past Emotions," *Sex Roles* (1995). A. R. Eisenberg, "Emotion Talk Among Mexican American and Anglo American Mothers and Children from Two Social Classes," *Merrill-Palmer Quarterly* 45, no. 2 (1999).

20. Sixty-two percent of kids think parents are too distracted to listen, based on *Highlights* magazine's "2014 State of the Kid" survey of 1,521 children ages six to twelve: "National Survey Reveals 62% of Kids Think Parents Are Too Distracted to Listen," *Highlights*, October 8, 2014, https://www.highlights.com/newsroom/national-survey-reveals-62-kids-think-parents-are-too-distracted-listen.

21. Jenny S. Radesky, C. J. Kistin, B. Zuckerman, K. Nitzberg, J. Gross, M. Kaplan-Sanoff, M. Augustyn, and M. Silverstein, "Patterns of Mobile Device Use by Caregivers and Children During Meals in Fast Food Restaurants," *Pediatrics* 133, no. 4 (March 10, 2014): pp. e843–49. Perri Klass, "Parents, Wired to Distraction," *New York Times*, March 10, 2014, http://well.blogs.nytimes.com/2014/03/10/parents-wired-to-distraction, accessed December 9, 2014.

22. Dimitri Christakis et al., "Audible Television and Decreased Adult Words, Infant Vocalizations, and Conversational Turns: A Population-Based Study," *Archives of Pediatrics and Adolescent Medicine* 163, no. 6 (2009): 554–58.

23. Christakis et al., "Audible Television."

24. Matthew A. Lapierre, Jessica Taylor Piotrowski, and Deborah L. Linebarger, "Background Television in the Homes of US Children," *Pediatrics* 130, no. 5 (September 2012): 1–8.

25. Marvin L. Simner, "Newborn's Response to the Cry of Another Infant," *Developmental Psychology* 5, no. 1 (July 1971): 136–50. Simner was first to demonstrate that newborns cry when listening to the recorded cries of other infants; he also established that crying

was not simply a response to a disturbing stimulus, because the infants did not cry as much when exposed to equally loud and intense nonhuman sounds.

26. G. B. Martin and R. D. Clark, "Distress Crying in Neonates: Species and Peer Specificity," *Developmental Psychology* 18, no. 1 (1987): 3–9.

27. Daniel Goleman, "Researchers Trace Empathy's Roots to Infancy," *New York Times,* March 28, 1989.

28. T. Farroni, G. Csibra, F. Simion, and M. H. Johnson, "Eye Contact Detection in Humans from Birth," *Proceedings of the National Academy of Sciences* 99, no. 14 (2002): 9602–5.

29. Richard J. Davidson with Sharon Begley, *The Emotional Life of Your Brain* (New York: Penguin, 2013), pp. 35–36.

30. Alison Gopnik, Andrew N. Meltzoff, and Patricia K. Kuhl, *The Scientist in the Crib: What Early Learning Tells Us About the Mind* (New York: Harper Perennial, 2001), p. 39.

31. Gopnik et al., *The Scientist in the Crib.*

32. Mary Gordon discipline suggestion from Maia Szalavitz, "How Not to Raise a Bully: The Early Roots of Empathy," *Time,* April 17, 2010, http://www.time.com/time/printout/0,8816,1982190,00.html.

33. Victoria J. Rideout, Ulla G. Foehr, and Donald F. Roberts, "Generation M2: Media in the Lives of 8- to 18-Year-olds," Menlo Park, CA: Kaiser Family Foundation, January 2010.

34. The six basic emotions are derived from the research of P. Ekman, "Facial Expression of Emotion," *American Psychologist* 48, no. 4 (1993), pp. 384–92.

35. Nancy Eisenberg and Paul H. Mussen, *The Roots of Prosocial Behavior in Children* (New York: Cambridge University Press, 1996), p. 61.

Chapter 2: Empathetic Children Have a Moral Identity

1. Reports of the Genovese incident that reexamined the murder fifty years later did find major discrepancies in police reports; there were witnesses, and some did help: Kevin Cook, *Kitty Genovese: The Murder, the Bystanders, the Crime That Changed America* (New York: W. W. Norton & Co., 2014).

2. Chesley Sullenberger, with Jeffrey Zaslow, *Highest Duty: My Search for What Really Matters* (New York: William Morrow, 2009), p. 152.

3. Sullenberger, *Highest Duty,* 152.

4. Sullenberger, *Highest Duty,* 2.

5. Six in ten American adults identified "as a very serious problem" young people's failure to learn fundamental moral values, including honesty, respect, and responsibility for others: Public Agenda, "Americans Deeply Troubled about Nation's Youth; Even Young Children Described by Majority in Negative Terms," press release, June 26, 1997, http://www.publicagenda.org.

6. Richard Weissbourd, *The Parents We Mean to Be* (New York: Mariner Books, 2009), pp. 41–42.

7. Nancy Eisenberg and Paul H. Mussen, *The Roots of Prosocial Behavior in Children* (New York: Cambridge University Press, 1996), p. 155.

8. Alice G. Walton, "Too Much Praise Can Turn Kids into Narcissists, Study Suggests," *Forbes,* March 9, 2015, http://www.forbes.com/sites/alicegwalton/2015/03/09/parents-stop-overvaluing-your-kid-you-may-create-a-future-narcissist-study-says/.

9. Study cited by Jean M. Twenge and W. Keith Campbell, *The Narcissism Epidemic: Living in the Age of Entitlement* (New York: Free Press, 2009), p. 34.

10. Twenge and Campbell, *The Narcissism Epidemic,* p. 13.

11. Narcissistic Personality Disorder increasing: F. S. Stinson, D. A. Dawson, R. B. Gold-

stein, S. P. Chou, B. Huang, S. M. Smith, W. J. Ruan, A. J. Pulay, T. D. Saha, R. P. Pickering, and B. F. Grant, "Prevalence, Correlates, Disability, and Comorbidity of DSM-IV Narcissistic Personality Disorder: Results from the Wave 2 National Epidemiologic Survey on Alcohol and Related Conditions," *Journal of Clinical Psychiatry* 69, no. 7 (2008): 1033–45.

12. Jeff Grabmeir, "How Parents May Help Create Their Own Little Narcissists," The Ohio State University, March 9, 2015, https://news.osu.edu/news/2015/03/09/little-narcissists/.

13. "Marking in Red Ink Banned in Case It Upsets Schoolchildren," *Telegraph*, December 26, 2008, accessed January 29, 2015, http://www.telegraph.co.uk/education/educationnews/3964683/Marking-in-red-ink-banned-in-case-it-upsets-schoolchildren.html.

14. Sherry Parmet, "Teachers Starting to Shun Red Pens," *San Diego Union-Tribune*, October 4, 2004, http://www.utsandiego.com/uniontrib/20041004/news_1m4pens.html, accessed January 29, 2015.

15. Ashley Merryman, "Losing Is Good for You," *New York Times*, September 24, 2013, http://www.nytimes.com/2013/09/25/opinion/losing-is-good-for-you.html.

16. Ellen Greenberger, Jared Lessard, Chuansheng Chen, and Susan P. Farruggia, "Self-Entitled College Students: Contributions of Personality, Parenting and Motivational Factors," *Journal of Youth and Adolescence* 37 (2008): 1193–1204.

17. Jeffrey Zaslow, "The Most-Praised Generation Goes to Work," *Wall Street Journal*, April 20, 2007, http://www.wsj.com/articles/SB117702894815776259, accessed January 27, 2015.

18. S. P. Oliner and P. M. Oliner, *The Altruistic Personality: Rescuers of Jews in Nazi Europe* (New York: Free Press, 1988), 164–68.

19. Samuel P. Oliner, "Ordinary Heroes," *Yes!*, November 5, 2001, http://www.yesmagazine.org/issues/can-love-save-the-world/ordinary-heroes.

20. S. P. Oliner, *Do Unto Others: Extraordinary Acts of Ordinary People* (Cambridge, MA: Westview Press, 2003), p. 43.

21. Thomas Lickona, *Character Matters* (New York: Simon & Schuster, 2004), p. 19.

22. Kristen Renwick Monroe, *The Heart of Altruism: Perceptions of a Common Humanity* (Princeton, NJ: Princeton University Press, 1996), p. 3.

23. Renwick Monroe, *The Heart of Altruism*, p. 220.

24. Anne Colby and William Damon, *Some Do Care: Contemporary Lives of Moral Commitment* (New York: Free Press, 1992), p. 27.

25. Colby and Damon, *Some Do Care*, p. 219.

26. Colby and Damon, *Some Do Care*, p. 304.

27. Oliner and Oliner, *The Altruistic Personality*, p. 3.

28. Weissbourd, *The Parents We Mean to Be*, p. 53.

29. Kim Clark, "Bringing Up Bold Babies," *U.S. News & World Report*, August 20–August 27, 2001, p. 76. Philip Zimbardo, *The Lucifer Effect* (New York: Random House, 2008), p. 451. A. Strenta and W. DeJong, "The Effect of a Prosocial Label on Helping Behavior," *Social Psychology Quarterly* 44, no. 2 (1981): 142–47.

30. Joan E. Grusec et al., "Modeling, Direct Instruction, and Attributions: Effects on Altruism," *Developmental Psychology* 14, no. 1 (1978): 51–57.

31. Christopher J. Bryan, Allison Master, and Gregory M. Walton, "'Helping' Versus 'Being a Helper': Invoking the Self to Increase Helping in Young Children," *Child Development* 85, no. 5 (September/October 2014): 1836–42.

32. J. E. Grusec and E. Redler, "Attribution, Reinforcement, and Altruism: A Developmental Analysis," *Developmental Psychology* 16, no. 5 (September 1980): 525–34.

33. J. Philippe Rushton, "Generosity in Children: Immediate and Long-Term Effects of Modeling, Preaching and Moral Judgment," *Journal of Personality and Social Psychology* 31, no. 3 (March 1975): 459–66.

34. John Wooden: Transcript from ESPN: "E-Ticket: The Wizard at 95," http://sports.espn.go.com/espn/eticket/story?page=wooden, accessed February 4, 2015.

35. William Lee Miller, *Lincoln's Virtues* (New York: Alfred A. Knopf, 2002).

36. Robert Coles, *Lives of Moral Leadership* (New York: Random House, 2000), p. xii.

37. Zimbardo, *The Lucifer Effect*, p. 474.

38. Bruce Feiler, *The Secrets of Happy Families* (New York: William Morrow, 2013), p. 70.

39. Laura A. King and Joshua A. Hicks, "Narrating the Self in the Past and the Future: Implications for Maturity," *Research in Human Development* 3, no. 2–3 (2006): 121–38.

40. Po Bronson, "How Not to Talk to Your Kids," *New York* magazine, August 3, 2007.

41. William Damon, "The Moral Development of Children," *Scientific American*, August 1999, pp. 72–78.

Chapter 3: Empathetic Children Understand the Needs of Others

1. J. Elliott discrimination lesson in William Peters, *A Class Divided: Then and Now* (New Haven, CT: Yale University Press, 1971). Peters, *A Class Divided*, p. 17.

2. Peters, *A Class Divided*, p. 51.

3. Peters, *A Class Divided*, p. 50.

4. Peters, *A Class Divided*, pp. 3–4.

5. Peters, *A Class Divided*, pp. 120–24.

6. Stephen G. Bloom, "Lesson of a Lifetime," *Smithsonian*, September 2005, pp. 82–92.

7. Peters, *A Class Divided*, p. 129.

8. Inductive reasoning produces children who are better adjusted, based on research by Nancy Eisenberg, Richard Fabes, and Martin Hoffman, cited by Dacher Keltner, "The Compassionate Instinct," in *The Compassionate Instinct*, ed. by Dacher Keltner, Jason Marsh, and Jeremy Adam Smith (New York: W. W. Norton & Co., 2010), pp. 13–14.

9. V. Slaughter, K. Imuta, C. C. Peterson, and J. D. Henry, "Meta-Analysis of Theory of Mind and Peer Popularity in the Preschool and Early School Years," *Child Development* 86, no. 4 (April 2015), pp. 1159–74.

10. Quote by A. Dixon, "Can Empathy Reduce Racism," Greater Good, July 21, 2011, http://greatergood.berkeley.edu/article/item/empathy_reduces_racism/, citing study: A. R. Todd, G. V. Bodenhausen, J. A. Richeson, and A. D. Galinsky, "Perspective Taking Combats Automatic Expressions of Racial Bias," *Journal of Personality and Social Psychology* 100, no. 6 (June 2011): 1027–42.

11. Fifty discipline encounters a day or more than 15,000 a year cited by M. L. Hoffman, *Empathy and Moral Development: Implications for Caring and Justice* (New York: Cambridge University Press, 2000), p. 140.

12. Susan Campbell, "Spare the Rod?" *Psychology Today*, September 2002.

13. C. A. Taylor, J. A. Manganello, S. J. Lee, and J. C. Rice, "Mothers' Spanking of 3-Year-Old Children and Subsequent Risk of Children's Aggressive Behavior," *Pediatrics* 125, no. 5 (2010): e1057–65, http://pediatrics.aappublications.org/content/125/5/e1057.full. L. J. Berlin, J. M. Ispa, M. A. Fine, P. S. Malone, J. Brooks-Gunn, C. Brandy-Smith, C. Ayoub, and Y. Bai, "Correlates and Consequences of Spanking and Verbal Punishment for Low-Income White, African American, and Mexican American Toddlers," *Child Development* 80, no. 5 (September–October 2009): 1403–20.

14. Elizabeth Thompson Gershoff, "Corporal Punishment by Parents and Associated Child Behaviors and Experiences: A Meta-Analytic and Theoretical Review," *Psychological Bulletin* 128, no. 4 (2002): 539–79.

15. Eighty-eight percent of parents yell at kids: M. A. Straus and C. J. Field, "Psychological Aggression by American Parents: National Data on Prevalence, Chronicity, and Severity," *Journal of Marriage and Family* 65 (November 2003): 795–808.

16. Hilary Stout, "For Some Parents, Shouting Is the New Spanking," *New York Times*, October 21, 2009, http://www.nytimes.com/2009/10/22/fashion/22yell.html.

17. Elizabeth Dougherty, "Cutting Words May Scar Young Brains: Parental Verbal Abuse of Child Appears to Damage Cerebral Pathways," Harvard Medical School, February 20, 2009, http://hms.harvard.edu/news/cutting-words-may-scar-young-brains -2-20-09.

18. Nancy Eisenberg, "Emotion, Regulation, and Moral Development," *Annual Review of Psychology* 51 (February 2000): 665–97.

19. S. P. Oliner and P. M. Oliner, *The Altruistic Personality: Rescuers of Jews in Nazi Europe* (New York: Free Press, 1988).

20. Daniel Siegel and Tina Payne Bryson, "Time-Outs Are Hurting Your Child," *Time*, September 23, 2014, http://time.com/3404701/discipline-time-out-is-not-good/.

21. Alfie Kohn, *The Brighter Side of Human Nature* (New York: Basic Books, 1990), p. 203.

22. M. L. Hoffman, *Empathy and Moral Development: Implications for Caring and Justice* (New York: Cambridge University Press, 2000), p. 143.

23. C. Zahn-Waxler, M. Radke-Yarrow, and R. A. King. "Child Rearing and Children's Prosocial Initiations Toward Victims of Distress," *Child Development* 50, no. 2 (1979): 319–30.

24. Julia Krevans and John C. Gibbs, "Parents' Use of Inductive Discipline: Relations to Children's Empathy and Prosocial Behavior," *Child Development* 67, no. 6 (December 1996): 3263–77.

25. R. B. Patrick and J. C. Gibbs, "Inductive Discipline, Parental Expression of Disappointed Expectations, and Moral Identity in Adolescence," *Journal of Youth and Adolescence* 41, no. 8 (August 2012): 973–83.

26. Nancy Eisenberg, *The Caring Child* (Cambridge, MA: Harvard University Press, 1992), p. 96.

27. Nancy Eisenberg, "Emotion, Regulation, and Moral Development," *Annual Review of Psychology* 51 (2000): 665–97.

28. Adam Grant, "Raising a Moral Child," *New York Times*, April 11, 2014, http://www .nytimes.com/column/adam-grant/.

29. N. Eisenberg and P. A. Miller, "The Relation of Empathy to Prosocial and Related Behaviors," *Psychological Bulletin* 101, no. 1 (1987): 91–119.

30. E. Stotland, "Exploratory Investigations of Empathy," in *Advances in Experimental Social Psychology*, ed. by Leonard Berkowitz, vol. 4 (New York: Academic Press, 1969), pp. 271–313.

31. M. A. Barnett, L. M. King, and J. A. Howard, "Inducing Affect About Self or Other: Effects on Generosity in Children," *Developmental Psychology* 15, no. 2 (1979): 164–67. D. Aderman, S. S. Brehm, and L. B. Katz, "Empathic Observation of an Innocent Victim: The Just World Revisited," *Journal of Personality and Social Psychology* 29, no. 3 (1974): 342–47.

32. J. Decety and P. L. Jackson, "The Functional Architecture of Human Empathy," *Behavioral and Cognitive Neuroscience Reviews* 3, no. 2 (2004): 71–100.

33. Jennifer Greenstein Altmann, "Meryl Streep Talks About the 'Mysterious Art of Acting,' "

News at Princeton, December 1, 2006, http://www.princeton.edu/main/news/archive
/S16/49/92S82/.

Chapter 4: Empathetic Children Have a Moral Imagination

1. Stuart J. Ritchie and Timothy C. Bates, "Enduring Links from Childhood Mathematics and Reading Achievement to Adult Socioeconomic Status," *Psychological Science* 24, no. 7 (July 2013): 1301–8.

2. Jonathan Douglas, "The Importance of Instilling a Need to Read," *Daily Telegraph,* May 4, 2013, http://www.telegraph.co.uk/education/educationopinion/10035473/The -importance-of-instilling-a-need-to-read.html.

3. Survey of 35,000 kids by the UK's National Literary Trust; screens don't seem to be improving children's reading experience: Asi Sharabi, "Tablets Make It Nearly Impossible for Kids to Get Lost in a Story," *The Atlantic,* December 18, 2013, http://www.theatlan tic.com/education/archive/2013/12/tablets-make-it-nearly-impossible-for-kids-to-get -lost-in-a-story/282469/.

4. Irene Picton, "The Impact of Ebooks on the Reading Motivation and Reading Skills of Children and Young People," National Literacy Trust, September 2014. Study was of children ages eight to sixteen.

5. Charlotte Alter, "Study: The Number of Teens Reading for Fun Keeps Declining," *Time,* May 12, 2014, http://time.com/94794/common-sense-media-reading-report-never-read, accessed August 22, 2015.

6. Fifty-four percent of kids surveyed said they preferred watching television to reading: Research by the National Literacy Trust based on survey of 21,000 children: "Children Are Reading Less," *The Independent,* September 14, 2012, http://www .independent.co.uk/news/education/education-news/children-are-reading-less -8113993.html.

7. Common Sense Media, "Zero to Eight: Children's Media Use in America 2013," October 23, 2013, http://www.commonsensemedia.org/zero-to-eight-2013-infographic.

8. The second most popular activity for kids behind watching TV (36 percent) is watching videos on YouTube (17 percent), and playing mobile games and apps (16 percent). Stuart Dredge, "Children's Reading Shrinking Due to Apps, Games and YouTube," *Guardian,* September 26, 2013, http://www.theguardian.com/technology/appsblog/2013/sep/26 /children-reading-less-apps-games.

9. About half of parents (49%) feel their children do not spend enough time reading books for fun—an increase from 2010, when 36% of parents were dissatisfied with time their children spent reading. Based on a national survey of kids ages six to seventeen and their parents. Press release, January 14, 2013, Scholastic, "New Study on Kids' Reading in the Digital Age: The Number of Kids Reading eBooks Has Nearly Doubled Since 2010," http:// mediaroom.scholastic.com/press-release/new-study-kids-reading-digital-age-number -kids-reading-ebooks-has-nearly-doubled-2010.

10. Liz Bury, "Children's Bedtime Stories on the Wane, According to Survey," *Guardian,* September 11, 2013, http://www.theguardian.com/books/2013/sep/11/children-bedtime -stories-on-wane-survey.

11. Greg Toppo, "Techie Tykes: Kids Going Mobile at Much Earlier Age," *USA Today,* November 2, 2015, 3B.

12. Julie Bosman, "Picture Books No Longer a Staple for Children," *New York Times,* October 7, 2010, http://www.nytimes.com/2010/10/08/us/08picture.html.

13. Common Core Standards shift to nonfiction: Joel Stein, "How I Replaced Shakespeare and Why Our Kids May Never Read a Poem as Lovely as a Tree," *Time,* December 10, 2012, p. 67.

14. Literary fiction, not popular fiction or nonfiction, boosts empathy best: Julianne Chiaet, "Novel Finding: Reading Literary Fiction Improves Empathy," *Scientific American,* October 4, 2013, http://www.scientificamerican.com/article.cfm?id=novel-finding-reading-literary-fiction-improves-empathy.

15. Annie Murphy Paul, "Reading Literature Makes Us Smarter and Nicer," *Time,* June 3, 2013, http://ideas.time.com/2013/06/03/why-we-should-read-literature.

16. Raymond A. Mar, Jennifer L. Tackett, and Chris Moore, "Exposure to Media and Theory-of-Mind Development in Preschoolers," *Cognitive Development* (January–March 2010): 69–78.

17. Chiaet, "Novel Finding: Reading Literary Fiction Improves Empathy," *Scientific American,* October 4, 2013. David Comer Kidd and Emanuele Castano, "Reading Literary Fiction Improves Theory of Mind," *Science* 342, no. 6156 (2013): 377–80, http://www.sciencemag.org/content/342/6156/377.abstract.

18. Quote by Gregory Berns, lead author of the study and director of Emory's Center for Neuropolicy: Gregory S. Berns, Kristina Blaine, Michael J. Prietula, and Brandon E. Pye, "Short- and Long-Term Effects of a Novel on Connectivity in the Brain," *Brain Connectivity* 3, no. 6 (2013): 590–600.

19. N. K. Speer, J. R. Reynolds, K. M. Swallow, and J. M. Zacks, "Reading Stories Activates Neural Representations of Perceptual and Motor Experiences," *Psychological Science* 20, no. 8 (2009): 989–99.

20. Tom Oswald, "Reading the Classics: It's More Than Just for Fun," *Michigan State University,* September 14, 2012, http://msutoday.msu.edu/news/2012/reading-the-classics-its-more-than-just-for-fun/.

21. Oatley describes his five-year-old daughter's imaginary game: "A Feeling for Fiction," in *The Compassionate Instinct,* ed. by Dacher Keltner, Jason Marsh, and Jeremy Adam Smith (New York: W. W. Norton & Co., 2010), p. 150.

22. Press release, Scholastic, "New Study on Reading in the Digital Age: Parents Say Electronic, Digital Devices Negatively Affect Kids' Reading Time," September 29, 2010, http://mediaroom.scholastic.com/node/378.

23. Mothers talk about mental states: T. Ruffman, L. Slade, and E. Crowe, "The Relation Between Children's and Mothers' Mental State Language and Theory-of-Mind Understanding," *Child Development* 73, no. 3 (2002): 734–51.

24. Theory of mind understanding at forty months was correlated with engagement in family talk about feelings and causality, and cooperative interaction with a sibling: J. Dunn, J. Brown, C. Slomkowski, C. Tesla, and L. Youngblade, "Young Children's Understanding of Other People's Feelings and Beliefs: Individual Differences and Their Antecedents," *Child Development* 62, no. 6 (1991): 1352–66.

25. One-fifth of kids find books embarrassing: Sam Parker, "Children Find Books 'Embarrassing' and Are Reading Less Than 7 Years Ago, Report Suggests," *Huffington Post,* United Kingdom, July 9, 2012, http://www.huffingtonpost.co.uk/2012/09/07/children-reading-rates-down_n_1863582.html.

26. This study of teen literature was by Sarah Coyne, a Brigham Young University professor who analyzed the use of profanity in forty books on an adolescent bestseller list. "Study Shows Vulgar Characters in Books Most Popular," May 19, 2012, *RedOrbit,* http://www.redorbit.com/news/science/1112538370/study-shows-vulgar-characters-in-books-most-popular/.

Chapter 5: Empathetic Children Can Keep Their Cool

1. Mayra Reyes's quotations based a phone conversation May 6, 2015, and class visit to Epiphany Prep Charter School in San Diego, California, June 10, 2014.
2. Jonah Lehrer, "Don't!" *The New Yorker*, May 18, 2009.
3. Terrie E. Moffitt et al., "A Gradient of Childhood Self-Control Predicts Health, Wealth, and Public Safety," *Proceedings of the National Academy of Sciences* 108, no. 7 (2011): 2693–98.
4. Lehrer, "Don't!" *The New Yorker*.
5. A review of the annual "Stress in America" survey: "Stress in America: Are Teens Adopting Adults' Stress Habits?" American Psychological Association, Washington, DC, February 11, 2014, http://www.apa.org/news/press/releases/stress/2013/stress-report.pdf.
6. "Stressed in America," *Monitor on Psychology*, January 2011, http://www.apa.org/monitor/2011/01/stressed-america.aspx.
7. Lawrence J. Cohen, "The Drama of the Anxious Child," *Time*, September 26, 2013, http://ideas.time.com/2013/09/26/the-drama-of-the-anxious-child/.
8. Robert M. Sapolsky, "When Stress Rises, Empathy Suffers," *Wall Street Journal*, January 16, 2015, http://www.wsj.com/articles/when-stress-rises-empathy-suffers-1421423942.
9. A. R. Todd, M. Forstmann, P. Burgmer, A. W. Brooks, and A. D. Galinsky, "Anxious and Egocentric: How Specific Emotions Influence Perspective Taking," *Journal of Experimental Psychology: General* 144, no. 2 (April 2015): 374–91.
10. Committee on Communications, American Academy of Pediatrics, "Media Violence," *Pediatrics* 95, no. 6 (June 1995): 949–51.
11. Number of violent acts on television by viewed by age eighteen quoted in Ron Taffel, *Nurturing Good Children Now* (New York: Golden Books, 1999), p. 18.
12. Nick Bilton, "Looking at Link Between Violent Video Games and Lack of Empathy," *New York Times*, June 15, 2014, http://bits.blogs.nytimes.com/2014/06/15/looking-at-link-between-violent-video-games-and-lack-of-empathy/.
13. I. Orue, B. J. Bushman, E. Calvete, S. Thomaes, B. Orobio de Castro, and R. Hutteman, "Monkey See, Monkey Do, Monkey Hurt: Longitudinal Effects of Exposure to Violence on Children's Aggressive Behavior," *Social Psychological and Personality Science* 2, no. 4 (July 2011): 432–37.
14. Alice Park, "How Playing Violent Video Games May Change the Brain," *Time*, December 2, 2011, http://healthland.time.com/2011/12/02/how-playing-violent-video-games-may-change-the-brain/.
15. Randy Vogt, "How Refs Can Deal with Spectator Abuse," *Soccer America*, April 10, 2012, http://www.socceramerica.com/article/46300/how-refs-can-deal-with-spectator-abuse.html.
16. Ellen Galinsky, *Ask the Children* (New York: Morrow, 1999), and Ellen Galinsky, "Do Working Parents Make the Grade?" *Newsweek*, August 30, 1999, pp. 52–56.
17. Bob Sullivan, "Students Can't Resist Distractions for Two Minutes . . . and Neither Can You," NBC News, May 18, 2013, http://www.nbcnews.com/business/consumer/students-cant-resist-distraction-two-minutes-neither-can-you-f1C9984270, accessed June 9, 2015.
18. Andrew K. Przybylski and Netta Weinstein, "Can You Connect with Me Now? How the Presence of Mobile Communication Technology Influences Face-to-Face Conversation Quality," *Journal of Social and Personal Relationships* 30, no. 3 (2012): 237–46.
19. Katrina Schwartz, "Age of Distraction: Why It's Crucial for Students to Learn to Focus,"

KQED News: "Mindshift," December 5, 2013, http://www.kqed.org/mindshift/2013/12/05/age-of-distraction-why-its-crucial-for-students-to-learn-to-focus/.

20. Dan Stober, press release, Stanford University, "Multitasking May Harm the Social and Emotional Development of Tweenage Girls, But Face-to-Face Talks Could Save the Day, Say Stanford Researchers," January 25, 2012, http://news.stanford.edu/news/2012/january/tweenage-girls-multitasking-012512.html.

21. Definition from the Inner Kids Program from Susan Kaiser Greenland: http://www.susankaisergreenland.com/inner-kids.html.

22. Y. Shoda, W. Mischel, and P. K. Peake, "Predicting Adolescent Cognitive and Self-Regulatory Competencies from Preschool Delay of Gratification," *Developmental Psychology* 26, no. 6 (1999): 978–86.

23. Terrie E. Moffitt, Richie Poulton, and Avshalom Caspi, "Lifelong Impact of Early Self-Control," *American Scientist*, September-October 2013, pp. 353–59.

24. Terrie E. Moffitt, Louise Arseneault, Daniel Belsky, Nigel Dickson, Robert J. Hancox, HonaLee Harrington, Renate Houts, Richie Poulton, Brent W. Roberts, Stephen Ross, Malcom R. Sears, W. Murray Thomson, and Avshalom Caspi, "A Gradient of Childhood Self-Control Predicts Health, Wealth, and Public Safety," *Proceedings of the National Academy of Sciences* 108, no. 7 (2011): 2693–98.

25. Lehrer, "Don't!" *The New Yorker*.

26. Terrie E. Moffitt et al., "A Gradient of Childhood Self-Control."

27. Richard J. Davidson with Sharon Begley, *The Emotional Life of Your Brain* (New York: Penguin, 2013), p. 161.

28. Mandy Oaklander, "Bounce Back," *Time,* June 1, 2015, p. 42.

29. R. J. Davidson, J. Kabat-Zinn, J. Schumacher, M. Rosenkranz, D. Muller, S. F. Santorelli, F. Urbanowski, A. Harrington, K. Bonus, and J. F. Sheridan, "Alterations in Brain and Immune Function Produced by Mindfulness Meditation," *Psychosomatic Medicine* 65, no. 4 (July-August 2003): 564–70.

30. Netta Weinstein, Kirk W. Brown, and Richard M. Ryan, "A Multi-Method Examination of the Effects of Mindfulness on Stress Attribution, Coping, and Emotional Well-Being," *Journal of Research in Personality* 43, no. 3 (2009): 374–85.

31. C. E. Kerr, "Effects of Mindfulness Meditation Training on Anticipatory Alpha Modulation in Primary Somatosensory Cortex," *Brain Research Bulletin* 85, no. 3–4 (May 2011): 96–103.

32. A. Moore, T. Gruber, J. Derose, and P. Malinowki, "Regular, Brief Mindfulness Meditation Practice Improves Electrophysiological Markers of Attention Control," *Frontiers in Human Neuroscience* 6 (February 10, 2012): 18, doi:10.3389/fnhum.2012.00018.

33. F. Zeidan, S. K. Johnson, B. J. Diamond, Z. David, and P. Goolkasian, "Mindfulness Meditation Improves Cognitive: Evidence of Brief Mental Training," *Consciousness and Cognition* 19, no. 2 (June 2010): 597–605.

34. Brigid Schulte, "Harvard Neuroscientist: Meditation Not Only Reduces Stress, Here's How It Changes Your Brain," *Washington Post*, May 26, 2015, http://www.washingtonpost.com/news/inspired-life/wp/2015/05/26/harvard-neuroscientist-meditation-not-only-reduces-stress-it-literally-changes-your-brain/.

35. Jennifer S. Mascaro, James K. Rilling, Lobsang Tenzin Negi, and Charles L. Raison, "Compassion Meditation Enhances Empathic Accuracy and Related Neural Activity," *Social Cognitive Affective Neuroscience* 8, no. 10 (January 2013): 48–55.

36. H. Y. Weng, A. S. Fox, A. J. Shackman, D. E. Stodola, J. Z. K. Caldwell, M. C. Olson, G. M. Rogerts, and R. J. Davidson, "Compassion Training Alters Altruism and Neural Responses to Suffering," *Psychological Science* 24, no. 7 (July 2013): 1171–80.

37. David L. Kirp, "Meditation Transforms Roughest San Francisco Schools," *San Francisco Chronicle*, January 12, 2014, http://www.sfgate.com/opinion/openforum/article /Meditation-transforms-roughest-San-Francisco-5136942.php.

38. Cynthia McFadden, Tim Sandler, and Elisha Fieldstadt, "San Francisco Schools Transformed by the Power of Meditation," NBC News, January 1, 2015, http://www.nbcnews .com/nightly-news/san-francisco-schools-transformed-power-meditation-n276301.

39. Adolescents reared in suburban homes with an average family income of $120,000 were found to have the highest stress levels: Amy Novotney, "The Price of Affluence," *Monitor on Psychology*, January 2009, http://www.apa.org/monitor/2009/01/teens.aspx.

40. Kimberly A. Schonert-Reichl, Eva Oberle, Molly Stewart Lawlor, David Abbott, Kimberly Thomson, Tim F. Oberlander, and Adele Diamond, "Enhancing Cognitive and Social-Emotional Development Through a Simple-to-Administer Mindfulness-Based School Program for Elementary School Children: A Randomized Controlled Trial," *Developmental Psychology* 51, no. 1 (2015): 52–56.

41. Maryanna Klatt, Karen Harpster, Emma Browne, Susan White, and Jane Case-Smith, "Feasibility and Preliminary Outcomes for Move-Into-Learning: An Arts-Based Mindfulness Classroom Intervention," *Journal of Positive Psychology* 8, no. 3 (2013): 233–41.

42. Willem Kuyken, Katherine Weare, Obioha C. Ukoumunne, Rachael Vicary, Nicola Motton, Richard Burnett, Chris Cullen, Sarah Hennelly, and Felicia Huppert, "Effectiveness of the Mindfulness in Schools Programme: Non-Randomised Controlled Feasibility Study," *British Journal of Psychiatry* 203, no. 2 (August 2013): 126-31.

43. D. S. Black and R. Fernando, "Mindfulness Training and Classroom Behavior Among Lower-Income and Ethnic Minority Elementary School Children," *Journal of Child and Family Studies* 22, no. 7 (2013): 1242–46, http://link.springer.com/article/10.1007 /s10826-013-9784-4.

44. Vicki Zakrzewski's advice on breathing to activate vagus nerve based on a personal phone conversation and email exchange, June 9, 2015.

45. Glitter Calming Jar recipe from doodlecraft, Instructables: http://www.instructables .com/id/DIY-Calming-Glitter-Jars/.

46. Kind wishes and thinking about helpers adapted from the Madison Metropolitan School District curriculum developed by Richard Davidson. Kelly April Tyrrell, "'Kindness Curriculum' Boosts School Success in Preschoolers," press release, University of Madison—Wisconsin, January 23, 2015, http://www.news.wisc.edu/23437.

Chapter 6: Empathetic Children Practice Kindness

1. Quotes from Su Chafin based on several personal phone, email, and Skyped conversations from February 2014 to January 2015.

2. Chaz Schmitt quoted by Maddy Lauria, "Spreading SMAK Throughout the State," *Beacon* (Georgetown, DE), February 6, 2014, http://www.milfordbeacon.com/article/20140206 /NEWS/140209804.

3. Hannah Knechel quote cited by Maddy Lauria, "Spreading SMAK Throughout the State," *Beacon* (Georgetown, DE), February 6, 2014.

4. Hannah Knechel's response, based on a public exchange on Twitter with the author on June 4, 2014.

5. Stephanie Castillo, "13 Ways to Be Nicer," *Prevention*, June 7, 2012, http://www.prevention .com/mind-body/emotional-health/doing-kind-acts-reduces-anxiety-study.

6. Madeline Levine, *The Price of Privilege: How Parental Pressure and Material Advantage*

Are Creating a Generation of Disconnected and Unhappy Kids (New York: HarperPerennial, 2008).

7. Richard Weissbourd and Stephanie Jones, "The Children We Mean to Raise: The Real Messages Adults Are Sending About Values," Making Caring Common Project (Cambridge, MA: Harvard Graduate School of Education, 2014), http://sites.gse.harvard.edu/sites /default/files/making-caring-common/files/mcc_report_the_children_we_mean_to _raise_0.pdf.

8. James H. Fowler and Nicholas A. Christakis, "Cooperative Behavior Cascades in Human Social Networks," *Proceedings of the National Academy of Sciences* 107, no. 12 (March 8, 2010): 5334–38.

9. University of California–San Diego, "Acts of Kindness Spread Surprisingly Easily: Just a Few People Can Make a Difference," *ScienceDaily*, March 10, 2010, www.sciencedaily .com/releases/2010/03/100308151049.htm, accessed January 1, 2015.

10. Quote from Christine Carter, *Raising Happiness: 10 Simple Steps for More Joyful Kids and Happier Parents* (New York: Ballantine, 2011). Cited by Eric Barker in "How to Raise Happy Kids: 10 Steps Backed by Science," *Time,* March 24, 2014, http://time.com/35496 /how-to-raise-happy-kids-10-steps-backed-by-science/.

11. Elizabeth Svoboda, "Pay It Forward," *Psychology Today,* July 2006, http://www .psychologytoday.com/articles/200607/pay-it-forward.

12. Sonja Lyubomirsky, *The How of Happiness: A Scientific Approach to Getting the Life You Want* (New York: Penguin, 2008), p. 130.

13. K. Layous, S. K. Nelson, E. Oberle, K. A. Schonert-Reichl, and S. Lyubomirsky, "Kindness Counts: Prompting Prosocial Behavior in Preadolescents Boosts Peer Acceptance and Well-Being," *PLoS ONE* 7, no. 12 (2012), e51380, doi:10.1371/journal.pone.0051380.

14. Nancy Eisenberg, *The Caring Child* (Cambridge, MA: Harvard University Press, 1992), pp. 91–97.

15. Eisenberg, *The Caring Child.*

16. E. Midlarksy and J. H. Bryan, "Affect Expressions and Children's Imitative Altruism," *Journal of Experimental Research in Personality* 6, no. 2–3 (1972): 195–203.

17. Emily Esfahani Smith, "Masters of Love," *The Atlantic,* June 12, 2014, http://www.the atlantic.com/health/archive/2014/06/happily-ever-after/372573/2/.

18. E. Staub, *The Development of Prosocial Behavior in Children* (Morristown, NJ: General Learning Press, 1975).

19. Kindness Jar developed by Shipley School teachers Tina Wattles and Linda Redding; empathy-stretching strategy from the author's visit to the school and email correspondence with Usha Balamore, January 9, 2015.

20. Marceen Farsakian, "Kind Kids Club," The Random Acts of Kindness Foundation, https:// www.randomactsofkindness.org/kindness-videos/6813-kind-kids-club.

21. Idea from Qualicum Beach Elementary School in Qualicum, British Columbia, based on author's school visit and correspondence with the staff member Cathy Van Herwaarden on September 26, 2010.

Chapter 7: Empathetic Children Think "Us" Not "Them"

1. Rebecca A. London, Sebastian Castrechini, Katie Stokes-Guinan, and Lisa Westrich, "Findings from an Experimental Evaluation of Playworks: Effects on Play, Physical Activity and Recess," Mathematica Policy Research, Robert Wood Johnson Foundation, May 2013.

2. Randi Hogan and Norris P. West, "Recess: The Fourth 'R'?," *Baltimore Sun*, August 25, 2014, http://articles.baltimoresun.com/news/bs-ed-playworks-recess-20140825_1_playworks-recess-playworks-schools-school-climate, accessed May 15, 2015.

3. Playworks quote by Chicago public school principal based on email exchange, and email conversation with Jeannette Claassen and Beth Kimberly, head of Digital Marketing for Playworks, May 11, 2015.

4. Jill Vialet comments based on a personal phone conversation with the author, May 16, 2015.

5. Richard Moss, "Muhammad Ali and the World's Shortest Poem," Physical Education Update Blog, March 10, 2008, http://blog.physical-education-update.com/?p=119.

6. Roman Krznaric, *Empathy: A Handbook for Revolution* (London: Rider, 2014), p. 73.

7. Alfie Kohn, *The Brighter Side of Human Nature* (New York: Basic Books, 1990), p. 93.

8. Richard Sennett, *Together: The Rituals, Pleasures and Politics of Cooperation* (London: Allen Lane, 2012), p. 6.

9. William J. Doherty, "Overscheduled Kids, Underconnected Families: The Research Evidence," Putting Family First, May 2006, http://web.archive.org/web/20060501041926.

10. Rhonda Clements, "Research Finds Decline in Outdoor Play," *Education Update*, June 2003, p. 11, http://www.educationupdate.com/archives/2003/june03/issue/assets/edupdate_june03.pdf.

11. Peter Gray quote cited by Christine Gross-Loh, *Parenting Without Borders: Surprising Lessons Parents Around the World Can Teach Us* (New York: Penguin, 2014), pp. 148–149.

12. Jeremy Rifkin, *The Empathic Civilization: The Race to Global Consciousness in a World in Crisis* (New York: Jeremy P. Tarcher, 2009), p. 94.

13. Barbara Bronson Gray, "Over-scheduling Kids May Be Detrimental to Their Development," CBS News, July 8, 2014: http://www.cbsnews.com/news/over-scheduling-kids-may-be-detrimental-to-their-development.

14. Jane E. Barker, A. D. Semenov, L. Michaelson, L. S. Provan, H. R. Snyder, and Y. Munakata, "Less-Structured Time in Children's Daily Lives Predicts Self-Directed Executive Functioning," *Frontiers in Psychology* 5 (June 17, 2014): 593, doi:10.3389/fpsyg.2014.00593.

15. Jane E. Barker et al., "Less-Structured Time in Children's Daily Lives Predicts Self-Directed Executive Functioning."

16. Forty percent of American schools either eliminated a daily recess period or have considering doing away with it, based on survey of 15,000 elementary school districts by the American Association for the Child's Right to Play and cited by Judith Newman, "How to Let Kids Be Kids," *Redbook*, August 2008, p. 188.

17. Centers for Disease Control and Prevention, *The Association Between School-Based Physical Activity, Including Physical Education, and Academic Performance* (Atlanta: US Department of Health and Human Services, 2010), April 2010, http://www.cdc.gov/HealthyYouth/health_and_academics/pdf/pape_executive_summary.pdf.

18. Clifton B. Parker, "School Recess Offers Benefits to Student Well-Being, Stanford Educator Reports," press release, Stanford University, February 11, 2015, http://news.stanford.edu/news/2015/february/recess-benefits-school-021115.html.

19. Kenneth R. Ginsberg, "The Importance of Play in Promoting Healthy Child Development and Maintaining Strong Parent-Child Bonds," *Pediatrics* 119 (January 2007).

20. Jamil Zaki, "Empathy: A Motivated Account," *Psychological Bulletin* 140, no. 6 (2014): 1608–47.

21. Alfie Kohn, "It's Hard to Get Left Out of a Pair," *Psychology Today*, October 1987, pp. 53–57.

22. Bullying statistics gathered from Stopbullying.gov, "Facts About Bullying," http://www
.stopbullying.gov/news/media/facts/#stats, accessed May 19, 2015.

23. Rose Schmidt and Greg Toppo, "Ripples of Racism Spur Campuses Into Action," *USA
Today*, Nov. 9, 2015, A1.

24. M. Sherif, O. J. Harvey, B. J. White, W. R. Hood, and C. W. Sherif, *Intergroup Conflict
and Cooperation: The Robbers Cave Experiment*, vol. 10 (Norman, OK: University Book
Exchange, 1961).

25. Sherif et al., *Intergroup Conflict*.

26. Sherif description of Greek brutality in Izmir, Turkey, May 15, 1919, described by Stefan
Klein, *Survival of the Nicest: How Altruism Made Us Human and Why It Pays to Get Along*,
(New York: The Experiment, 2014), pp. 154–55; Paul Bloom, *Just Babies: The Origins of
Good and Evil* (New York: Crown Publishers, 2013), pp. 115–18.

27. M. Sherif and C. W. Sherif, *Groups in Harmony and Tension: An Integration of Studies
on Intergroup Relations* (New York: Harper and Bros., 1953). M. Sherif, "Experiments in
Group Conflict," in Jennifer M. Jenkins et al., eds., *Human Emotions: A Reader* (Oxford:
Blackwell, 1998), pp. 245–52. M. Sherif et al., *Intergroup Conflict and Cooperation: The
Robbers Cave Experiment*.

28. "Muzafer Sherif, 82, Psychologist Who Studied Hostility of Groups," *New York Times*,
October 27, 1988, http://www.nytimes.com/1988/10/27/obituaries/muzafer-sherif-82
-psychologist-who-studied-hostility-of-groups.html.

29. M. Sherif and C. W. Sherif, *Groups in Harmony and Tension*. M. Sherif, "Experiments in
Group Conflict," *Scientific American* 195, no. 5 (1956).

30. Joseph Adelson, "The Psychology of Altruism," *Commentary*, November 1988, p. 42.

31. Kohn, *The Brighter Side of Human Nature*, p. 94.

32. Susan Gilbert, "A Conversation with Elliot Aronson: No One Left to Hate: Averting
Columbines," *New York Times*, March 27, 2001.

33. E. Aronson and N. Osherow, "Cooperation, Prosocial Behavior, and Academic Performance: Experiments in the Desegregated Classroom," *Applied Social Psychology Annual* 1
(1980): 163–96.

34. D. M. Desforges, C. G. Lord, S. L. Ramsey, J. A. Mason, M. D. Van Leeuwen, S. C. West,
and M. R. Lepper, "Effects of Structured Cooperative Contact on Changing Negative
Attitudes Toward Stigmatized Social Groups," *Journal of Personality and Social Psychology* 60, no. 4 (1991): 531–44; R. Lazarowitz, R. Hertz-Lazarowitz, and J. H. Baird,
"Learning Science in a Cooperative Setting: Academic Achievement and Affective Outcomes," *Journal of Research in Science Teaching* 31, no. 10 (1994): 1121–31; S. Sharan,
"Cooperative Learning in Small Groups: Recent Methods and Effects on Achievement,
Attitudes, and Ethnic Relations," *Review of Educational Research* 50, no. 2 (1980): 241–
71; I. Walker and M. Crogan, "Academic Performance, Prejudice, and the Jigsaw Classroom: New Pieces to the Puzzle," *Journal of Community & Applied Social Psychology* 8,
no. 6 (1998): 381–93.

35. Gilbert, "A Conversation with Elliot Aronson," *New York Times*.

36. Elliot Aronson, *Nobody Left to Hate: Teaching Compassion After Columbine* (New York:
Worth Publishers, 2000), pp. 149–51.

37. Gilbert, "A Conversation with Elliot Aronson," *New York Times*.

38. Norah Rabiah, "School-wide Morning Meetings," *The Maury Messenger*, March 2015, http://
mauryelementary.com/wp-content/uploads/2015/04/March_2015.pdf, p. 3, accessed
May 21, 2015.

39. Sara Bullard, *Teaching Tolerance* (New York: Doubleday, 1996), pp. 180–81.

40. Richard Weissbourd and the Making Caring Common Team, "Leaning Out: Teen Girls

and the Leadership Bias," Making Caring Common Project (Cambridge, MA: Harvard Graduate School of Education, August 2015), http://sites.gse.harvard.edu/sites/default /files/making-caring-common/files/mcc_leanout_report.pdf.

41. Kathleen T. Horning, Merri V. Lindgren, and Megan Schliesman, "A Few Observations of Publishing in 2012," Cooperative Children's Book Center, 2013, http://ccbc.education .wisc.edu/books/choiceintro13.asp, accessed May 19, 2013.

42. KidsHealth Survey: Kendall Marcocci, "HealthAmerica KidsHealth Poll Finds Kids Feel Too Busy," August 17, 2006, http://businesswire.com/news/home/20060817005326/en /HealthAmerica-KidsHealth-Poll-Finds-Kids-Feel-Busy.

Chapter 8: Empathetic Children Stick Their Necks Out

1. Andrew Martin, "Courage in the Classroom: Exploring a New Framework Predicting Academic Performance and Engagement," *School Psychology Quarterly* 26, no. 2 (June 2011): 145–60, http://psychnet.apa./psycinfo/2011-09696-001.

2. Po Bronson and Ashley Merryman, "The Creativity Crisis," *Newsweek*, July 10, 2010.

3. Students present 88 percent of bullying episodes on school playground: D. Lynn Hawkins, Debra J. Pepler, and Wendy M. Craig, "Naturalistic Observations of Peer Interventions in Bullying," *Social Development* 10, no. 4 (2001): 512–27. Wendy M. Craig and Debra J. Pepler, "Peer Processes in Bullying and Victimization: An Observational Study," *Exceptionality Education Canada* 5, no. 3–4 (1995): 81–95.

4. Wendy M. Craig and Debra J. Pepler, "Observations of Bullying and Victimization on the Playground," *Canadian Journal of School Psychology*, 2, 41–60. Richard Weissbourd and Stephanie M. Jones, "Preventing Bullying Begins with Us," *Huffington Post,* February 28, 2012.

5. Dacher Keltner and Jason Marsh, "We Are All Bystanders," in Dacher Keltner, Jason Marsh, and Jeremy Adam Smith, eds., *The Compassionate Instinct* (New York: W. W. Norton & Co., 2010), p. 189.

6. G. R. Janson and R. J. Hazler, "Trauma Reactions of Bystanders and Victims to Repetitive Abuse Experiences," *Violence and Victims* 19, no. 2 (2004): 239–55. I. Rivers, V. P. Poteat, N. Noret, and N. Ashurst, "Observing Bullying at School: The Mental Health Implications of Witness Status," *School Psychology Quarterly* 24, no. 4 (2009): 211–23.

7. B. Latané and J. Darley, "Bystander 'Apathy,'" *American Scientist* 57, no. 2 (1969): 244–68.

8. J. M. Darley and C. D. Batson, " 'From Jerusalem to Jericho': A Study of Situational and Dispositional Variables in Helping Behavior," *Journal of Personality and Social Psychology* 27, no. 1 (1973): 100–108.

9. Maria Plötner, Harriet Over, Malinda Carpenter, and Michael Tomasello, "Young Children Show the Bystander Effect in Helping Situations," *Psychological Science* 26, no. 4 (2015): 499–506.

10. Ervin Staub, D. Fellner Jr., J. Berry, and K. Morange, "Passive and Active Bystandership Across Grades in Response to Students Bullying Other Students," in *The Psychology of Good and Evil: Why Children, Adults, and Groups Help and Harm Others*, ed. Ervin Staub (New York: Cambridge University Press, 2003), pp. 240–43.

11. Kim Clark, "Bringing Up Bold Babies," *U.S. News & World Report*, August 20–27, 2001, pp. 76–77.

12. John Darley quote cited by: Dacher Keltner and Jason Marsh, "We Are All Bystanders," in Dacher Keltner, Jason Marsh, and Jeremy Adam Smith, eds., *The Compassionate Instinct*.

13. Ron Arias, "Five-Year-Old Rocky Lyons, Son of the Jets' Star, Thought He Could Save His

Mom's Life—and He Did," *People*, December 14, 1987, http://www.people.com/people/archive/article/0,20097833,00.html.

14. Esther Davidowitz, "Children of Courage," *Woman's Day*, March 20, 1990, pp. 92 and 135. Jack Canfield and Mark Victor Hansen, *Chicken Soup for the Soul: 101 Stories to Open the Heart and Rekindle the Spirit* (Deerfield Beach, FL: Health Communications, Inc., 1993), pp. 153–55. (I contributed the story to this volume.)

15. Ron Arias, "Five-Year-Old Rocky Lyons," *People*.

16. Samuel P. Oliner and Pearl M. Oliner, *The Altruistic Personality* (New York: Touchstone, 1992).

17. D. Lynn Hawkins, Debra J. Pepler, and Wendy M. Craig, "Naturalistic Observations of Peer Interventions in Bullying," *Social Development*.

18. Michael Phelps, *No Limits: The Will to Succeed* (New York: Free Press, 2008), p. 9.

19. Described as "Combat Lamaze" by Amanda Ripley, *The Unthinkable: Who Survives When Disaster Strikes—and Why* (New York: Harmony, 2009), p. 75.

20. Quote based on author's personal conversation with Travis Price, September 20, 2014, at the Hero Round Table Conference in Flint, Michigan.

21. Ira Berkow, "Two Men Who Did the Right Thing," *New York Times*, November 2, 2005, http://www.nytimes.com/2005/11/02/sports/baseball/two-men-who-did-the-right-thing.html.

22. Mohandas K. Gandhi, *Gandhi: An Autobiography* (Boston: Beacon Press, 1993), p. 6.

23. Description of Rosa Parks culled from her obituaries and described by Susan Caine in *Quiet: The Power of Introverts in a World That Can't Stop Talking* (New York: Broadway Paperbacks, 2013), p. 2.

24. Description of Captain Sullenberger: Chesley Sullenberger, *Highest Duty*, p. 10.

25. *We Bought a Zoo*, screenplay by Aline Brosh McKenna and Cameron Crowe, 20th Century Fox, April 3, 2012. PG rating. Based on the book by Benjamin Mee, *We Bought a Zoo* (New York: Weinstein Books, 2011). Video clip: http://www.hitfix.com/videos/we-bought-a-zoo-20-seconds-of-courage.

Chapter 9: Empathetic Children Want to Make a Difference

1. Art Carey, "A Child's Kindness Matures," December 18, 2003, *Philadelphia Inquirer*, http://articles.philly.com/2003-12-18/news/25470498_1_homeless-man-trevor-s-campaign-trevor-ferrell.

2. Frank and Janet Ferrell, *Trevor's Place: The Story of the Boy Who Brings Hope to the Homeless* (San Francisco: Harper & Row, 1985), p. 114.

3. Ferrell and Ferrell, *Trevor's Place*.

4. Ronald Reagan, Address Before a Joint Session of Congress on the State of the Union, February 4, 1986.

5. Description of Trevor's Campaign for the Homeless on http://www.trevorscampaign.org/12/30/14.

6. Harry Readhead, "Boy, 8, Raises $1 Million to Help Research Best Friend's Incurable Disease," *Metro News*, December 17, 2014, http://metro.co.uk/2014/12/17/boy-8-raises-1million-to-help-research-best-friends-incurable-disease-4990465/, accessed August 25, 2015.

7. Mary Murray, "American Girl, Just 12, Builds 27 Homes in Haiti," NBC News, November 14, 2011, http://dailynightly.nbcnews.com/_news/2011/11/14/8800940-american-girl-just-12-builds-27-homes-in-haiti, accessed August 25, 2015.

8. CNN Staff, "3 Young Wonders Changing the World," CNN, December 16, 2013, http://www.cnn.com/2013/12/16/world/cnnheroes-young-wonders/, accessed August 25, 2015.

9. Erin Anderssen, "Doing Good Deeds Can Improve Health, Make You Happier, Scientists Suggest," *Globe and Mail,* January 15, 2005.

10. Allan Luks, *The Healing Power of Doing Good* (New York: iUniverse, 2000); Allan Luks, "What Satisfies Us Today?" *Western Journal of Medicine* 174, no. 1 (January 2001): 78.

11. Sara Konrath, Andrea Fuhrel-Foris, and Alina Lou, "Motives for Volunteering Are Associated with Mortality Risk in Older Adults," *Health Psychology* 31, no. 1 (2011): 87–96.

12. Lara B. Aknin, J. Kiley Hamlin, and Elizabeth W. Dunn, "Giving Leads to Happiness in Young Children," *PLoS ONE* 7, no. 6 (2012), e39211, doi:10.1371/journal.pone.0039211.

13. J. M. Twenge, S. M. Campbell, B. J. Hoffman, and C. E. Lance, "Generational Differences in Work Values: Leisure and Extrinsic Values Increasing, Social and Intrinsic Values Decreasing," *Journal of Management* 36, no. 5 (2010): 1117–42; J. M. Twenge, S. Konrath, J. D. Foster, W. K. Campbell, and W. B. Bushman, "Egos Inflating over Time: A Cross-Temporal Meta-Analysis of the Narcissistic Personality Inventory," *Journal of Personality* 76, no. 4 (2008): 875–903.

14. Keith Perry, "One in Five Children Just Want to Be Rich When They Grow Up," *Telegraph,* August 5, 2014, http://www.telegraph.co.uk/news/newstopics/howaboutthat/11014591 /One-in-five-children-just-want-to-be-rich-when-they-grow-up.html.

15. Emma Brockes, "I Want to Be Famous," *Guardian,* April 16, 2010, http://www.theguard ian.com/lifeandstyle/2010/apr/17/i-want-to-be-famous.

16. Y. T. Uhls and P. M. Greenfield, "The Rise of Fame: An Historical Content Analysis," *Cyberpsychology: Journal of Psychosocial Research on Cyberspace* 5, no. 1 (2011): article 1.

17. S. D. Boon and C. D. Lomore, "Admirer-Celebrity Relationships Among Young Adults," *Human Communication Research* 27, no. 3 (July 2001): 432–65, http://onlinelibrary.wiley .com/doi/10.1111/j.1468-2958.2001.tb00788.x/abstract, accessed July 9, 2015.

18. Philip Zimbardo quoted by Kendra Cherry, "Teaching Heroism," *About Health* http://psy chology.about.com/od/socialpsychology/a/teaching-heroism.htm, accessed July 9, 2015.

19. Sharon Jayson, "Generation Y's Goal? Wealth and Fame," *USA Today,* January 10, 2007, http://usatoday30.usatoday.com/news/nation/2007-01-09-gen-y-cover_x.htm, accessed July 8, 2015.

20. Paul K. Piff, Daniel M. Stancato, Stéphane Côté, Rodolfo Mendoza-Denton, and Dacher Keltner, "Higher Social Class Predicts Increased Unethical Behavior," *Proceedings of the National Academy of Sciences* 109, no. 11, 4086-91. Daisy Grewal, "How Wealth Reduces Compassion," *Scientific American,* April 10, 2012, http://www.scientificamerican.com /article/how-wealth-reduces-compassion/.

21. P. K. Piff, M. W. Kraus, S. Cote, B. H. Cheng, and D. Keltner, "Having Less, Giving More: The Influence of Social Class on Prosocial Behavior,"*Journal of Personality and Social Psychology* 99, no. 5 (November 2010): 771–84.

22. Maia Szalavitz, "The Rich Are Different: More Money, Less Empathy," *Time,* November 24, 2010, http://healthland.time.com/2010/11/24/the-rich-are-different-more -money-less-empathy/.

23. Lisa Esposito, "Unhappy Kids Are More Materialistic, Study Finds," HealthDay, August 21, 2012, http://health.usnews.com/health-news/news/articles/2-12/08/21/unhappy-kids-are -more-materialistic-study-finds, accessed July 29, 2015.

24. J. M. Twenge and T. Kasser, "Generational Changes in Materialism and Work Centrality, 1976–2007: Associations with Temporal Changes in Societal Insecurity and Materialistic Role Modeling," *Personality and Social Psychology Bulletin* 39, no. 7 (2013): 883–97.

25. Lara B. Aknin, Elizabeth W. Dunn, and Michael I. Norton, "Happiness Runs in a Circular Motion: Evidence for a Positive Feedback Loop between Prosocial Spending and Happiness," *Journal of Happiness Studies* 13, no. 2 (April 2012): 347–55. Kathryn E. Buchanan

and Anat Bardi, "Acts of Kindness and Acts of Novelty Affect Life Satisfaction," *Journal of Social Psychology* 150, no. 3 (2010): 235–37.

26. The survey of 300 college students was conducted in 2010 by psychology professor Neil Montgomery of Keene State College in New Hampshire and cited in: Rachael Rettner, "'Helicopter' Parents Have Neurotic Kids, Study Suggests," *LiveScience*, June 3, 2010, http://www.livescience.com/10663-helicopter-parents-neurotic-kids-study-suggests.html.

27. A study of 438 college students: L. M. Padilla-Walker and L. J. Nelson, "Black Hawk Down? Establishing Helicopter Parenting as a Distinct Construct from Other Forms of Parental Control During Emerging Adulthood," *Journal of Adolescence* 35, no. 5 (October 2012): 1177–90.

28. Terri LeMoyne and Tom Buchanan, "Does 'Hovering' Matter? Helicopter Parenting and Its Effect on Well-Being," *Sociological Spectrum: Mid-South Sociological Association* 31, no. 4 (2011): 399–418.

29. Julie Lythcott-Haims, "Kids of Helicopter Parents Are Sputtering Out," *Slate*, July 2015, http://www.slate.com/articles/double_x/doublex/2015/07/helicopter_parenting _is_increasingly_correlated_with_college_age_depression.2.html, accessed July 24, 2015.

30. "Born Good? Babies Help Unlock the Origins of Morality," CBS News, November 18, 2012, https://www.youtube.com/watch?v=FRvVFW85IcU.

31. J. Kiley Hamlin, Karen Wynn, and Paul Bloom, "Social Evaluation by Preverbal Infants," *Nature* 450, no. 2 (2007): 557–59.

32. Paul Bloom, "The Moral Life of Babies," *New York Times*, May 5, 2010, http://www .nytimes.com/2010/05/09/magazine/09babies-t.html.

33. "Roots of Altruism Show in Babies' Helping Hands," Associated Press, March 2, 2006, http://www.nbcnews.com/id/11641621/ns/health-childrens_health/t/roots-altruism -show-babies-helping-hands/#.VphINvkrk02/. Felix Warneken, "The Development of Altruistic Behavior: Helping in Children and Chimpanzees," *Social Research* 80, no. 2 (Summer 2013): 431–42.

34. F. Warneken and M. Tomasello, "Helping and Cooperation at 14 Months of Age," *Infancy* 11, no. 3 (2007): 271–94.

35. Rick Weissbourd and Stephanie Jones, "The Child We Mean to Raise: The Real Messages Adults Are Sending About Values," Making Caring Common Project (Cambridge, MA: Harvard Graduate School of Education, 2004), http://sites.gse.harvard.edu/sites /default/files/making-caring-common/files/mcc_report_the_children_we_mean_to _raise_0.pdf.

36. Alfie Kohn, *The Brighter Side of Human Nature* (New York: Basic Books, 1990), p. 203.

37. Karina Schumann, Jamil Zaki, and Carol S. Dweck, "Addressing the Empathy Deficit: Beliefs About the Malleability of Empathy Predict Effortful Responses When Empathy Is Challenging," *Journal of Personality and Social Psychology* 107, no. 3 (2014): 475–93.

38. Nancy Eisenberg and Paul H. Mussen, *The Roots of Prosocial Behavior in Children* (New York: Cambridge University Press, 1996), p. 155.

39. Author's personal interview with Marilyn Perilyn on February 11, 2014. Lisa Goddard, "All in the Family," *Sun-Sentinel*, December 22, 1996, http://articles.sun-sentinel .com/1996-12-22/news/9612190172_1_needy-children-children-s-home-society-kids, accessed July 22, 2015.

40. David C. McClelland, "Characteristics of Successful Entrepreneurs," *Journal of Creative Behavior* 21, no. 3 (1987): 219–33. Cited by David Bornstein in *How to Change the World* (New York: Oxford University Press, 2007), p. 238.

41. Craig Kielburger and Marc Kielburger, *Me to We: Finding Meaning in a Material World* (New York: Simon & Schuster, 2006), p. 13.

42. Tracy Rysavy, "Free the Children: The Story of Craig Kielburger," *Yes!*, September 30, 1999, http://www.yesmagazine.org/issues/power-of-one/free-the-children-the-story-of-craig-kielburger.

43. Rysavy, "Free the Children."

44. ABC News, "California Teen Collects 25,000 Books in Book Drive, Inspires Others," July 22, 2015, https://gma.yahoo.com/california-teen-collects-25-000-books-book-drive-110819383.html, accessed July 27, 2015.

45. Paul Slovic, " 'If I look at the mass I will never act': Psychic Numbing and Genocide," *Judgment and Decision Making* 2 (2007): 79–95.

46. Paul Slovic quote cited by Shankar Vedantam, "Why Your Brain Wants to Help One Child in Need—But Not Millions," NPR, November 5, 2014, http://www.npr.org/sections/goatsandsoda/2014/11/05/361433850/why-your-brain-wants-to-help-one-child-in-need-but-not-millions, accessed August 16, 2015.

47. Amber Melke-Peters, "Pay It Forward: No Kid Goes Hungry," *FundRazr*, Howell, MI, Michigan Radio, "Third Grader Raises Money for Hot School Lunches for Low-Income Kids," March 7, 2014, http://michiganradio.org/post/third-grader-raises-money-hot-school-lunches-low-income-kids#stream/0.

48. Craig and Marc Kielburger, "How to Discuss the News with Your Kids," *Canadian Living*, February 2007, p. 140.

49. Not for Sale, "Bay Area 8-Year-Old Makes a (Lemonade) Stand to End Slavery," June 27, 2012, https://notforsalecampaign.org/stories/2012/06/27/bay-area-8-year-old-makes-a-lemonade-stand-to-end-slavery/, accessed August 5, 2015.

50. GreatSchools video: *Empathy by Example*, http://www.greatschools.org/gk/videos/empathy-by-example/.

51. Jennifer Marino Walters, "Buddy Bench," *Scholastic*, December 13, 2013, http://magazines.scholastic.com/news/2013/12/Buddy-Bench, accessed September 29, 2014.

52. Kevin Curwick's "Nice It Forward Campaign," based on phone interview and email exchange with the author, January 7, 2015.

53. " 'Saint Trevor' Still Cares for the Less Fortunate," Associated Press, December 13, 2003, http://www.nbcnews.com/id/3692534/.

54. Schumann, Zaki, and Dweck, "Addressing the Empathy Deficit."

55. Kimberly Yam, "Boy Collects 79 Coats for Homeless Families, Inspired by a Random Act of Kindness," *Huffington Post*, December 17, 2017, http://www.huffingtonpost.com/2014/12/17/boy-donates-79-coats_n_6342764.html.

Epilogue: The Empathy Advantage

1. Fiona Macdonald, "The Skate Girls of Kabul," BBC, May 5, 2015, http://www.bbc.com/culture/story/20150501-the-skate-girls-of-kabul. Orlando von Einsiedel, "Skateistan: To Live and Skate Kabul," January 2010, http://aeon.co/video/society/skateistan-kabul-skateboarding-afghanistan/. Jessica Fulford-Dobson, *Skate Girls of Kabul*, http://www.jessicafd.com BBC World Services.

2. Personal and phone interview with Noah Abrams, November 16, 17, and 18, 2014.

3. Shia Rubin, "Arab-Jewish Preschool Oasis Amid Violence," *USA Today*, Nov 1, 2015, B1.

4. Rubin, "Arab-Jewish Preschool Oasis Amid Violence."

5. Matthew Diebel, "Multitasking Teens Pick Texting Over Sleeping," *USA Today,* Nov. 4, 2015, B1.

6. R. Aciego, L. Garcia, and M. Betancort, "The Benefits of Chess for the Intellectual and Social-Emotional Enrichment in Schoolchildren," *Spanish Journal of Psychology* 15, no. 2 (2012): 551–59.

7. Chrissy Garten, "Beyond Peek-a-Boo: Mastering More Complex Lessons, Like Teaching Empathy," *Christian Science Monitor,* November 3, 2014, http://www.csmonitor.com /The-Culture/Family/Modern-Parenthood/2014/1103/Beyond-peek-a-boo-Mastering -more-complex-parenting-lessons-like-teaching-empathy.

8. Susan Pinker, *The Village Effect: How Face-to-Face Contact Can Make Us Healthier, Happier and Smarter* (New York: Random House, 2014).

9. Maia Szalavitz and Bruce D. Perry, *Born for Love: Why Empathy Is Essential—and Endangered* (New York: William Morrow, 2010), p. 6.

INDEX

UnSelfie

Michele Borba, Ed.D.

Teens today are 40 percent less empathetic than they were thirty years ago, with dangerous implications for children. First, it hurts children's academic performance and leads to bullying behaviors. Also, it correlates with more cheating and less resilience as well as hampering their ability to collaborate, innovate, and problem-solve—all vital skills for the global economy. *UnSelfie: Why Empathetic Kids Succeed in Our All-About-Me-World,* pinpoints the forces causing the Empathy Crisis and shares a revolutionary, researched-based, nine-step parenting plan for reversing what Dr. Borba calls the Selfie Syndrome. This guide is designed to help parents discuss how to apply the strategies in *UnSelfie* to raise empathetic, courageous, caring children with skills to thrive in a twenty-first-century, digital-driven world.

HOW TO START AND FACILITATE AN
UNSELFIE PARENT BOOK GROUP

- Identify parents interested in forming a book club to discuss *UnSelfie*.

- Determine the specific days, times, places, and frequency for your group meeting. There are several ways to divide your discussion content. Here are four possibilities, but choose the number of total book sessions based on group consensus and needs.

  ▷ Nine meetings discussing one chapter per month: Most book clubs meet once a month and discuss a different chapter in *UnSelfie*. Since there are nine chapters, the meetings would take nine months total.

  ▷ Traditional book club; one meeting total: Meet just once and discuss issues participants find most relevant.

  ▷ Two chapters per meeting; four meetings total: You might divide *UnSelfie* into four sections and discuss two chapters at each meeting.

  ▷ Three total sessions divided into discussing how to Develop Empathy, Practice Empathy, and Live Empathy: The first meeting would discuss Developing Empathy (Chapters 1, 2, 3, 4); Session two: Practicing Empathy (Chapters 5, 6, 7); Session three: Living Empathy (Chapters 8, 9, Epilogue).

- Assign a discussion leader or rotate the role at each discussion.

- Use the questions provided to facilitate discussion. Some groups ask each participant to develop one question for each meeting. The key is to make your meetings meaningful for parents.

INTRODUCTION: THE HIDDEN ADVANTAGE OF EMPATHY AND WHY IT MATTERS FOR OUR CHILDREN

1. What about *UnSelfie* piqued your interest? What do you hope to gain from these discussions?

2. How would you answer this question: "What do kids really need to be happy and successful?" (p. xiii). Do you believe empathy is integral to children's future success happiness and well-being? Despite science, why do many think empathy to be a soft skill?

3. Teens today are 40 percent less empathetic than thirty years ago. Have you seen a change in your child or his friends' character and behavior that might indicate the Selfie Syndrome?

4. *UnSelfie* describes several factors that contribute to the Empathy Deficit. Which cultural factors/parenting styles do you think affect kids' empathy capacities? Which factors can parents really control?

5. Step into the shoes of today's kids: What *invisible* and *visible* messages would you read about our culture? Are they ones that would nurture empathy and help to produce a generation of "Unselfies" or are they more likely to exacerbate the Selfie Syndrome?

6. Which of the nine essential habits do you feel are most crucial for today's twenty-first-century kids? Which habits are you instilling in your child? Which might you be overlooking?

7. How could parents teach empathy habits in such a way that their children master them and no longer need our reminders?

How might you network with other parents to cultivate children's empathy?

8. What skills will our children need to succeed in the global economy when jobs of today don't exist tomorrow? What should parents be doing to prepare kids for a world of rapid change?

9. How would you define an "Unselfie world"? What would an empathetic family, school, community, nation look and sound like? How do we create empathy in those teachable parent-child moments?

10. What behaviors would adults display in an empathetic culture? How often is your child seeing adults model courage, empathy, and compassion? How often does your child see *you* model empathy?

11. What is your hope in cultivating empathy in your children?

PART ONE: DEVELOPING EMPATHY

Chapter 1: Empathetic Children Can Recognize Feelings

1st EMPATHY HABIT: Teaching emotional literacy to help children recognize and understand the feelings and needs of others

1. Common Sense Media finds that the average child is plugged into digital devices about nine hours a day. What impact do dig-

ital devices have on kids' empathy? How do you know if your family is "too plugged in"?

2. How can parents reclaim conversation with children in a digital-driven world? How are you setting digital limits? How do we help children develop healthy relationships with peers, especially when face-to-face contact is breaking down and the internet is becoming meaner?

3. One study found that 62 percent of kids said their *parents* were too plugged in. How would your kids describe your digital habits? How can parents set a better example for their kids?

4. Why was Mary Gordon's Roots of Empathy approach successful in increasing children's empathy? What are meaningful ways to help your child experience empathy?

5. Mothers are more likely to discuss emotions with daughters than sons. What impact does it have on boys? Do you notice the tendency in your friends or yourself? What will you do to reduce the pink/blue emotion divide?

6. Tuning in to feelings is an essential part of good parenting and lays the groundwork for developing close relationships with our kids. How could developing empathy enhance your relationship with your child? How can parents cultivate their empathy so that they model empathy to their children?

7. Emotional literacy is cited as a key to motivating kids to care. How can you can help your digital native understand feelings and tune into others?

Chapter 2: Empathetic Children
Have a Moral Identity

2nd EMPATHY HABIT: Helping children develop an ethical code so they will adopt caring values that guide their integrity and activate empathy to help others

1. How have cultural values changed in ways that might affect today's children's character? What factors are increasing narcissism? Do you see a rise in youth entitlement? If so, why is this?

2. Our messages help with "depositing prosocial images in our children's identity banks so they can define themselves as caring, responsible people who value others' thoughts and feelings" (p. 27). What kinds of daily actions can parents do to nurture positive Moral Identities in their children?

3. Why do "two-thirds of adolescents rank their own personal happiness as more important than their goodness"? (p. 27). What are you doing to help your child recognize the value of caring?

4. How can parents help their children find their "respectful voice" in a disrespectful world?

5. How we praise helps kids define the type of people they believe themselves to be. Wrong praise can increase narcissism. How might you use the science-backed strategies?

6. How do you think your child would describe your family's values? What do you hope your child would say? How could you apply the steps to creating a caring family mantra?

7. "If I were the only example my child had to learn moral iden-

tity, what did she learn today?" (p. 42) How can parents tune up their behavior to exemplify social responsibility and caring?

Chapter 3: Empathetic Children Understand the Needs of Others

3rd EMPATHY HABIT: Instilling perspective taking so children can step into others' shoes to understand another's feelings, thoughts, and views

1. Do you agree that "Children's empathy is sparked by active, face-to-face experiences—not from worksheets or lectures" (p. 49)? Can you recall a teacher's lesson that helped you understand another's perspective? If so, why was it memorable? How can you provide such authentic experiences for your child?

2. "It's easier for children to empathize with people they know, or are similar to, so widen your child's perspective by exposing him to people of different backgrounds" (p. 70). How could you expand your children's social hubs so they are more likely to empathize with people who are "different" or "not like them"? What are you doing to broaden your child's empathy horizons?

3. Science finds that discipline can stretch or shrink children's perspective-taking abilities. Where on the "stretch or shrink" spectrum would you say your discipline practices fall? Which practices do you believe parents should use to nurture empathy? Are they different from how you were raised?

4. Which age-by-age strategy would you consider using or adapting (pp. 66–70) to expand your child's perspective-taking abilities? What other strategies might you consider?

Chapter 4: Empathetic Children
Have a Moral Imagination

4th EMPATHY HABIT: Instilling a moral imagination so children can use literature, films, and emotionally charged images as a source of inspiration to feel with others

1. "Books can be portals to understanding other worlds and other views, to helping our children be more open to differences and cultivate new perspectives." Which books were your childhood favorites? Which resonate with your child? Were you surprised about the power of literary fiction to activate empathy? How can you find books that pull your child's heart strings?

2. Posing the right questions can help kids vicariously step into someone else's place. What strategies might help your child see the world from other perspectives?

3. Around eight years old is generally when kids stop reading for enjoyment, and also when we typically stop reading aloud to them. How can you use the ideas outlined on pp. 85–87 to instill in your child a greater love of reading?

4. Have you considered starting a parent-child book club? If so, how would you start?

PART TWO: PRACTICING EMPATHY

Chapter 5: Empathetic Children Can Keep Their Cool

5th EMPATHY HABIT: Mastering self-regulation to help children learn to manage strong emotions and reduce personal distress so they can help others

1. Research shows that self-control is a better predictor of adult wealth, health, and happiness than grades or IQ. Do you agree? If so, why? Are today's children being raised to have self-control?

2. Are you noticing a change in children's (and adults') ability to regulate their self-control? If so, to what do you attribute the increase? How well do your children manage their emotions? What are you doing to help your children learn habits of self-regulation?

3. *UnSelfie* describes approaches that nurture children's self-regulation (like stress-management, yoga, meditation, mindfulness). Do any interest you? Have you considered a parent-child yoga group?

4. Many schools are embracing mindfulness practices. Would you consider adopting the approach in your home? How might you start? Are there ways you might join other parents (such as in playgroups, scouting, play dates) to teach self-regulation practices to your children together?

5. Which age-by-age strategy would you consider using with your children? What other self-regulation strategies have you tried? How would you know if they worked?

Chapter 6: Empathetic Children Practice Kindness

6th EMPATHY HABIT: Developing and exercising compassion to increase children's concern about the welfare and feelings of others

1. Did Harvard's survey as to the values teens deem "most important" surprise you? What values would your child say matter? Do you agree that "achievement and success" are trumping "kindness and character"? How can parents help kids realize that kindness matters?

2. Do you agree that kindness can be stretched, like a muscle? Why do many parents think that kindness is a fixed trait? How can you help your child practice kindness?

3. Jessica and Mark initiated Secret Kindness Buddies to focus on kindness and giving. Are there other family rituals (such as those on pp. 135–139) you would like to try with your kids?

4. "Kids learn kindness best through example" (p. 134). If your child had only your example to watch, would he catch kindness? How can parents be more intentional about modeling kindness?

5. Were you surprised by the findings from random acts of kindness studies with children? How could you apply Sonja Lyubomirsky's findings with your family?

6. What books and films help kids understand kindness? How could parents share selections among friends so more children can be exposed to their messages about kindness?

7. Is starting a Kid Kind Club something you might consider? If so, how might you begin?

Chapter 7: Empathetic Children
Think "Us" Not "Them"

7th EMPATHY HABIT: Cultivating collaboration to activate empathy and help children work with others to achieve shared goals for the benefit of all

1. How has the decline of unstructured play affected childhood? How much free time does your child have to learn collaborative skills?

2. How might parents join forces to use the cooperative game ideas and mix up the social scene or movie nights to boost their children's cooperative skills?

3. How are you strengthening your child's collaborative skills (playgroups, team membership, family meetings)? What family projects might help your family work together?

4. How could you use family meetings to polish your child's social-emotional skills?

5. How has stiff competition affected empathy? Are you more likely to praise "the win" or your child's camaraderie? How can parents help kids grasp that teamwork counts?

6. We empathize with those like us. How can you expand your child's circles of caring?

7. What community resources might you use to expose your child to more diversity? How do we help children understand racism and injustice happening in the world?

Chapter 8: Empathetic Children Stick Their Necks Out

8th EMPATHY HABIT: Promoting moral courage to embolden kids to speak out, step in, and help others

1. Which parenting styles curtail or strengthen children's moral courage? How does over-rescuing or a helicopter style of parenting impede? What is your style? If you are mostly in a rescue mode, how might you step back?

2. The story of Kelly and Rocky Lyons describes how a parent helped her child find his inner hero. How are you helping your child develop moral courage? What else might you do?

3. Which of the six reasons as to why kids are bystanders rather than upstanders (outlined on pp. 172–175) curtails your child and their peers from helping bullied peers? What can parents do so kids feel more comfortable coming to you or other adults for help?

4. What family courage ritual could you use to empower your child to face setbacks? How can parents help children be more likely to step in to help or comfort others?

5. Kids need heroes to inspire their moral courage. Who are your child's heroes?

6. Which books or films could help kids learn to stick their necks out for others?

7. Which moral courage builders might you use with your child? How could parents join forces to help children learn upstander strategies?

Chapter 9: Empathetic Children Want to Make a Difference

9th EMPATHY HABIT: Cultivating altruistic leadership abilities to motivate children to make a difference for others and become Changemakers

1. Do you believe that empathy is something kids are born with, or a trait that can be developed? How could that answer have a surprising impact on whether children become Changemakers?

2. Does your child (or you) believe that empathy is something you're born with, or something that can be developed? How can you use the steps on pp. 201–202 to teach your child that empathy stretches?

3. Do you agree that fame-driven "heroes," a materialistic world, and an over-helping parenting style can limit a child's altruistic potential? What else can shortchange altruistic urges?

4. How might you use the Perlyns' six steps (pp. 205–206) to help your child become a Changemaker?

5. What community resources might offer meaningful service opportunities for your child?

6. How might you use the eight strategies on pp. 208–212 to help your child develop altruistic leadership?

7. How could you stretch your child's comfort zone to include "different" experiences?

8. How can parents work together to raise kids who want to better the world?

TEACHING CHILDREN THE EMPATHY SKILLS AND HABITS IN *UNSELFIE*

Dozens of empathy-building skills are provided throughout *UnSelfie*. Parents should choose those deemed important for their children. Use this model to teach each skill.

- SHOW. A skill is learned best if you *show* (not tell or lecture) what it looks like. So model it for the child! Point it out in context. Provide examples so the child can see it and copy it.

- ROLE PLAY. Role play the skill with the child so he understands what it looks like in action.

- PRACTICE. Skills are learned best through repetition and generally take around twenty-one days of practice to be mastered. Find various ways for the child practice the skill.

- REINFORCE OR CORRECT. Correct any errors in context and praise your child's skill-building efforts.

- STEP BACK. Once your child has mastered the skill and can use it without your guidance, teach the next empathy-builder and then the next and the next!

Chapter 1: Empathetic Children Can Recognize Feelings

EMPATHY SKILLS TO BOOST EMOTIONAL LITERACY

1. 4T Rule: No Texting, Tapping, Talking on a cell, or TV viewing when others are present: To tune in to emotions and not let digital devices hinder face-to face connections.

2. Always Look at the Color of the Talker's Eyes: To pick up on facial expressions, voice tone, and emotional cues.

3. Name the Feeling, Pose Questions that Tune In to Feelings, or Match the Word with the Gesture: To build a feeling vocabulary and help children recognize feelings and needs of others.

Chapter 2: Empathetic Children Have a Moral Identity

EMPATHY SKILLS TO BOOST MORAL IDENTITY

1. How to REFUSE Temptations: To buck peer pressure and stick up for beliefs.

2. "Is that me?" tests: To stick to moral identity and conscience in trying times.

3. Self-Talk: To counter taunts and adhere to personal code of ethics.

4. The KIND Rule: To guide an inner moral compass, both online and off.

Chapter 3: Empathetic Children Understand the Needs of Others

EMPATHY SKILLS TO BOOST PERSPECTIVE TAKING

1. **SOLER:** Five key listening skills to boost empathy and paying attention to the other.

2. **Look and Listen for the Feeling:** Playing detective to look and listen for the feeling.

3. **Put Yourself in Their Shoes:** To imagine the other person's perspective.

4. **Describe Their Side:** To paraphrase a speaker's perspective and increase empathy.

5. **"I Wonder":** To stretch perspective taking when encountering someone new.

Chapter 4: Empathetic Children Have a Moral Imagination

EMPATHY SKILLS TO BOOST MORAL IMAGINATION

1. **Ask "What If?":** To think about a character from the child's perspective.

2. **"How Would *You* Feel?":** To help reflect as to whether the child shared a similar experience.

3. **Switch from "Me" to "You":** To switch from "me" thinking to "we" thinking.

Chapter 5: Empathetic Children Can Keep Their Cool

EMPATHY SKILLS TO BOOST SELF-REGULATION

1. "Just Breathe": To learn mindful breathing and increase self-regulation abilities.

2. Belly Breathing: To learn breath control to create an instant relaxation response.

4. Learn a Cool-Down Strategy (Imagine a Calm Place, Self-Talk, or "1 + 3 + 10"): To adopt a self-regulation habit when stress kicks in.

5. Gratitude Breathing: To use mindful breathing to increase compassion and gratitude.

Chapter 6: Empathetic Children Practice Kindness

EMPATHY SKILLS TO CULTIVATE KINDNESS

1. The Two Kind Rule: To help children practice kindness and expand their kindness muscles. *This skill has five steps; teach each step separately.*

2. Kindness Rituals: To practice kindness and help children adopt a caring mindset.

Chapter 7: Empathetic Children Think "Us" Not "Them"

EMPATHY SKILLS TO BOOST COLLABORATION

1. "Take a STAND" to Solve Problems: To learn to solve problems peacefully and consider other people's feelings and needs. *Each of the five steps should be taught as a separate habit.*

2. Take a Reality Check: To learn to listen for categorical statements and halt stereotypes.

3. Encouragers: To support others, inspire collaboration and be a team player.

4. FACT Conversation Starters: To start dialogues, build relationships, and focus on others.

5. Disagreeing Respectfully: To learn to disagree respectfully and keep communication open.

6. Decision Makers and Deal Breakers: To resolve conflicts and boost cooperation.

Chapter 8: Empathetic Children Stick Their Necks Out

EMPATHY SKILLS TO BOOST MORAL COURAGE

1. STANDUP for Others: To mobilize moral courage and step in to reduce bullying. *Each strategy should be taught as a separate skill.*

2. Positive Self-Talk: To override the fear response and build moral courage.

3. Mental Rehearsal: To use visualization in reviewing an activity so reduce stress.

4. Chunk It: To set goals in extremely short chunks to reduce stress.

5. 2-3-4 Breathing or Dragon Breathing: To get oxygen to the brain for instant relaxation.

6. Use Your HEART: To help those who are distressed. *Each strategy should be taught as a separate skill.*

7. S.O.S. Safety Smarts: To avert danger and decide if it's safer to step in or wiser to get help.

Chapter 9: Empathetic Children Want to Make a Difference

EMPATHY SKILLS TO BOOST ALTRUISTIC LEADERSHIP

1. FACE: To show concern and close the empathy gap. *Each skill should be taught separately.*

2. ABCs of Stress Management: To cope with emotional distress and fight the empathy gap.

3. Start with One: To build self-efficacy and realize "I can make a difference."

START AN UNSELFIE REVOLUTION

Here's how to give children the Empathy Advantage in your home, school, or community, and create a more just and caring world.

- To watch videos of Michele's latest talks and media appearances and to read her blog, where she discusses the latest in cultivating empathy, character, parenting, and preventing bullying, visit her website: www.micheleborba.com.

- Follow Michele's musings and photo posts about empathy building, and join her on her round-the-world adventures on Twitter: www.twitter.com/micheleborba.

- Join Michele on Facebook to chat with other parents and educators about empathy-building strategies: www.facebook.com/drmicheleborba.

- Bring Michele as a guest speaker to your school, conference, or company event and hear her practical, proven, and inspiring empathy-building examples. Learn more at www.micheleborba.com/workshops-speaking/ or contact the American Program Bureau to invite Michele to speak to your parents, teachers, students, or community: http://apbspeakers.com/speaker/michele-borba.

- Contact Michele to arrange a virtual book club meeting via Skype: http://micheleborba.com/contact-dr-michele-borba/.